THE NATIONAL ELECTION OF 1964

The National Election
of 1964

PAUL TILLETT

STANLEY KELLEY, JR.

NELSON W. POLSBY

CHARLES A. H. THOMSON

HERBERT E. ALEXANDER

MILTON C. CUMMINGS, JR.

ANGUS CAMPBELL

Edited by MILTON C. CUMMINGS, JR.

THE BROOKINGS INSTITUTION
Washington, D. C.

© 1966 by

THE BROOKINGS INSTITUTION
1775 Massachusetts Avenue, N. W., Washington, D. C.

Published July 1966

Library of Congress Catalogue Card Number 66-23335

THE BROOKINGS INSTITUTION is an independent organization devoted to nonpartisan research, education, and publication in economics, government, foreign policy, and the social sciences generally. Its principal purposes are to aid in the development of sound public policies and to promote public understanding of issues of national importance.

The Institution was founded December 8, 1927, to merge the activities of the Institute for Government Research, founded in 1916, the Institute of Economics, founded in 1922, and the Robert Brookings Graduate School of Economics and Government, founded in 1924.

The general administration of the Institution is the responsibility of a self-perpetuating Board of Trustees. The trustees are likewise charged with maintaining the independence of the staff and fostering the most favorable conditions for creative research and education. The immediate direction of the policies, program, and staff of the Institution is vested in the President, assisted by the division directors and an advisory council, chosen from the professional staff of the Institution.

In publishing a study, the Institution presents it as a competent treatment of a subject worthy of public consideration. The interpretations and conclusions in such publications are those of the author or authors and do not purport to represent the views of the other staff members, officers, or trustees of the Brookings Institution.

Foreword

This volume on the national election of 1964 was designed to incorporate some of the more significant, and possibly less obvious, information on the presidential and congressional elections of that year. It is one of a number of studies published by Brookings on aspects of nominating and election politics. Among the earlier volumes are: *The Presidential Election and Transition 1960-1961* (Paul T. David, ed., 1961); *The Politics of National Party Conventions* (1960), by Paul T. David, Ralph M. Goldman, and Richard C. Bain; *Presidential Transitions* (1960), by Laurin L. Henry; *The 1956 Presidential Campaign* (1960), by Charles A. H. Thomson and Frances M. Shattuck; and *Convention Decisions and Voting Records* (1960), by Richard C. Bain.

Milton C. Cummings, Jr., now teaching at The Johns Hopkins University, served as editor of the 1964 election book and wrote two of the chapters while he was a member of the Brookings senior staff. Other contributors were: Herbert E. Alexander, director of the Citizens' Research Foundation, Princeton, New Jersey; Angus Campbell, director of the Survey Research Center, The University of Michigan; Stanley Kelley, Jr., chairman of the department of politics, Princeton University; Nelson W. Polsby, Wesleyan University; Charles A. H. Thomson, the RAND Corporation, Santa Monica, California; and Paul Tillett, Eagleton Institute of Politics, Rutgers University. The Institution would also like to express its gratitude to Paul T. David, chairman of the department of political science, University of Virginia, who did much of the initial work involved in designing and planning the study. The project was conducted under the general supervision of George A. Graham, Director of Governmental Studies at Brookings.

During the preparation of this volume, many valuable suggestions for improving the manuscript were received from an advisory committee consisting of: Clarence A. Berdahl, department of political science, University of Illinois; Austin Ranney, department of political science, University of Wisconsin; and Richard M. Scammon, director of the Elections Research Center, Washington, D. C. The contributors and the editor are deeply indebted to these readers for their help.

The contributors express their appreciation to a number of persons for assistance and comment. Stanley Kelley received suggestions and criticisms from Walter F. Murphy, Edward V. Schneier, Charles J. Peischl, and George Will, Princeton University; Richard Ayres and Melvin Masuda, Yale Law School; Mrs. Margaret Ayres; Mrs. Edith Jeffrey; Mrs. Rosalie Feltenstein. Nelson Polsby acknowledges comments from H. Douglas Price, Charles O. Jones, John Kessel, John Manley, Linda O. Polsby, Raymond E. Wolfinger, Paul A. Smith, Milton C. Cummings, Elizabeth Brenner Drew, Aaron B. Wildavsky, and Robert L. Peabody; assistance from Karl Lamb in securing Republican National Convention delegate lists; and editorial advice from Miriam Gallaher. Herbert Alexander received information and explanations from many persons—too many to acknowledge individually. Milton Cummings had the benefit of review and criticism from Robert L. Peabody, The Johns Hopkins University; Barbara J. Maly assisted with the statistical analyses and other assignments. Mr. Cummings is also indebted to Thomas N. Schroth, Executive Editor of Congressional Quarterly, for permission to use material from its publications. Miss Maly and Mrs. Elizabeth Patton typed the manuscript, and the index was prepared by Florence Robinson. To Frances M.

Shattuck, who edited the manuscript for publication with patience, skill, and unflagging good humor, the authors are especially grateful.

Chapter 5 (Financing the Parties and Campaigns) will be published by the Citizens' Reseach Foundation in an expanded and revised form, with additional supporting details and documentation; the pamphlet will be entitled "Financing the 1964 Election." The Foundation will also publish a separate study, "Financing the 1964 Congressional Elections: The Role of National-Level Party and Non-Party Committees."

The study on which Chapter 8 (Interpreting the Presidential Victory) is based was made possible by a grant from the Carnegie Corporation of New York.

The Brookings Institution appreciates the support of the Ford Foundation, which financed this study.

The views expressed in this book are those of the authors, and do not purport to represent the views of the Ford Foundation, or of other staff members, officers, or trustees of the Brookings Institution.

Robert D. Calkins
President

January 1966
Washington, D. C.

Contents

Introduction

In a sense the presidential campaign of 1964 began on November 9, 1960, or as soon thereafter as the Republicans were willing to acknowledge defeat. John F. Kennedy's extremely narrow margin of victory encouraged the opposition to believe that he might be a one-term President, and it is clear that a number of leading Republicans regarded their party's nomination as a prize worth fighting for in 1964.

Among the Republicans, New York's liberal Governor Nelson Rockefeller—who President Kennedy reportedly believed would have beaten him had he been the Republican nominee in 1960—was one obvious contender for the Republican nomination. Rockefeller's prospects suffered a sharp setback in the spring of 1963, however, when he married a recent divorcée with several small children. At the other end of the ideological spectrum within the Republican party, a strong movement sprang up among conservatives to win the nomination for Senator Barry Goldwater of Arizona. Others who were talked of as possible candidates, despite their early denials of any interest in actively seeking the nomination, were Governor George Romney of Michigan, former Vice President Richard M. Nixon, and Pennsylvania's Governor William Scranton.

On the Democratic side everyone assumed that President Kennedy would want and would receive the Democratic nomination. He was in fact attempting to mend some political fences in Texas when he was assassinated in

November 1963. His successor, Lyndon B. Johnson, inherited both the Presidency and, after a series of swift moves that established his intention to be a decisive and a liberal Democratic President, the presumption of the nomination.

The Republican preconvention campaign opened early, with Governor Rockefeller announcing his candidacy on November 7, 1963. In December ex-President Dwight D. Eisenhower suggested that Henry Cabot Lodge should make himself available. Senator Goldwater made his formal announcement on January 3, 1964, and on January 27 Senator Margaret Chase Smith of Maine declared that she also was a candidate.

The presidential primary procession began on March 10 in New Hampshire, where both Rockefeller and Goldwater were on the ballot. Goldwater entered the campaign as the favorite, but appeared to lose support as the campaign progressed, in part because of adverse reaction to some of his off-the-cuff remarks. Yet many New Hampshire voters also appeared unwilling to vote for Rockefeller, and in the end the election was won on a dramatic write-in vote by Lodge, who was serving as United States Ambassador to Vietnam and had not entered the primary. These New Hampshire results appeared to make Lodge the leading choice of many Republican liberals and moderates across the nation in opposition to the strong conservative movement for Goldwater.

The next primary in which there was a confrontation of the candidates was in Oregon on May 15, where state law required that all genuine candidates be on the ballot. This time a Lodge victory was predicted by most observers—as well as by several well-known pollsters; but when the ballots were counted Rockefeller emerged the winner, followed by Lodge, Goldwater, Nixon, Smith, and Scranton.

Attention now focused on the climactic and potentially crucial primary on June 2 in California, where there was a direct contest between Rockefeller and Goldwater, with no other candidates on the ballot. Two events that may have had an impact on the balloting received widespread press and television coverage during the last ten days of the California campaign. On May 24 Eisenhower issued a statement urging the Republican party to name a candidate who would uphold "Republican principles" spelled out in the party platforms in 1956 and 1960—a statement that was widely interpreted as fitting all of the potential Republican candidates except Barry Goldwater. Two days before the primary, however, Eisenhower declared that his statement had been misinterpreted and denied that he had meant to read Goldwater out of the party. The other event—the announcement that the second Mrs. Rockefeller had given birth to a baby on the final weekend before the election—served to remind the public once again of the Rockefeller divorce and remarriage.

The final vote in California was close, but Goldwater won all 86 of the state's delegates to the Republican National Convention while winning 51.6 percent of the popular vote. Meanwhile, Goldwater supporters had been extremely successful in obtaining pledged delegates in the states where delegates were selected by state and local conventions or by party committees. With this support, plus California, victory now seemed almost within the Arizona Senator's grasp.

Rockefeller's California defeat ended whatever chances he had had of obtaining the nomination (and his chances had never been bright). Ironically, it also underscored the strategic importance of the Rockefeller victory over Lodge in Oregon some two and a half weeks earlier. If Lodge had won in Oregon, as had been expected, he might have provided the focal point for a final, last-ditch attempt to stop Goldwater. As it was, other Republican moderates and liberals, although clearly distressed over the prospect of a Goldwater nomination, were left without an avowed leader for ten days after the California primary. During this period there was considerable confusion among Goldwater's potential Republican opponents, as each tried to get the other to declare that he was an active candidate. Governor Scranton of Pennsylvania finally determined to make a stand and announced his candidacy on June 12. Rockefeller immediately made a formal withdrawal and gave his support to Scranton, who hastily organized a campaign and made a strenuous effort to do the impossible. But with only a month before the Republican National Convention, it was too late. Senator Everett Dirksen of Illinois saw the handwriting on the wall. On July 1 he declared that no one could stop Goldwater and announced that he would place the Arizona Senator's name in nomination.

When the Republican platform committee met in San Francisco during the week preceding the convention, it was immediately apparent that the Goldwater forces were in complete command. All significant attempts by Republican liberals to alter the platform were defeated, both in drafting the platform and later in the convention itself, where Governor Rockefeller was booed as he attempted to speak. On July 15 Goldwater was nominated with ease on the first ballot, collecting 883 votes when only 655 were needed for the nomination. Governor Scranton then moved to make it unanimous. For his running mate, Goldwater selected the chairman of the Republican National Committee, Representative William E. Miller of New York, like himself a strong conservative.

Even with the nomination firmly in hand, Goldwater appeared to be in no mood to conciliate the moderates with the customary gestures toward party unity that usually conclude a major party nominating convention. Goldwater's acceptance speech mentioned unity, but it was most notable for its assertion that "extremism in defense of liberty is no vice." A conference at Hershey, Pennsylvania, on August 12, when the two candidates met with fourteen Republican governors, Eisenhower, Nixon, and other party leaders, produced a momentary show of unity, sufficient to elicit a statement of satisfaction from General Eisenhower and to give hope of party harmony during the conduct of the campaign. Nevertheless, some prominent Republican office-seekers declined to associate themselves with the Goldwater candidacy, and charges by Goldwater partisans that they were receiving inadequate support from the regular Republican organizations in some states were heard right up until election day.

Although the identity of the Democratic presidential candidate appeared certain, two developments that had a possible bearing on Democratic prospects in the general election attracted considerable attention. The Republicans endeavored to embarrass the President for his past association with Robert G. (Bobby) Baker when it became known that Baker, the former Secretary of the Senate, had given Johnson an expensive stereophonic phonograph. Alabama's Democratic Governor George Wallace, seeing possible advantage in the white reaction to Negro gains and civil rights demonstrations, entered the Democratic presidential primaries in Wisconsin (April 7), Indiana (May 5), and Maryland (May 19), as well as backing unpledged Democratic presidential electors in his own state. In these primaries Wallace won 34 percent of the Democratic vote in Wisconsin, 30 percent in Indiana, and nearly 43 percent in Maryland. Johnson, however, in addition to profiting from the public's reaction to the Kennedy assassination, had all the advantages of an incumbent President. During the 1964 session of Congress he also began to win some impressive legislative victories.

The main question of interest among the Democrats centered on who would be selected as the party's candidate for Vice President. There were a number of would-be candidates, either known or suspected, including Attorney General Robert Kennedy, Senator Hubert Humphrey of Minnesota, and Senator Eugene McCarthy of Minnesota. Kennedy was effectively and adroitly eliminated by the President on July 30, when Johnson declared that he felt that no member of his cabinet ought to be the nominee—a move that prompted Robert Kennedy to say shortly thereafter that he was "sorry to take so many good men over the side" with him. Otherwise the suspense over the Vice-Presidency continued until the President flew to the Democratic Convention in Atlantic City, where he announced that Hubert Humphrey was his man. The convention, which met from August 24 to 27, was also enlivened briefly by dissension over the credentials of the Alabama and Mississippi delegations; but there was never any doubt of the firm Johnsonian control.

For a while it appeared that there might be three candidates, rather than two, who stood a chance of polling a significant vote on election day. On June 7, Alabama's Democratic Governor George Wallace said that he would stand as a third-party presidential candidate in every state where he could get on the ballot. Three days later, however, Goldwater voted in the Senate against invoking cloture, which would permit a vote on the administration's Civil Rights bill; and as it became increasingly clear that Goldwater would win the Republican nomination, pressure on Wallace to withdraw mounted among conservatives, on the grounds that both he and Goldwater were likely to draw support from the same sources. On July 19, shortly after Goldwater was nominated, Wallace withdrew, declaring that he had accomplished his mission by serving as the "instrument" through which the leaders of both parties had been "conservatized." Thus he provided a clear confrontation in the South between a Democratic nominee and a conservative Republican opposed on the race issue.

The main events in the campaign itself need not be detailed at any length here. If the public opinion polls could be believed, Johnson, the incumbent, maintained a commanding lead throughout. He clearly had more support from newspapers and backing from normally Republican voters than any Democratic presidential nominee had had in a generation. Although there was some discrepancy between what Goldwater was saying during the campaign and the positions some Democratic orators attributed to him, there was considerable evidence that many voters felt that there was a real difference between the candidates on domestic social welfare policies and on the relative restraint with which the two candidates would approach vital decisions involving questions of peace or war. And always looming in the background, though usually discussed only gingerly by the candidates themselves, were the different postures the two men had taken on the potentially explosive issue of civil rights.

Whatever the reasons were, it soon became evident that the alternatives given the voters in the campaign were exerting a strong tug on normal partisan loyalties. In South Carolina Senator J. Strom Thurmond switched from the Democratic party to the Republican to campaign actively for Goldwater. Meanwhile, in other parts of the country, many regular Republicans, including prominent businessmen and several former members of President Eisenhower's cabinet, declared for Johnson. These departures from more normal political preference patterns were reflected in the voting, when the nation as a whole gave a landslide victory to Johnson, with 61 percent of the vote. Goldwater carried

only the five once heavily Democratic states of South Carolina, Georgia, Alabama, Mississippi, and Louisiana, plus
his home state of Arizona. Moreover, in the North, Maine
was even more Democratic than New York State, while the
most Republican state of all in the presidential balloting was
Mississippi, where Goldwater received 87 percent of the
total vote.

The following volume is not a comprehensive survey of
the primary and general election campaigns of 1964, a
task to which a number of other books have been devoted.
The aim, rather, is to present several interpretive and analytical essays that probe into selected aspects of those political
events.

In the first chapter, Paul Tillett comes to the conclusion
that the two national party conventions reached completely
different results in several highly important respects. The
Democrats achieved a nearly all-embracing consensus, while
one faction of the Republicans imposed an agreement that
excluded many party members. A notable interchange was
visible in the changed role of the South: the dominant
Republican faction received the support of the old-line
southern Democrats and rejected the Negro; the Democrats
took a firmer hold on the image of the national party and
championed the cause of the Negro minority. Moreover,
the consequences of these decisions, Tillett feels, may haunt
the Republican party for years to come, for the Republicans
face the danger that they may flounder for some time in
minority status, plagued by all the Democratic weaknesses
of the past—factionalism, bitter fights, interminable convention ballots, and the assaults of adventurers willing
to work four long hard years to gain a nomination almost
certain to meet defeat.

The basic strategy of the Goldwater presidential campaign,
as viewed by Stanley Kelley, differed in only some respects

from what would have been adopted by a moderate Republican nominee. His appeal for the votes of southern whites was almost certain to alienate the Negro; and his attack on big government, bureaucracy, and spending lacked compensating assurances that there would be no drastic change in federal domestic policy and programs. Nevertheless, his overwhelming defeat cannot be easily attributed to any particular feature of his campaign strategy. He was running against a popular incumbent President of the majority party. And he was a far from ideal standard-bearer for the conservative Republican cause. Actually, the strategy may have helped to save the party from an even more severe defeat. The greater activity for the Republican ticket at the grassroots level may be related to his ideological appeal. Goldwater's strategy may have been a desperate one, but it was not an unreasonable response to the situation in which any Republican candidate would have found himself in 1964.

Nelson Polsby assesses the possible reasons why Goldwater won the Republican nomination and concludes that Goldwater was successful in part because his avowed opponents were weak, because the chances of winning the Presidency seemed sufficiently remote to discourage much competitive effort by candidates who might otherwise have contested the nomination more effectively, because the Republican party organizations in many states were particularly susceptible to preconvention campaigning, and because he reflected the policy preferences of many party activists and leaders. He also appealed to amateurs (who showed up at the convention in unusually large numbers) because of his ideological purity and his emphasis on issues of morality and rightness. The amateurs were moved by passionate conviction and were relatively insensitive to demands for compromise or the necessities of team play with others whose political orientation differed from their own.

It may also be, Polsby believes, that some Goldwater Republicans recognized that their chances of winning the election were slim, but felt that even a debacle in 1964 would enhance their long-run chances of controlling the party and in possibly pushing political dialogue in the country to the right. This seems to have been a gross miscalculation. Prompt and meaningful measures were taken to try to mend the damage caused by the Republican electoral disaster, but they may be insufficient to prevent an effective shift to a one-and-a-half party system. Ultimately, Polsby feels, the health of a two-party system depends on the capacity of the two parties to agree on most issues and at the margins to offer alternatives attractive to slightly different components of the population. This makes for disagreement on live issues, not on issues already settled and part of an overriding national consensus. The Republicans' danger now is that they may not soon be able to capture the long-time loyalties of enough voters to return them to power for any lengthy period of time.

The most important development in 1964 among the news media, in the judgment of Charles A. H. Thomson, was the new collaboration achieved between television and the printed press. Television inaugurated a comprehensive and accurate Network Election Service for the reporting of returns, and in addition launched services of prediction and analysis of returns (such as CBS's Vote Profile Analysis) that vastly improved television's capability to do its job of immediate reporting and commentary. Both these services were put at the disposal of the nation's major news agencies and newspapers, much to the improvement of their natural functions of reporting in depth and providing an enduring record of event, analysis, and evaluation. The book and pamphlet also achieved unusual prominence, but television played a major role, both in the immediate electoral process and in contributing to public understanding of the process.

Herbert Alexander delves into the financial aspects of the campaign and finds that 1964 was undoubtedly the most expensive election year in history. Both parties spent more and raised more than ever before, and both made successful use of fund-raising techniques previously tried but unproductive. Future campaigns will bring new challenges, including the provision of more democratic ways to finance American politics.

In addition to electing a President, voters in federal elections in 1964 elected 35 United States Senators and 435 members of the House of Representatives. Milton Cummings analyzes these House and Senate voting results and concludes that although the voting left a potentially decisive majority of liberal members in both the House and Senate, these consequences were achieved in the two chambers in different ways. In the Senate there was very little net change in the balance of party strength; the Democratic victories in those races, where the Democrats were defending an unusually large number of potentially vulnerable seats, were primarily defensive victories, and probably assured the Democrats of continued control of the Senate for the following six years. In the House, however, the Democrats were on the offensive; and the net Democratic gain of 38 seats resulted in a marked change in the balance of power between opponents and supporters of President Johnson's domestic program in the House.

Angus Campbell, in the concluding chapter, examines the presidential results, and on the basis of preliminary survey findings reports that President Johnson was far more favorably perceived by the electorate than Goldwater and that the images of the two parties also showed a clear Democratic preference—both stronger differentiations than found in 1960. Two major issues in the campaign, civil rights and governmental welfare activities, aroused contrasting reactions in different sections of the electorate, favoring Johnson in the North and Goldwater in the South. Attitudes on issues and toward the candidates can be major short-term forces in any presidential contest, and their impact has been visible in earlier election studies, often favoring the Republican candidate. But the earlier years did not show a change in the basic distribution of party identification such as was found in 1964—when a modest shift toward the Democratic party manifested itself. If this shift should turn out to be the first sign of an enduring realignment of party attachments, the consequences of 1964 for future elections in the United States may be far-reaching.

These findings by Angus Campbell point to the larger question of what were the broad general consequences of the 1964 election for American politics. One immediate consequence was certain. By sweeping into office a heavy Democratic majority in the House, by retaining a large Democratic majority in the Senate, and by giving Lyndon Johnson a full presidential term by a decisive margin, the election made possible the passage of a series of domestic measures that two Democratic Presidents had been advocating and the Congress had been resisting for several years. To the extent that there had been deadlock in Washington on these issues before, it was removed. The way was thus paved for a series of legislative victories for an activist Democratic President in 1965, the like of which had not been seen for a generation. Any possible longer-term results for the Democratic party, however, were quite thoroughly overshadowed by speculation concerning the Republican party.

The consequences of the 1964 election for the Republicans were problematical, and depended upon the unfolding of subsequent events to establish whether they would be of long-term importance. Although in the nation as a whole the

1964 balloting pushed the Republican vote well below recent more normal levels of strength, in the South the Republican party succeeded in opening up new areas for two-party competition—both at the presidential and the congressional level. In Mississippi, Alabama, and Georgia, and throughout the black belt generally—once the hard core of traditional southern Democratic voting strength—the Republicans polled a larger vote than at any other election since Reconstruction. It remained to be seen, however, whether this new Republican strength in these areas would last, or whether many of them would revert to Democratic voting habits.

Another major problem for the Republican party raised by the 1964 electoral verdict was what would be the political future of rising younger Republicans, such as Charles Percy of Illinois and Robert A. Taft, Jr., of Ohio, whose public careers were at least slowed down by the election results. Would they be able to regain the lost ground and achieve the positions that had appeared to be in prospect for them?

A further problem is brought up by Angus Campbell's finding, already cited, that there was a small but noticeable change in 1964 in the underlying balance in the electorate between the proportion of persons who consider themselves Democrats and the proportion who consider themselves Republicans. This shift was to the disadvantage of the Republican party, which already has been outnumbered in the electorate for many years. If the new balance of party identifiers is maintained, it would place additional difficulties on the ability of the Republicans to play their role effectively as a counterweight to the Democrats in a two-party system. A related problem was the success Lyndon Johnson demonstrated in persuading some Republicans, including a substantial number of business leaders, to vote for and to provide financial support for the Democratic presidential ticket. For the GOP it was a matter of legitimate concern whether this development would last, or whether it was merely an aberration of the 1964 campaign year.

Finally, and perhaps most important of all, were the conclusions Republicans would draw about the meaning of the 1964 results, and the consequences these conclusions would have for the selection of future Republican presidential nominees. Would the selection of a right-wing Republican nominee, followed by a GOP electoral disaster of the magnitude of 1964, lead many Republicans to say, "Never again," and assure that the moderates and liberals in the Republican party would be in control of the party's conventions for many years to come? Or should 1964 be read as a dramatic indication of the potential power of the dedicated conservatives in the GOP, and merely a foretaste of more captures of Republican National Conventions by the right wing of the party?

To pose these questions, one does not have to answer the antecedent question whether the fact that Senator Goldwater was a conservative caused the unusual severity of the 1964 Republican losses (although a definitive answer to that question might influence the conclusions Republicans will draw about 1964). A parallel might be drawn with the nomination and subsequent defeat of Al Smith in 1928, which undoubtedly hurt the chances any subsequent Roman Catholic had of obtaining the Democratic nomination for a generation, despite the fact that some more recent analyses have suggested that Smith was a relatively strong Democratic nominee, given the political circumstances of that year. Yet, whatever the answers to these questions are, the way Republicans read the meaning of 1964 will be of great importance; and subsequent decisions taken by them, plus the inevitable and often uncontrollable flow of events, will determine some of the more long-term consequences of the national election of 1964.

1

The National Conventions

PAUL TILLETT

An examination of the two national party conventions of 1964 must surely lead to astonishment at the difference in purpose and results of two apparently similar gatherings. Will Rogers' quip, "I belong to no organized party, I'm a Democrat," hardly applied to the Democrats at Atlantic City, who discovered a consensus that embraced nearly everybody between there and Hawaii. The Republicans, on the other hand, meeting earlier in San Francisco, reached an agreement so exclusive that it shut out many who were present as well as nearly everyone else.

In certain ways the conventions of 1964 strengthened trends made especially apparent since the end of World War II. Paul David and his colleagues have remarked upon the "recent and continuing increase in the amount of work transacted prior to the convention in the national committee and both before and during the session in the credentials, rules, and resolutions committees. . . ." [1] This tendency continued strong in 1964 both in San Francisco and Atlantic City. Naturally, these developments have helped to expedite

---

[1] Paul T. David, Ralph M. Goldman, Richard C. Bain, *The Politics of National Party Conventions,* paperback edition edited by Kathleen Sproul (Brookings Institution, 1960), p. 202.

the dispatch of business before the convention and have also made more critical than before the question of the representativeness of committees. No movement within either party has yet appeared, however, to raise the issue of representativeness. There continued also the proliferation of conventions —that of the professionals and leaders before the convention opened; the convention of the delegates and their families; the television convention or the mass media convention; and the Pepsi-Cola convention. There was a further divorcement of the representation of interest groups before the platform committees from the real work of those committees.

In a genuine exchange of image and practice, the parties reflected a change in the role of the South in American politics. At the convention and in the campaign, the dominant Republican faction behaved like old-line rural southern Democrats and received the support of these vociferous, but disappearing, types. The Democrats took a firmer hold on the image of the national party, championing the cause of the Negro minority. Finally, formal changes were entirely beaten off in the case of the Republicans; but two were made by Democrats—an enlarged convention, and the promise for a future convention unstained by racism in the selection of delegates. At every point, both conventions displayed a high degree of outside control, accepted willingly enough to be sure, but observable nonetheless.

Selection of Presidential Candidates

The excitement at San Francisco over a foregone conclusion —that is, the nomination of Barry Goldwater as the presidential standard-bearer for the GOP—is readily understandable when one comes to comprehend that the victorious faction had begun its preconvention campaign four years earlier. The campaign resembled, if it was not deliberately modeled on, that waged by John F. Kennedy for the Democratic nomination in 1960. Mr. Goldwater's success exceeded Mr. Kennedy's triumph in Los Angeles, because it represented not only the ascension of a man or a personality, but the triumph of a party faction which considered that it had been neglected for a quarter of a century.[2] Some of those who had first felt the sting of rejection, like Senator Everett Dirksen, were present to savor the sweet smell of victory and had a hand in bringing it about.

Goldwater and his immediate associates arrived in San Francisco with the situation firmly in hand. It may be too much to say that with William Miller occupying the chairmanship of the Republican National Committee, Goldwater and his group were able to control the convention much after the fashion of an incumbent President. However, no one would pretend that this was an open convention, and the statement is closer to the mark than the assumption that Goldwater's control of the party was always symmetrical; that is, neatly matched by his control over delegates.[3] Perhaps the appropriate perspective on preconvention activities can be obtained by considering a remark from one delegate to another at San Francisco: "If Goldwater had lost the California primary, Scranton might have won the nomination but it would've been a hell of a fight."

Some commentators have emphasized that a high proportion of the Republican delegates were attending a national

[2] One should not conclude without further evidence that the Goldwater nomination represented the ascendancy of an ideological faction alien to the party. After all, McCloskey and his collaborators have suggested that "Republican followers . . . disagree far more with their own leaders than with leaders of the Democratic party," an observation that may have been confirmed in part by the 1964 election. Herbert McClosky, Paul J. Hoffmann, Rosemary O'Hara, "Issue Conflict and Consensus Among Party Leaders and Followers," *American Political Science Review*, Vol. 54 (June 1960), p. 426.

[3] Charles O. Jones, "The 1964 Presidential Election—Further Adventures in Wonderland," in Donald G. Herzberg (ed.), *American Government Annual 1965-66* (Holt, Rinehart and Winston, 1965), pp. 2-4.

convention for the first time.[4] This seemed not nearly so significant as that they were newcomers to politics, and that they had arrived instructed. Ordinarily new people expect to follow the orders of the state leader, but a number of state leaders were surprised to find in their delegations individuals they hardly recognized who would not take their instructions but were set upon an independent, pro-Goldwater path. In many such cases one can say that, in effect, the party was infiltrated from below. This had a curious result in states like Florida and Minnesota, where pro-Goldwater slates had been defeated, but dedicated pro-Goldwater delegates turned up in the victorious delegation.[5] The casualness which typically surrounds the process of delegate selection at the lower levels permitted this infiltration to take place without challenge and almost unnoticed.

However, it was not all that way. The southern states, where John Grenier, the organizational genius behind Goldwater's southern strategy, was influential, openly carried much of the planning and the work of the national "Draft Goldwater" committee.[6] Several southern Republican leaders attended the meeting in Chicago in December 1962 to plan the organization; and when the committee was formed in April 1963, Peter O'Donnell of Texas was made its chairman. Youth, vigor, and an uninhibited conservative appeal went into the task of building a southern Republican organi-

---

[4] Chap. 3, below, pp. 100-01; Richard H. Rovere, "Letter from San Francisco," *New Yorker*, Vol. 40 (July 25, 1964), p. 80; Karl A. Lamb, "Under One Roof: Barry Goldwater's Campaign Staff," unpublished study, the Eagleton Institute of Politics Case Studies Program. David, Goldman, and Bain estimate that about 40 percent of the delegates at both 1952 conventions had served at least once before; *op. cit.*, p. 185.

[5] This occurred also in New Jersey, New York, and South Dakota.

[6] For the material on the South, I have drawn heavily on a paper by Bernard Cosman, University of Alabama, "The Deep South at the Republican National Convention: The Goldwater Delegates." Professor Cosman was an Eagleton-National Center for Education in Politics (NCEP) Fellow to the Republican National Convention in San Francisco, 1964.

zation at the grass roots for the convention and the election. John Grenier became regional coordinator, and the movement to recruit delegates swept Alabama, Louisiana, Mississippi, and South Carolina. In these states, the Goldwater faction became the Republican party. After a hard fight, they won control of the party in Georgia at the May convention in Atlanta.

At San Francisco, what had been the Gas Buggy Room in the Jack Tar Motel—the accommodations of a number of southern delegations—became the headquarters for southern Republicans for Goldwater. Headquarters employed a staff of fifty at the height of the convention activities, aided and abetted by twenty or more volunteers from Bay area party groups. A communications blanket covered the southern delegates, keeping them in contact with headquarters at all times. Delegations were divided into teams of five, each with a captain. Six regional directors were appointed. From a trailer outside the Cow Palace linked by telephone to headquarters and by walkie-talkie to the convention floor, the southern group was able to maintain command of its troops. From this network, Goldwater and his advisers received continuous reinforcement and assurance that a majority of the delegates were and would be his. Early in the game their organizational perfectionism gave rise to considerable confidence. As one Deep South delegate said to someone who asked him about Scranton: "Hell, they're not organized. We'll win this thing on the first ballot."

Organized they were—down to the last detail. Delegates were urged to read the Goldwater convention newsletter and the *Oakland Tribune,* former Senator William F. Knowland's paper; to look at the Goldwater television programs broadcast three times a day; and to keep their car radios tuned to the Goldwater radio programs emanating five times daily. What happened in the South was imitated in the other regions to a greater or lesser extent, depending on enthusiasm for the candidate. In most of the regions, that enthusiasm was intense.

The small, isolated state of South Dakota offers considerable contrast to the tightly organized enthusiasm of the southern delegations.[7] South Dakota was one of those states where a Goldwater slate had been defeated in the primary, but where, nonetheless, the Senator from Arizona was the favorite of more than one-half of the state's delegates at the convention.[8] He had their favor even though less than a majority believed that he represented the choice of the South Dakota voters and only two out of fourteen thought that he would become the nation's favorite. Very little happened in the South Dakota delegation itself. On Monday, at a caucus, their division—nine for Goldwater, five for Scranton—was duly noted. On Thursday morning after the Goldwater nomination, the delegates held a desultory conversation about the vice-presidential nomination. Turning to the man he called "Goldwater's contact man for South Dakota" for a report, the chairman was told: "Well, we'll get the word when we get to the convention floor. Why worry about it now?" Between those two occasions the only thing of any consequence the delegation had done was to discuss a request for an audience from an organization they called the "Negro Republican headquarters." After due consideration, they decided not to respond to the request in any form. They listened without sympathy to a report from their platform committee representative on charges that minorities were not

[7] For an account of the activities of the South Dakota delegation, I am indebted to Alan L. Clem, University of South Dakota, an Eagleton-NCEP Fellow to the 1964 Republican National Convention, on whose paper, "No Runs, No Hits, No Errors: National Convention Impact on Small State Politics," I have drawn heavily.

[8] After the regular slate was announced, more conservatively oriented interests formed a second slate committed to Goldwater, even though the regular slate contained a good number of his supporters. In the primary, the regular slate won by a margin of more than 2 to 1.

given fair treatment in the platform. It was quite clear that they could not make out what the fuss was all about and didn't really care to know.

More important things happened by virtue of South Dakota's connection with so-called Region V of the Goldwater organization, comprising the states of Iowa, Missouri, North Dakota, Nebraska, Kansas, Oklahoma, and Colorado as well. The instructions here contrast sharply with the casual quality of the deliberations in the state delegation. The chairman of Region V told the assembled group of delegates it had been given a quota of 152 votes; a Goldwater chairman was named for each state; one team captain was assigned to every four uncommitted delegates; known Scranton delegates were to be covered at convention sessions; each state was asked to provide two delegates as runners; and telephones were set up on the floor. Finally, the chairman said: "On pages, check their background and be sure they're loyal to Goldwater. . . . At the committee meetings Monday, vote with Frank Whetstone of Montana in the credentials committee and with Claude Jasper of Wisconsin in the rules committee. . . . Report to me as soon as possible the delegation's voting preferences. . . ."

The South Dakota delegates began the week 9-5 in favor of Mr. Goldwater, and supported him on the first official ballot by a 12-2 vote. They felt a faint sense of loss that it was South Carolina and not South Dakota which put Goldwater over the top and assured him the nomination.

As a political phenomenon, the process by which the convention of Democrats nominated Lyndon B. Johnson was fairly obvious. It may be that, as Justice Holmes once observed, we need more insight into the obvious, less elaboration of the obscure, but an adequate treatment of Mr. Johnson's bold venture into unexplored realms of political kitsch is far beyond the scope of this paper.

The Vice-Presidential Nominations

If what preceded the presidential nomination showed an essential disdain for the concerns of any but the dominant Goldwater faction at San Francisco, the selection of the Republican vice-presidential nominee and the method by which it was done rubbed salt into open wounds. So far as one can determine, there was no consultation among party leaders, at least none out of the Goldwater faction, and the selection of Representative William P. Miller as the candidate seemed calculated to exacerbate party differences and to demonstrate the degree of control of the convention by the triumphant conservative faction. Miller was demanded by conservative stalwarts who pleaded with Mr. Goldwater, "Don't give in to the liberals!" He was a Roman Catholic and was possessed of a photogenic family. Beyond that, he had a vitriolic tongue and it was said Goldwater liked him because "he gives Johnson fits." Very little was said about his qualifications to succeed to the Presidency if that were necessary.

Among the Democrats, efforts to seek the vice-presidential nomination were shaped rather decisively by: (1) a feeling among the delegates that it was all up to President Johnson; (2) the President's lukewarm reaction to the Attorney General, Robert F. Kennedy; (3) Johnson's statement of July 30 ruling out cabinet members or those who sat regularly with the cabinet, eliminating Dean Rusk, Robert McNamara, Orville Freeman, Sargent Shriver, Adlai Stevenson, as well as the young Attorney General; (4) the absence of a faction in the party demanding or obviously requiring representation or recognition to balance the ticket, satisfy dissidents, cement alliances, or extend appeal.[9]

[9] In what follows, I have drawn on Gerald Pomper, "The Nomination of Hubert H. Humphrey," unpublished paper. Professor Pomper was an Eagleton-NCEP Convention Fellow in 1964.

Hubert Humphrey, popular with liberals, labor, civil rights leaders, had significant support among congressional southerners though he was weak among city bosses and business-statesmen. To many, he seemed to live up to the line he and his staff had hit upon as the focus for his efforts: namely, to look upon the selection of the vice-presidential candidate as the search for the "next best man." He and his aides put on a discreet, low-pressure campaign, much below the decibel level they were prepared to create. But his advisers lived in fear of an emotional tidal wave for John F. Kennedy that would redound to the benefit of his younger brother Robert. After July 30, Hubert Humphrey took on a few speaking engagements, and appeared in shallow, milk-fed, wholesome, complacent contrast to James Baldwin in a television spectacular, "My Childhood." With presidential approval, perhaps at executive command, Humphrey continued his television contract with the American Broadcasting Company, journeyed to Atlantic City as a delegate from Minnesota, and took to the floor before his nomination. On convention eve, he wound up with the support of the cabinet, forty senators, "nearly all significant party figures in 26 states and the District of Columbia, and a clear majority [of delegates] in six additional states," according to a White House survey.[10] He had, in addition, considerable press support, and in the polls led Robert Kennedy and Adlai Stevenson both in popularity and in the voters' view of him as best qualified for the job.[11] He had been aided by the nomination of Goldwater, which made the Midwest the battleground; he was strong among Negroes, farmers, and labor unions.

At Atlantic City, it was felt necessary to put the dampers on to avoid offending the President. Headquarters reserved for Humphrey were turned over to the Minnesota delega-

[10] *New York Times,* Aug. 17, 1964.
[11] See poll data collected in *Congressional Quarterly Weekly Report,* June 19, 1964, pp. 1213-14, 1232.

tion. Other steps were taken to lie low. While thus modestly waiting to be asked, the aspiring Senator was thrust into the limelight at the President's own request. Working out a compromise to the dispute over the seating of delegates of the Mississippi Freedom Democratic party was assigned to him. This, the only issue of consequence, and the only significant decision not made personally by Lyndon Baines Johnson, involved the claim of an integrated delegation of Mississippians, selected at a rump election which followed procedures laid down in state statutes and party rules but departed from practice by permitting Negroes to vote. The slate thus elected sought recognition in Atlantic City as the Democratic delegation. They were opposed by a lily-white regular Democratic delegation, chosen by the usual procedures, in the official forms, which excluded Negroes. The conduct of the regular Democrats gave rise to a strong presumption that they would defect from the national ticket in November. From Humphrey's standpoint, the conflict contained great personal risk—the decision had to fit the moral temper of the convention, that is, recognize the claim of the Freedom Democrats to the equal participation of Negroes in Mississippi political life, for any eleven states could have a roll call on the issue. Moreover, Humphrey could not afford to alienate the southern states. The successful compromise was effected with the loss only of those who had been lost already, and it put Humphrey in a commanding position.[12] From this point, the affair was stage-managed by the President so as to announce his choice of running mate while acknowledging his own nomination by the convention, ignoring the tradition of consulting leaders after the nomination, thus overturning another precedent from the pre-television era. Although this had the effect of keeping attention focused on the presidential nominee, in his remarks about

[12] The terms of the compromise are given below, p. 32.

Humphrey, August 26, 1964, the President at least showed a decent respect for the proprieties: "I thought the people of this country and the people of the free world were entitled to a man as Vice President of the United States who would be the best equipped man in this nation to be President if something happened to the President." [13]

The process by which Hubert Humphrey was selected showed Johnson's consummate political skill. In the end, the President got the man he wanted who was also the choice of the convention and popular in nearly every section of the party and the country—in short, a consensus candidate.

The Platforms

The two great moral poseurs who have offered themselves as candidates for the Presidency have had radically different views of the party platforms. To Woodrow Wilson, the Democratic candidate in 1912, "the platform is meant to show that we know what the nation is thinking about, what it is most concerned about, what it wishes corrected, and what it desires to see attained that is new and constructive and intended for its long future." [14] No pioneering, forward-looking, direction-setting platform for Senator Goldwater in 1964. "At best," he said, "political platforms are a packet of misinformation and lies." For this reason and others, he desired to see the party in 1964 run on a brief declaration of principles, of about 250 words.[15] The Republican platform of 1960 had contained 12,485 words. Platform committee chairman Melvin Laird hoped to bring in the 1964 platform under a ceiling of about 7,000 words; the final product weighed in at a plump 9,000.

[13] *New York Times,* Aug. 27, 1964.
[14] Quoted in Marvin R. Weisbord, "Again the Platform Builders Hammer Away," *New York Times Magazine,* July 5, 1964, p. 29.
[15] *Congressional Quarterly Convention Guide,* June 12, 1964, p. 1127.

The national chairman, William Miller, had chosen Representative Melvin Laird of Wisconsin for the platform job in January.[16] Laird had the assistance of a Critical Issues Council headed by former President Eisenhower's brother, Milton, the president of Johns Hopkins University, and a Party-to-People program which held hearings in various places in the country and collected responses to questionnaires about what should be in the platform. The platform committee which assembled in San Francisco consisted of 100 members, basically one man and one woman from each state or territory.[17]

Among the committee members there emerged three approaches to platform construction. First, there were the ideologues who wanted and received some satisfaction in breaking the hold of the eastern establishment on the party and in having the convention accept their principles even at the risk of losing the election. These individuals appear to have comprised a majority of the platform committee. A second group may be identified as orthodox party members who wanted to win or at least do well in the election and therefore were given to negotiating, compromising, and muting discord. They were open to persuasion on the ground of the effect of any particular plank on the national ticket or on state and local races. These individuals were in a hopeless minority. A third group actually did the work of the platform committee—the leadership group, which was largely congressional. Members of the House and Senate filled eleven of thirteen positions on the executive committee. Though largely conservative and supporters of the Gold-

---

[16] For information relating to the drafting of the Republican platform, I have relied on an unpublished paper by Kenneth M. Dolbeare, "The Republican Platform Committee of 1964: The Emergence of the New Non-Politics." Professor Dolbeare attended the 1964 Republican Convention as an Eagleton-NCEP Fellow.

[17] Some states sent only one member, which reduced the number to 100.

water candidacy, these professionals concerned themselves primarily with seeking consensus in the committee. Such moderation as the 1964 platform reflects is their handiwork.

At their first meeting in the week before the opening of the convention, Chairman Laird proposed a four-part platform stating basic Republican principles, indicting Democratic performance, setting forth the Republican position on foreign policy and on domestic issues. And so it was. Panels numbered one, two, three, and four held hearings, but were not permitted to specialize and the witnesses were scattered among them without rhyme or reason. Appearances before the platform committee were almost entirely exercises in futility. At all committee hearings the galleries appeared to be for Scranton while seventy to eighty of the committee members were shown by early votes and by their responses to witnesses to be firmly committed to Goldwater and following the leadership of Senator John Tower of Texas.

Probably there have been few moments of such complete failure to communicate as occurred when civil rights leaders appeared before a panel of the platform committee and attempted to discuss issues which went beyond the Civil Rights Act of 1964. Virtuoso performances by James Farmer of CORE and Dick Gregory, the comedian, attempting to explain the sources of frustration of Negroes in American life, left the committee unmoved and seemingly a little confused. They did not, however, change their opinions.

The state of affairs became clear early in the week. Governor Nelson Rockefeller of New York was a lead-off witness before the platform panel considering civil rights. His own low-keyed remarks, his reception, and the vote later in the day all indicated that his views had no chance of becoming part of the platform in the drafting process. On that day, July 6, the moderates on the platform committee—Senator Hugh Scott of Pennsylvania, New York Republican state leader Joseph Carlino, Representatives Peter Frelinghuysen of New Jersey and Abner Sibal of Connecticut—agreed among themselves that civil rights and the anti-John Birch Society extremism planks had the best chance of winning broad support in the convention. They concentrated on those issues.

The platform presented to the delegates came from the hands of a committee on style and language which included Bryce Harlow, a former special assistant and speech writer for President Eisenhower; one Goldwater man, Carl Hess, a former editor of *Newsweek* magazine; and a political science professor at Johns Hopkins, Malcolm Moos, another former Eisenhower assistant and in 1964 a Scranton supporter.

The whole experience leads to the question whether Laird represented Goldwater from the start. Perhaps so, but he seemed to restrain the rabid ideologues in the party and on his committee. The efforts of the moderates to have an anti-extremism plank and a plank on civil rights adopted may have helped Laird considerably in this task by capping off or diverting the effervescence of the Goldwater men on the platform committee who would have gone further had they not been distracted. Unwittingly, then, the moderates aided the consensus-seeking leadership. Only four committee votes were registered against the final document, which contained no major substantive changes from the material offered to the committee by Laird and which had withstood an attempt to reaffirm presidential control of atomic arms, to affirm the constitutionality of the civil rights act, denounce extremism, and broaden immigration laws. It was, nonetheless, a platform more moderate than the convention from which it emanated.

On the floor, the moderates lost all five skirmishes, only one of which went to the point of a roll call; an amendment to the civil rights plank was crushed, 897-409. The way was clear for the war hawks of Goldwater and the evangelical politics of the right; but there was not much left to be done. Thereafter, not much was heard about the platform.

In this respect, the Democratic experience was similar. The platform did not appear to play a great part in the campaign—old Goldwater speeches being far more significant and useful to campaigning Democrats. The Democratic platform was also completely packaged outside the convention city, under the placid chairmanship of Representative Carl Albert of Oklahoma. Most of the hearings were held in Washington during the week preceding the convention, with some in Atlantic City. The theme of the platform appeared from its title, "One Nation, One People." In some respects it provided a reverse image of the Republican effort, with the Democrats adopting some of the planks rejected after much travail at San Francisco. For example, the Democrats declared: "We condemn extremism, whether from the Right or Left, including the extreme tactics of such organizations as the Communist party, the Ku Klux Klan, and the John Birch Society." The Democrats also included a promise to give municipal home rule to the District of Columbia, a subject not mentioned in the Republican platform because, it is said, Laird took offense at the questioning of Senator Goldwater by George Parker, a Negro delegate from the District of Columbia, who pressed the candidate on his attitude toward enforcement of the Civil Rights Act.[18] When the Democratic platform builders' work was complete, a committee member epitomized their achievement by saying, "There's no unhappiness about anything."

Governing the Party

Only one change appears to have been attempted by the victorious Goldwater forces at San Francisco; this was a pro-

18 *Election '64*, A Ripon Society Report (Cambridge, Mass., 1965), p. 18.

posal to the rules committee to make members of the Republican National Committee voting delegates to the national convention. The proposed change lost by a vote of 81-20, just as nearly every proposal to alter the work of the committee leadership lost. One other issue caused very little difficulty—that was the settlement of the dispute over the blocking of George W. Lee from the Tennessee delegation, allegedly because of his race. Mr. Lee had been a delegate to every Republican convention since 1940, but he was excluded in 1964 after a new group took over control of the state party. Race may, indeed, have lain at the bottom, but the changes made were so subtle that the exclusion of Mr. Lee from the delegation looked very much like the penalty of losing a factional fight. In any case, the credentials committee voted 66-19 against his seating, and after Senator Carl Curtis appealed to the delegates as "the salt of the earth" and "the hope of mankind," a resolution on behalf of Mr. Lee on the convention floor was overwhelmingly defeated. A resolution barring delegates chosen by practices which had the purpose or effect of discriminating on grounds of race, color, creed, or national origin, was shouted down by the convention without a roll call.

In the Democratic convention two structural changes were made, one of which may have lasting influence. On January 11, 1964, the Democratic National Committee adopted a new formula for the allocation of delegates and convention votes and at the same time raised the total number of votes. The formula favored states which had supported Kennedy in 1960: for each electoral vote three convention votes; one vote for every 100,000 popular votes for the 1960 nominee; ten more votes if the state's electoral votes went to Kennedy; and one vote for each national committeeman and committeewoman. The formula resulted in 2,316 convention votes as against 1,521 in 1960. A minor population explosion also came about by application of the new formula. In 1960 there had been a maximum of 2,394 delegates, 1,467 alternates, and 108 national committee members for a grand total of 4,509. The 1964 scheme allowed for 2,944 delegates, 2,208 alternates and 108 national committee members —a total of 5,260.[19] By contrast, the 1964 Republican convention contained 1,308 delegates and an equal number of alternates, for a total of 2,616.

Far more significant and more controversial: the call to the 1964 convention issued by the Democratic National Committee contained a loyalty pledge just as it had in 1956 and 1960. The gist of the pledge was that the state party by the act of sending delegates to the national convention undertook to assure that the voters in that state would have the opportunity to cast their ballots for the presidential and vice-presidential nominees of the convention under the label of the Democratic party. In the absence of credentials contests, no further demonstration of loyalty was to be required.

Prior to the opening of the 1964 convention, National Chairman John Bailey advised the chairmen of all state delegations that contested delegations would be omitted from the temporary roll of the convention until their cases had been settled by the credentials committee headed by former Pennsylvania Governor David L. Lawrence. As explained previously, controversy over the seating of the delegation from Mississippi became the outstanding issue, in fact the only issue not directly settled by President Johnson at the Democratic convention; and its solution played a role in enhancing the stature of Hubert Humphrey and consolidating his hold on presidential favor leading to his nomination for Vice President. The confrontation within the party of the Negroes and the southern Democrats provided a more convincing demonstration of the party's intentions toward civil rights than anything that could have been said in a platform.

[19] For details, see *Congressional Quarterly Convention Guide,* June 12, 1964, p. 1140.

The changed position of the lily-white segment of the Democratic party was brilliantly illuminated for all to see.

Technically, the challenge to the seating of the Mississippi delegation came from the Mississippi Freedom Democratic party on the basis of discriminatory voting practices in the state of Mississippi and of disloyalty of the delegates elected on that basis. In response, the regular Democratic party delegates maintained that the regular party had pledged to put Johnson's name on the ballot and thus had complied with the loyalty requirements. Moreover, they argued, the MFDP had not held elections throughout the state and thus its delegates were not representative of the Democratic party. The compromise that ensued retained the majority of the southern delegates without antagonizing the Negro vote. The credentials committee decided: (1) regular Democratic party delegates would be seated if each member signed a personal loyalty pledge (complying with the party rule in cases of credentials contests that a delegate would be seated after stating his position as a member of the party); (2) two of the MFDP delegates would be seated at large with one vote each (this rule pertained only to the 1964 convention); (3) the rest of the MFDP members would be welcomed as "honored guests" of the convention; and (4) a recommendation would be submitted for the 1968 Democratic convention outlining an additional loyalty requirement of nondiscrimination in the states. Upon adoption by voice vote of the credentials committee report on Mississippi, the two MFDP delegates were seated (not with the Mississippi delegation) and all but three of the Mississippi delegates refused to take the loyalty pledge, left the convention, and returned home.

A second contest involved the Alabama delegates, whose credentials were challenged on the ground that the state party would not comply with the loyalty obligation. The basis for this was the election, at the same May primary in which the delegates were selected, of a slate of unpledged presidential electors (strongly backed by Governor George Wallace) to appear under the Democratic symbol on the ballot in the November general election, thus depriving President Johnson, the party's nominee, of a place on the ballot. The credentials committee decided that the seating of the Alabama delegation would be contingent upon individual signing of a loyalty oath, which would pledge each delegate to support the convention nominees and to attempt to induce the presidential electors to cast their votes for the party's candidates. The Alabama delegation reacted in the same manner as the Mississippi delegation, leaving only eleven out of 53 delegates or alternates who signed the pledge and participated actively in the convention.

An indication of a possible change in the loyalty oath came with the request that the loyalty oath be administered to all the delegates. Despite a "no additional assurances" phrase contained in the convention call, on August 25 Representative John McCormack of Massachusetts, permanent chairman of the convention, asked all delegates in the hall to take a pledge similar to the one requested of the Mississippi and Alabama delegations, as a condition of being seated, indicating their support of the party nominees by rising. The vast majority did so. (No official count was taken.)

The Conventions as Party Rallies

On the day before the opening of the Republican convention, Senator Goldwater's headquarters announced that he had 739 votes, nearly 100 more than the 655 required to win the nomination on the first ballot. He looked like a sure thing, and few observers of any objectivity would have quarreled with his estimate. The stage seemed set, then, for a week of harmony and love feasts, a toast to the successful candidate, of scourges and threats for the Democratic opposition, of Republicans girding for battle by asking for the support of fellow Republicans. Then the delegates would head for home and the hustings, heads high, hearts filled with hope, pledged to fight as brothers for their candidates until victory. That something like this did not happen seemed almost incredible to seasoned observers of conventions. Event after event, however, finally bore in upon them the conclusion that the Goldwater tribe represented a new breed of politicians, or perhaps they were not politicians at all. The affronts to the defeated wing of the party, an important and substantial wing, became too deliberate and sharp to be accidental; and there was besides an ambiance about the Cow Palace that bespoke a victory soured in the achievement of it, a disbelief that victory had come at last, and a churlish and paranoid desire for vengeance rather than for accommodation and a closing of ranks against the Democrats. There was disappointment in everything. Aside from the well-paced and well-organized (but ill-fitting) keynote speech of Governor Mark Hatfield of Oregon, the proceedings at San Francisco had a *noli-me-tangere* aspect, visible nationally in the rough reception given Governors Rockefeller and Romney during the debate on the platform,[20] and in the nominee's acceptance speech, but in full

[20] What purports to be an eyewitness account of what went on in the trailer outside the Cow Palace has it that when a Goldwater aide, Clif White, heard the booing of Governor Rockefeller, he immediately called all stations within the Cow Palace and asked them to silence anyone in their vicinity who was booing. He received the report that the booing came not from the floor, but from the galleries. It was pinpointed, and runners were dispatched to attempt to bring it under control. *New York Times,* July 16, 1964.

In light of the impression made by the Goldwater convention on those who observed it, especially on television, these instructions to the delegates emanating from Goldwater headquarters are very interesting:

DO be friendly and courteous to everyone,

DO be very thoughtful and careful when talking to anyone representing the press . . .

DON'T boo anyone or anything.

view of on-the-spot observers most of the week. Before the television cameras the victorious faction made the handful of Negro delegates and alternates so uncomfortable, and so obviously unwanted, that they considered a walkout.[21] All this was made explicit in Goldwater's acceptance speech:

> Anyone who joins us in all sincerity we welcome. Those, those who do not care for our cause, we don't expect to enter our ranks in any case. And let our Republicanism so focused and so dedicated not be made fuzzy and futile by unthinking and stupid labels.
>
> I would remind you that extremism in the defense of liberty is no vice.
>
> And let me remind you also that moderation in the pursuit of justice is no virtue.

The wounds opened in San Francisco were not cured by a meeting of party bigwigs at Hershey, Pennsylvania, several weeks later and, indeed, continued to harass the Republican party and its candidate throughout the election campaign and afterward.

By contrast, the celebration in Atlantic City had all the harmony of "Naughty Marietta," with the same depth of plot and much of the same triteness. From the moment of the keynote speech by Senator John C. Pastore of Rhode Island, however, it was clear that the enemy lay outside the party in the shape of the Republicans, and within the convention hall there was nothing but love for fellow Democrats. Just as a happy marriage rarely makes news, a novel, or a play, the harmonious convention did not make news. After the second day, it was obvious that things were beginning to pall; the President had attempted to induce interest by keeping his choice of running mate a secret. He began to liven things up by putting in a personal appearance and suc-

[21] See *Election '64*, p. 18, for documentation on physical attacks on Negro delegates on the convention floor.

ceeded at the end in focusing the attention of the television cameras on the proceedings of the convention. In the final session, all television personnel and equipment were barred from the convention floor, leaving very little for the cameras to focus on except the rostrum. The decision to banish the ubiquitous television interviewer suited the purposes of the President, though, fortunately, secret service and security needs could take the responsibility. Thus, viewers and most spectators in convention hall did not know that six Freedom Democrats remained throughout the evening in the space reserved previously for the regular Mississippi Democrats (who had left Atlantic City) surrounded by a group of white men, convention officials, to prevent enlargement of the Freedom delegation or other disturbance. For one evening only the rostrum held the center of the video set. Many people thought it an improvement. With eulogies to the party's fallen heroes, John F. Kennedy and Mrs. Eleanor Roosevelt, with an animated acceptance speech by the vice-presidential candidate attacking the Republican nominee vigorously and humorously, and in spite of a tediously expansive acceptance speech by the President, the crowd left convention hall on the upswing, ready for the long hard pull to November 3.[22]

The Impact of Television

In 1964 television had an impact on the organization of the conventions that went beyond matters of adaptation, such as controlling the length of demonstrations, the number and length of speeches, to affecting matters of form with tactical

[22] Richard H. Rovere, "Letter from Atlantic City," *New Yorker,* Vol. 40 (Sept. 5, 1964), p. 112.

implications.[23] For example, the Republicans, in their anxiety to conserve prime television viewing time, recombined the roles of temporary chairman and keynote speaker into one person. Moreover, at a critical point in the Republican convention, in order to delay the controversy over the platform until such time as most television viewers in the East and Midwest would have gone to bed, a decision was made to present President Eisenhower earlier than he had been scheduled to appear and to read the entire proposed Republican platform word for word.[24] Both parties employed experienced television executives as their program directors.

The New Jersey delegation, playing host at Atlantic City, found itself assigned choice seats up front but out of sight of the rostrum or even the large movie screen behind the rostrum because of the huge platform erected in the middle of the convention floor to hold television equipment and reporters. After protest, they were moved.

Perhaps understandably television often yielded to the impulse to cover itself, notably in the memorable shot of a newsman being carried from the convention floor at San Francisco after the manner of a nonviolent demonstrator. In the search for news, the television newsmen hooked upon every rumor, every stray breeze, every scent of controversy, and at times blew these wisps of difference out of all proportion. About the time that it was becoming perfectly apparent that the Mississippi Freedom Democrat compromise was acceptable to all but a tiny handful of the delegates (and these were restricted to the Mississippi and Alabama delegations), television reporters accosting David Lawrence, chair-

---

[23] Much of the information which follows is drawn from a paper by Herbert Waltzer, "In the Magic Lantern: Television Coverage of the 1964 National Conventions." Professor Waltzer was an Eagleton-NCEP Fellow at the 1964 Democratic Convention and also attended the Republican Convention as an observer.

[24] The platform session of the Republican convention did not wind up until 4:30 a.m. Eastern Daylight Time.

man of the credentials committee, in search of controversy drew from him the rebuke, "That's a damned stupid question."

But any medium which can bring the proceedings of a political convention to 83 million viewers, as was the case with the 1964 Republican convention, or gather for one session 41 million viewers, as for the third session of the Democratic convention, is a force to be reckoned with. What appears to be happening in the long run is that the parties are gradually yielding to the demands of the medium and making their conventions telegenic, planning and programming them so as to use the free television time to kick off the campaign. More and more the serious work, the often delicate work, of forming the essential party coalition, of reaching agreement on basic issues, selecting the candidates, and determining the strategy of the campaign goes on during the period immediately preceding the convention, before the cameras and cables and personnel necessary for television have been brought to the convention city and placed in operation.

The Future of Conventions

If this assessment of the long-term influence of television on conventions is correct or near the mark, it is consonant also with what appears to be a development of convention style, or better, approaches to the nomination. The 1960 Democratic convention and the 1964 Republican convention seemed to suggest, as James Reston has said, that "an attractive, industrious, single-minded man can slowly gather enough delegates in party conventions and caucuses to put himself within reach of the nomination, if only his opponents do not organize from the beginning to stop him." [25] That is to say,

25 *New York Times,* July 15, 1964.

at any given time, especially in the minority party in any state, there are probably enough vacant local party posts which can be quietly taken up by the supporters of an individual candidate to gain a considerable voice in party councils.

Such an effort, combined with a genuine attempt to curry favor with party leaders throughout the country and success in at least one important primary, may add up to a successful assault on the presidential nomination from outside the convention. When everybody competes in the same fashion, however, the situation is bound to become more complicated. Decisions which are now made by the rules, credentials, and platform committees during the week before the convention meets and which are now accepted without much regard to the representativeness of the committees, may become subject to serious question.

Thus, the politicians—Kennedy, Nixon, and Goldwater— have done what political scientists have shrunk from suggesting. They have devised a substitute for the national party convention as a means of selecting presidential candidates. Whether the new method is better, more democratic, more rational than what it displaced, is problematic; it is more expensive, more modern (principally in its use of the techniques of communication and the pointing of the conventions to television), more complicated, more independent of local domination. It is not more open, and seems no more susceptible to popular control, though popularity demonstrated in an important presidential primary is one ingredient in the new scheme. If there are smoke-filled rooms, they exist far from the convention city and meetings in them take place before the convention assembles. Will the new form last? When competition takes place along similar lines among several candidates within a given party, all of whom arrive at convention city strong but not in control, will the convention be restored? [26]

The new convention seems a further trend toward the nationalization of American politics. A candidate who is known nationally, more likely a senator than a governor, will stand a better chance of securing a nomination by this route.

In the past the national conventions served to balance the ticket and come up with candidates who could satisfy most of the factions of their parties and prevent them from splintering during the hard-fought election campaigns. To be sure, the system did not always work this way, the conventions of 1912 and 1924 providing examples. But the old pros, it might be argued, were unburdened by any ideological preconceptions and had a vested interest in selecting a candidate who would do their party the most good (or hurt it the least) back home. The new pros lay less stress on such considerations in their single-minded assault on the presidential nomination from outside the convention, with important and sometimes drastic consequences for their parties and for the political system.

The nationalizing trend continued in other directions, also, especially visible in the Republican party which in 1964 broke from its dependence upon the East and successfully invaded the Deep South. It must be admitted that the party lost considerably at the state and local level in what

26 Is such an approach to the nomination new? It bears a superficial resemblance to Jefferson and Madison's "botanical expedition" of the preconvention era. Among more recent efforts to secure the nomination from the outside, or by weaning delegates from leaders, the spadework of James A. Farley in 1932 on behalf of Franklin D. Roosevelt and the whirlwind campaign of Wendell Willkie in 1940 may be closer. Yet Donald B. Johnson has written of the latter: "The entire movement truly became 'an uprising of the people' such as the nation had never before seen. If anyone was directing it, it was not apparent then, and it has been neither proved nor admitted since 1940." *The Republican Party and Wendell Willkie* (University of Illinois Press, 1960), pp. 80-81. Farley attempted to enlist 1,000 potential delegates; he was frustrated by favorite-son strategies of several states, and while Roosevelt went into the Chicago convention with the support of a majority of delegates, he did not have the then necessary two-thirds.

might be called the unfanatic South, Florida and North Carolina, for example. And it all but cut itself off absolutely from the votes of Negroes. By the same token, the Democratic party cast off the southern bond, perhaps for good; at any rate, it needs in the future to take seriously inside the party only those moderate national elements in the Democratic parties of southern states.

Many of these reflections, however, apply with peculiar force only to the out-party. The Republicans may be taking on characteristics long associated with the Democratic party, but genuinely belonging to a minority party. One may expect that so long as the Democrats occupy the White House a rather high degree of control will be exercised over the convention in the shaping of the platform, the naming of the candidates, and other details, even though this control may be severely challenged no later than 1972. In the disarray that greets the observer of the Republican scene in 1966, there is still hope, for a major political party is a protean organization, not easily destroyed, even when it seems dominated by the death-wish. Yet for the Republicans the danger clearly is that for a generation or more they may flounder in minority status, plagued by all the Democratic weaknesses of the past—factionalism, bitter fights, interminable ballots, open disagreements openly arrived at, the prey of adventurers willing to work four long hard years to gain a nomination almost certain to meet defeat.

2

The Presidential Campaign

STANLEY KELLEY, JR.

The 1964 Republican campaign for the Presidency was conceived and conducted in defiance of a widely accepted view of the realities of American politics. That view has been succinctly put by the late V.O. Key:

> Each party leadership must maintain the loyalty of its own standpatters; it must also concern itself with the great blocks of voters uncommitted to either party as well as with those who may be weaned away from the opposition. These influences tend to pull the party leaderships from their contrasting anchorages toward the center. In that process, perhaps most visible in presidential campaigns, the party appeals often sound much alike . . .[1]

In 1964 things did not happen quite that way. Senator Barry Goldwater, who had pledged himself to offer the American people "a choice, not an echo," won the Republican nomination on July 15. For the first time in many years the country faced the prospect of a campaign which would pit against each other candidates apparently committed to radically different philosophies of government.

[1] V. O. Key, Jr., *Politics, Parties, and Pressure Groups* (Thomas Y. Crowell, 1964), p. 220.

What followed was important not only because it ended in so decisive a victory for the Democratic forces of Lyndon Baines Johnson, but also because it affords us an opportunity to reexamine, in the light of experience, some of our assumptions about the way leaders of major parties "must" act, and what happens when they do not act that way. At the very least, the events of the 1964 presidential campaign suggest some conclusions about the problems that beset a minority party, about difficulties that attend efforts to realign forces in party politics, and about the forms assumed by political discussion in a campaign where voters are given a "real choice."

Before any opinions on these issues are given, however, it is useful to review the facts of the case—in this instance particularly, for to date there has been far more agreement on what the Goldwater experiment proved than on what it was. In telling the story of the 1964 campaign, I will discuss some of those features of the situation immediately preceding the campaign that established the terms on which the rival camps would have to compete; outline the strategies that each side had settled on as the campaign opened, insofar as those strategies may be discerned; and identify the events of the campaign itself that modified the expectations and conduct of the campaigners.

The Precampaign Situation

In the spring of 1964 virtually every factor known to be related in an important way to the outcome of elections favored a landslide victory for Lyndon Johnson.

Voters who considered themselves Democrats far outnumbered those who considered themselves Republicans. Dr. George Gallup put the ratio at over 2 to 1;[2] the University of Michigan's Survey Research Center reported it to be about 5 to 3.[3] Moreover, while some 24 percent of the nation's voters felt themselves to be strong Democrats, only 11 percent felt themselves to be strong Republicans.[4]

The federal government was in Democratic hands. Democratic majorities in Congress meant, among other things, that the Republicans could not use congressional investigatory powers to generate and publicize facts or allegations damaging to the Johnson candidacy. The party's control of the executive branch put vast research facilities at the disposal of Democratic campaigners. Because Lyndon Johnson was the incumbent President, he had the heightened ability to command respect, attract attention, and order events that accrues to any Chief Executive.

Democrats held about two-thirds of the governorships, controlled the majority of state legislatures, and held the office of mayor in considerably more than half the nation's large cities. The Democratic party almost certainly, therefore, had patronage resources and resources in disposable favors superior to those available to the Republican party.

President Johnson stood very high in public favor, far higher than his opponent. His handling of his job was approved by 74 percent of the voters and disapproved by only 13 percent.[5] He was, much more than Senator Barry Goldwater, a known quantity to voters.[6] Johnson's image was that

[2] American Institute of Public Opinion (AIPO), press release, July 5, 1964.

[3] Data made available to the author, courtesy of the Survey Research Center, University of Michigan.

[4] See below, Chap. 8, Table 8.11, p. 278.

[5] AIPO press release, June 11, 1964.

[6] Seventeen percent of the voters thought they knew a great deal about the President, 59 percent thought they knew a fair amount, and 25 percent thought they knew very little. The comparable figures for Senator Goldwater were 10 percent, 41 percent, and 49 percent. The sources for these figures are exhibits 10 and 11 in "Public Opinion Trends . . . Their Meaning for the Republican Party," a mimeographed report prepared by Opinion Research Corporation of Princeton, New Jersey, at the request of the Republican National Committee staff and presented to the Republican National Committee at a meeting in Chicago, Jan. 22-23, 1965.

of a "warm and friendly person with good judgment," who was "progressive and forward looking"; relatively few voters credited the Senator with these qualities, although many did see him as a man of strong convictions, willing to speak his mind.[7] Johnson's "enthusiasm quotient" (E.Q.) was 59, Goldwater's 21.[8] In the period between President John F. Kennedy's assassination and Goldwater's nomination, no Republican leader won the support of more than 30 percent of the voters in Gallup poll trial heats against Johnson.[9] The first Gallup poll after Goldwater's nomination showed Johnson leading Goldwater, 59 percent to 31 percent, with 10 percent of the voters undecided.[10]

Mass opinion on issues of public policy favored Johnson and the Democrats. Large numbers of voters thought that racial antagonism or the international situation posed the most serious of the nation's problems.[11] Johnson's handling of racial problems was approved by 57 percent of the voters and disapproved by 21 percent (the comparable figures for southern voters alone were 36 percent and 39 percent).[12] Thirty-four percent of voters thought the Democrats more likely than the Republicans to keep the United States out of World War III, as compared to 21 percent who thought the Republicans the better guardians of peace.[13] The Democrats

---

[7] *Ibid.*

[8] AIPO press release, June 16, 1964. E.Q., as defined in Dr. Gallup's poll, is that percentage of persons who, on a ten-point scale ranging from "extremely favorable" to "extremely unfavorable," give a candidate at least a "highly favorable" rating. The E.Q. ratings for Richard Nixon and John F. Kennedy at the start of the 1960 campaign were 48 and 42 respectively. See Paul T. David (ed.), *The Presidential Election and Transition 1960-1961* (Brookings Institution, 1961), pp. 58-59.

[9] In one trial heat Henry Cabot Lodge won the support of just 30 percent of those polled. AIPO press release, April 18, 1964.

[10] AIPO press release, Aug. 6, 1964.

[11] AIPO press release, May 19, 1964.

[12] AIPO press release, May 23, 1964.

[13] AIPO press release, March 4, 1964.

were favored to keep the nation prosperous, and by a very large margin.[14]

Finally, the Republicans had come to the San Francisco convention badly divided and had left it so. After the convention the discourtesies to Governor Nelson Rockefeller in the course of the fight over the platform and Senator Goldwater's pronouncement on the virtue of extremism remained with moderate Republican leaders as irritating memories, and many of the moderates appeared to be unready to commit themselves to anything but nominal support of their party's candidate. Superficially, the situation was like that immediately following the Republican convention of 1952, when Senator Robert A. Taft had shown an initial reluctance to give an unequivocal pledge of support for General Dwight D. Eisenhower's candidacy. But there was an important difference. In 1952, anti-Eisenhower, conservative Republicans had nowhere to go; in 1964, anti-Goldwater moderates were not similarly restricted.

This state of affairs left little to feed the hopes of Senator Goldwater's followers, but it did leave something. A significant number of potential Republican votes might be turned into actual ones by determined efforts at the grass roots. The electorate's highly favorable estimate of Johnson could change, if sufficient publicity were given the President's alleged involvement in the shady operations of Robert G. (Bobby) Baker and others.[15] If Governor George Wallace of Alabama could be prevailed upon to abandon his candidacy for the Presidency, the support of southern Democratic leaders might be won for Goldwater. The Democratic ad-

---

[14] *Ibid.*

[15] At the beginning of the campaign 21 percent of the voters thought President Johnson was "too much of a politician," 16 percent thought he would promise "anything to get votes," 12 percent thought him too willing to compromise, and 7 percent cited him as "known for shady deals." "Public Opinion Trends . . . Their Meaning for the Republican Party," exhibit 16.

vantage might be dissipated by events: some new scandal might outrage voters; or an incident in one of the world's trouble spots could reveal (or seem to reveal) fatal mismanagement of foreign affairs; or race riots in the North could suddenly inflate northern white opposition to the civil rights policies of the Kennedy-Johnson administration. These possibilities made the election of Barry Goldwater conceivable, and they were real enough to figure importantly in the calculations of both Republican and Democratic strategists.

The Republican Strategy

Although there have been extensive accounts of the Republican strategy, they have been conflicting. What Republican campaigners did, however, makes fairly evident most of the basic elements of the strategy that guided their activities.

In the first place, plans called for a drive to identify those who were disposed to vote for Senator Goldwater and to get them to the polls.[16] The techniques employed—recruiting volunteers; setting vote quotas, precinct by precinct; and organizing extensive door-to-door canvassing and telephoning campaigns—had been tested in Goldwater's fight to win the California primary. The Republican drive to get out the vote assumed impressive proportions in the two months before election day. Dr. Gallup reported Republican workers to have reached some 12.2 million households by the middle of October, about four million more than the Democrats had reached. He estimated that the Republicans had 3.9 million persons working at the grass-roots level during the campaign, compared to a Democratic force of 2.5 million.[17]

[16] See the *New York Times,* Sept. 6, 1964, for John Grenier's statement announcing the drive.

[17] AIPO press release, Oct. 22, 1964. Cf. Stephen Shadegg, *What Happened to Goldwater?* (Holt, Rinehart and Winston, 1965), pp. 4, 180-81, 201.

Secondly, Republican strategists decided to portray Lyndon Johnson as a politician of dubious ethics, questionable associations, and brutal egoism. One Goldwater speech after another implied that Johnson either condoned or was blind to the cynicism, radicalism, and corruption of his close associates, whom Goldwater termed the President's "curious crew." In one particularly sharp attack, the Senator said:

To Lyndon Johnson, running a country means . . . buying and bludgeoning votes. It means getting a TV monopoly . . . and building a private fortune. It means surrounding himself with companions like Bobby Baker, Billie Sol Estes, Matt McCloskey and other interesting men. . . . It means craving and grasping for power—more and more and more, without end.[18]

Not in a great many years has a candidate for President described his rival in terms so personally derogatory. Usually a presidential candidate leaves disparagement of his opponent's character to others.

What Goldwater said about himself was calculated to give additional force to this attack on the President. The Senator presented himself as a straightforward and principled man, one who felt deeply that public service was too important to be left to the politicians. "What does *politics,* the ward heeler politics of something for everyone," he asked on one occasion, "have to do with the American Presidency?" [19] On another occasion he explained why he had gone to down-and-out West Virginia to speak against the "phony war" on poverty: "If I had to cater to every special interest in the country to get elected, I wouldn't want the job. . . . I, for one, am an ordinary mortal who cannot bring himself to

---

[18] Republican National Committee (RNC) press release, transcript of speech at Pikesville, Md., Oct. 21, 1964.

[19] RNC press release, transcript of address, ABC telecast, Oct. 9, 1964 (former Vice President Nixon appeared with Senator Goldwater on this telecast).

make these unkeepable promises." [20] Goldwater's nonpoliti-
cal pose was similar to the one which former President Eisenhower had frequently adopted; and in a televised conversation with the Republican candidate, the former President put
into words the image of Goldwater that Republican propa-
gandists were trying to project: "Now certainly the country
recognizes you," he said, "as a man of integrity, of goodwill,
honesty and dedication to his country." [21]

Republican propaganda made Johnson and Goldwater ac-
tors in a drama with a social message and a political point.
"There is a stir in the land," said the Senator. "There is a
mood of uneasiness . . . Why do we see wave after wave of
crime in our streets and in our homes? . . . A breakdown of
the morals of our young people? . . . A flood of obscene
literature? Corruption around our highest offices? . . . The
moral fiber of the American people is beset by rot and de-
cay." [22] These evils were attributed at times to "the philosophy of modern liberalism," and at times to the bad example of those in high places, including, presumably, the
President.[23] What did the Senator propose to do? "We want

[20] RNC press release, transcript of speech at Madison Square Garden,
New York City, Oct. 26, 1964.

[21] RNC press release, transcript of General Eisenhower-Senator Goldwater "Conversation at Gettysburg," NBC telecast, Sept. 22, 1964.

[22] RNC press release, transcript of speech at the Tabernacle, Salt Lake
City, Utah, Oct. 10, 1964.

[23] Russell Walton, public relations director of the Citizens for Goldwater-Miller, put the objective of Republican use of the so-called morality issue as follows: "We find that there are three major issues in this
campaign. (1) The nuclear syndrome. (2) The cost of living. (3) The
whole moral issue, juvenile delinquency, crime, violence, immorality in
government, immorality in the highest places, influence peddling. How
do we get back? We want to make them angry. Of immediate importance is the threat involved, the fact that they have to lock their doors at
night . . . We want to incite the people to feel that Lyndon Johnson is
incapable of coping with these problems because of the Bobby Baker
scandal, because of the Billie Sol Estes affair, because of the $14 million
that was made while he was on the public payroll, because of the
McCloskey kickbacks . . ." Transcript of an informal conference held at
the Beverly Carlton Hotel, Beverly Hills, Calif., Sept. 22, 1964. This

lights turned *on* in the White House," he told one campaign audience, "lights of honesty, lights of leadership." [24]

A third basic element in Republican plans for the cam-paign was the so-called southern strategy. The National Draft Goldwater Committee had circulated a highly publi-cized exposition of this scheme in the spring of 1963. At this early date, the committee claimed that the 128 electoral votes of the eleven southern states could be won for Gold-water in a Goldwater-Kennedy race. Among the fourteen states the committee was willing to concede to Kennedy were New York, Pennsylvania, New Jersey, and Michigan— all states which are usually hotly contested by both parties, and three of which had Republican governors in 1964. In-deed, the Draft Goldwater Committee wrote off the entire Northeast, except for Maine, Vermont, and New Hamp-shire; treated California as doubtful; and still found more than enough electoral votes to put Barry Goldwater in the White House.[25]

By the spring of 1964 the southern strategy had been substantially modified. Senator Goldwater and his advisers abandoned earlier notions of forsaking voters in the big northeastern industrial states. "Let's face it," the *Wall Street Journal* quoted him as saying, "that's where the people live . . . . I go for this attitude: Go shooting where the ducks are,

---

document was circulated by the Democratic National Committee during the campaign, but its authenticity was confirmed by Mr. Walton. It consisted of a verbatim report of a discussion of the aims and content of the documentary film, "Choice," which was to be used to dramatize the morality issue. The film was produced and scheduled for a showing on NBC television, but Senator Goldwater vetoed its release. The Senator was reported to have thought it "racist."

[24] RNC press release, transcript of speech at Milwaukee Arena, Mil-waukee, Wis., Oct. 13, 1964.

[25] For the best summation of the Draft Goldwater statement see Robert D. Novak, *The Agony of the G.O.P. 1964* (Macmillan, 1965), pp. 135-37.

where the people live." [26] The *Journal's* account of the Senator's intentions checks well with later events.[27] The states that claimed the greatest amounts of his scheduled time—collectively, about 55 percent—were California, Texas, Ohio, Illinois, Pennsylvania, New York, and New Jersey, in that order.[28] It is reasonable to assume that they were also the principal geographical targets of the overall effort on the Senator's behalf, insofar as this was controlled by his headquarters organization.[29] A presidential candidate's time is a

[26] *Wall Street Journal,* July 17, 1964.

[27] Not all accounts do. A *U.S. News and World Report* story on Republican strategy listed 28 states counted on by Republican strategists to provide them with the electoral votes needed for victory. If the story reported Republican intentions accurately, the Goldwater campaign was monumentally irrational, since more than half of Senator Goldwater's campaigning was done in states not among those listed. See *U.S. News and World Report,* July 20, 1964, pp. 37-40. The account of the 1964 campaign written by the staff of the *New York Times* includes a statement that Republican strategy involved "virtually writing off the big states that most candidates had traditionally contested most fiercely in the past: New York, New Jersey, Pennsylvania, and Michigan." Harold Faber (ed.), *The Road to the White House* (McGraw-Hill, 1965), p. 141. Senator Goldwater's schedule called for him to spend about 17 percent of his time in these four states, however, and Pennsylvania, New York, and New Jersey were among the seven states that consumed the largest amounts of his scheduled time, ranking fifth, sixth, and seventh respectively. Theodore H. White also reports that the Republican strategy called for Pennsylvania and New York "to be kissed off"; *The Making of the President 1964* (Atheneum, 1965), p. 316.

[28] Figures on the scheduling of campaign time for the presidential and vice-presidential candidates were derived from hour-by-hour schedules provided through the courtesy of Jack Valenti, aide to President Johnson; Ronald Stinnett, aide to Vice President Humphrey; and the Republican National Committee. The figures account only for time actually spent in campaigning in a state and do not include noncampaigning activities such as sleeping. In the case of the few days for which exact hour-by-hour schedules were not available, estimates were made on the basis of *New York Times* reports on the candidates' schedules and of patterns revealed by the hour-by-hour schedules themselves. Time spent in the District of Columbia was not included in the calculations since almost none of it was out-and-out campaigning. I am indebted to Melvin M. M. Masuda, Yale Law School, for assembling this data.

[29] In Representative William Miller's schedules as in Senator Goldwater's, for example, California, Pennsylvania, Ohio, New York, and Texas were among the states claiming the largest amounts of campaign time.

scarce resource. Given a modicum of rationality on the part of the strategists of a presidential campaign, the way the candidate's time is distributed among the states should reflect, at least roughly, the allocation of the other scarce campaign resources which can be transferred from state to state—money, for example.

The amount of attention Senator Goldwater eventually gave to New York, Pennsylvania, New Jersey, and other highly urbanized states suggests that the southern strategy, 1964 model, was designed not only to win the votes of southern whites but also to capitalize on the resentment of the civil rights movement by northern whites. The southern strategy had become, in other words, a southern-backlash strategy.[30] The Senator's stance on the civil rights issue is stronger evidence for the same conclusion. He assigned primary responsibility for handling "problems of social relations" to "the people" and to the governmental level closest to the people. This position had been envisioned as an essential feature of the southern strategy from its inception, and many southern whites doubtless found it a lesser evil than the position taken by Johnson.[31] Two other frequent themes of Goldwater's speeches, however, seemed designed primarily for the ears of northern whites. The Senator opposed bussing children out of their neighborhoods "for the sake of achieving 'racial balance' "[32] in the schools, and he denounced political leaders who had sought "political advan-

---

[30] Jerry Landauer observed that the civil rights issue was handled by the Republicans in a manner roughly comparable to John F. Kennedy's handling of the Catholic issue in 1960. Kennedy never asked explicitly for the Catholic vote but he "plotted the route of his campaign appearances in a way well designed to get it." Similarly, Goldwater had "no need to call the attention of disturbed white folk to himself" and was "bound to get whatever 'backlash' vote there may be" because of his vote against the Civil Rights Act of 1964. *Wall Street Journal*, July 17, 1964.

[31] Novak, *op. cit.*, p. 63.

[32] RNC press release, transcript of speech, Cleveland, Ohio, Oct. 27, 1964.

tages by turning their eyes from riots and violence." [33] This latter remark, and others like it, were widely taken to refer to the rioting of Negroes in New York and other eastern cities and to imply hostility toward demonstrations as well as riots. The conservatism of Goldwater's civil rights stand was moderated only by his stated opposition to racial discrimination as such and his pledge (voiced infrequently) to enforce the 1964 Civil Rights Act.

The southern-backlash strategy was a break with the Republican past, but an understandable one, given the circumstances confronting the party's candidate in 1964. Four years earlier, Richard Nixon had gone after the votes of both southern whites and northern Negroes. In 1960, however, there had been no third presidential candidate willing and able to make a strong appeal to southern segregationist sentiment. In 1964, there was. The Republicans could not, with realism, hope to find a civil rights stand that would attract the support of northern Negroes without losing the votes of segregationists in the South either to Governor George Wallace or to President Johnson. The Republican party had to choose. The party's chances to win the votes of northern Negroes were poor, whoever its candidate might be. Negroes could be expected to give a large percentage of their votes to Lyndon Johnson both because the President had sponsored the Civil Rights Act of 1964 and because he promised to continue and extend the federal welfare programs identified with the Democratic party. The Republicans were in a better position to win the votes of southern whites. Considerable numbers of southerners were not simply segregationist but were also conservative in their views on issues of economic and welfare policy.

As originally formulated, the southern strategy seems to have appealed to Senator Goldwater's backers for reasons

[33] RNC press release, transcript of nationwide address, ABC telecast, Oct. 22, 1964.

substantially like those just offered.[34] It became even more attractive when surveys of opinion and Governor Wallace's unexpectedly strong showing in the Wisconsin, Indiana, and Maryland primaries demonstrated the existence of strong anti-civil rights sentiment in the North. In 1963 the Draft Goldwater Committee was ready to count on the electoral votes of the southern states, while conceding those of Michigan and the larger states of the Northeast, because it had assumed that a conservative stance on civil rights would lose votes in industrial areas. With the wildfire spread of Negro demonstrations, this view began to appear unduly pessimistic. It seemed possible, early in 1964, that a conservative civil rights stand would be productive of votes in North and South alike.

A fourth major strategy decision was implicit in Senator Goldwater's prenomination promise to offer voters "a choice, not an echo." This meant redefining Republicanism to sharpen its differences from New Deal and post-New Deal Democracy, and attacking assumptions basic to administration policies, both foreign and domestic. The Senator ruled out, or seemed to rule out, any move toward accommodation with Communist governments, counting even Franklin Roosevelt's recognition of the Soviet Union as an act inspired by the false theory that Communist hostility could be placated.[35] Republican policy under Goldwater would be one of "peace through preparedness," of standing up to Communist efforts to push America around. Communist reversals, he told American Legion members, "have been brought about by the use or threatened use of military forces." [36] He found the Kennedy-Johnson policies with respect to Cuba, Vietnam, Berlin, Laos, the Congo, and toward weapons de-

---

[34] See Novak, *op. cit.,* pp. 60-65.

[35] RNC press release, transcript of speech at National American Legion Convention, Dallas, Texas, Sept. 23, 1964.

[36] *Ibid.*

velopment, trade with Communist nations, and defense expenditures, all examples of a record in foreign affairs of "drift, deceptions, and defeat." [37]

Goldwater's criticism of domestic policy put him into more fundamental opposition to the Democrats than did his foreign policy statements. Like Johnson, Senator Goldwater was for prosperity, encouragement of education, "an expansion of real jobs and real wages," and "a society in which all may be well fed, clothed and housed." [38] Unlike the President, however, Goldwater saw virtually no place for positive governmental action in furthering these aims. The real need, he argued, was to cut the federal government down to size and to free private enterprise from bureaucratic shackles. "Freedom," and programs handled principally at the levels of government closest to the people, were to be the key to progress. In opposing big government, Goldwater attacked not only the administration but the Supreme Court, particularly its decisions with respect to legislative apportionment and prayers in the public schools.

In two important respects the Republican presidential candidate qualified his objections to the domestic policies of the Democrats. He said that the task of cutting the government down to size would proceed with care and that a Republican administration could not in honesty fail to honor "the commitments government has made to all areas of the economy, whether explicit or implicit." [39] He also affirmed repeatedly and in the strongest terms his support of the Social Security system. By doing so, he was undoubtedly trying to recover

---

[37] See, for instance, Goldwater's speeches before the Veterans of Foreign Wars, Municipal Auditorium, Cleveland, Ohio, Aug. 25, 1964; at Peoria, Ill., Oct. 2, 1964; and at Houston, Texas, Oct. 15, 1964.

[38] RNC press release, transcript of speech at Toledo, Ohio, Sept. 30, 1964.

[39] RNC press release, transcript of speech beginning the campaign at Prescott, Ariz., Sept. 3, 1964.

ground lost earlier when he had suggested that participation in Social Security should be voluntary.

What was the basis for the decision to present voters a choice of programs and policies of the sort just described? The reasoning most commonly attributed to the strategists of the Goldwater campaign goes something like this: the Republicans had been defeated in presidential elections after 1936 largely because Republican candidates had failed to propose any genuine alternative to the economic policies and social welfare programs of New Deal Democracy. "Me-too" campaigns had not won the support of liberals, who continued to vote Democratic, and had lost the support of conservatives, who found nothing in the platform of either of the major parties to attract them to the polls. These stay-at-home conservatives would turn out on election day in sufficient numbers to put a Republican in the White House, if, and only if, the Republican party offered them a "real choice," that is, a choice between a conservative Republican program on the one hand and a liberal Democratic program on the other.[40]

That there were some in the Goldwater camp who accepted this diagnosis of Republican ills is doubtless true; that it was taken seriously by all, or even most, of the architects of the Senator's campaign, however, seems unlikely. Some of those in the Goldwater camp were probably quite aware that there was little or no evidence to suggest that stay-at-home conservatives existed in any significant numbers.[41] Furthermore, one did not have to believe in the existence of such a potential conservative vote to conclude that the Republican party, if it wanted to win elections, ought to distinguish its

[40] Cf. Novak, *op. cit.,* p. 62; Faber (ed.), *The Road to the White House,* p. vii; and Robert Donovan, *The Future of the Republican Party* (New American Library, 1964), pp. 58-59.

[41] Robert Novak observes that ". . . hardly anyone could accept the woodwork theory of hidden conservatives, probably not even the conservatives mouthing it." *Op. cit.,* p. 61.

program more sharply from that of the Democrats than it had in the period from 1940 to 1960.

That conclusion could also be reached by reasoning as follows: the Republican party is at a serious competitive disadvantage in presidential races because it lacks manpower for the kind of registration and get-out-the-vote drives that can be mounted by the Democrats and their allies in the trade unions. The Republican party can greatly improve its grassroots organization if it offers potential party workers an ideological incentive, and, given the composition of the party's clientele, such an incentive must be conservative in character. An explicit conservative appeal designed to attract volunteer workers to the Republican standard need not hurt the party at the polls, since the votes that decide presidential elections come mainly from persons who know or care little about issues of public policy. There is evidence for each of the foregoing propositions, and all were current in conservative Republican thought in 1964 and earlier.[42] It is reasonable to suppose, therefore, that they may have played at least as great a part in the thinking of Goldwater's strategists as did the doctrine of a hidden conservative vote.

Two final comments on the strategy of the 1964 Republican presidential campaign are in order. First, it is difficult to ascertain what importance Senator Goldwater and his staff attached to their postconvention efforts to win the support of moderate Republican leaders. The length to which the Senator went to win such support in the two months after the

---

[42] Republican professional politicians have long cited poor organization as one of the chief sources of the party's weakness at the polls. Nixon's defeat in 1960, as Robert Novak notes, was attributed to poor organization by Senator Thruston Morton, then chairman of the Republican National Committee, and other party professionals. See Novak, *op. cit.*, pp. 53-55. Stephen Shadegg, who was closely associated with Senator Goldwater from 1952 to 1962, is one of those who have emphasized the importance of ideological incentives in the recruitment of volunteer workers and the usefulness of volunteer workers in winning the votes of the politically indifferent. See his *How to Win an Election* (Taplinger Publishing Company, 1964), pp. 105-37 *passim*.

Republican convention was in striking contrast to the treatment that the moderates received from the Goldwater forces both earlier and later. Second, it is probable that at least some of the Goldwater inner circle set control of the Republican party—not winning the Presidency—as their principal objective in 1964. That is the implication, certainly, of Senator Goldwater's statement that the conservative cause would be strengthened if he could win as much as 45 percent of the vote.[43] Control of the party, moreover, would have been a reasonable objective for the Senator and his friends, given the political situation in 1964—more reasonable, at least, than the defeat of Lyndon Johnson.

The Democratic Response

Democratic campaign plans, unlike those of the Republicans, seem to have involved no unconventional assumptions about how votes are won, but the result was not a conventional Democratic campaign. The Democratic strategy was a carefully constructed response to the Goldwater experiment and was characterized, therefore, by a kind of mirror-image unorthodoxy. The Goldwater candidacy's imprint on that strategy was particularly evident in the way President Johnson and his running mate defined the choice facing voters.

Johnson declared that the nation was not presented with a choice between parties and that voters were "laying down their partisanship." Certainly the President and Senator Hubert Humphrey very largely abandoned the language of partisanship, with only a few lapses into old habits.[44]

[43] See Shadegg, *What Happened to Goldwater?* p. 8.

[44] The President occasionally predicted that November 3 would be "a great Democratic day" or that the election would see the American people choose "the leadership of the Democratic party." Senator Humphrey's speeches had a somewhat more partisan tone than Johnson's and included some jibes at Republicans. Both Johnson and Humphrey typically had good words to say on behalf of Democratic candidates for Congress and for state and local offices.

The opening speech of the Johnson campaign—his speech on Labor Day in Cadillac Square in Detroit—was without references to either party. Later in the campaign, the President's nonpartisanship was frequently expressed in words of tribute for Republicans and the GOP. He told an audience in Rockford, Illinois:

> I am proud that I have always been the kind of Democrat who could work with my fellow Americans of the party of Lincoln and McKinley, Herbert Hoover and Dwight Eisenhower, Robert Taft and Everett Dirksen.[45]

Senator Humphrey, following the President's lead, urged his Democratic friends to "extend a true hand of friendship and fellowship" to Republicans who put country before party.[46]

Four years earlier the Kennedy-Johnson campaign had been conducted on a very different basis. Kennedy declared then that "no Democratic candidate for President has ever run and said 'Parties don't matter,' because we are proud of our record. We want to be identified with it." [47] Again and again he invoked the name of the Democratic party and attacked the Republican party—with all the greater vigor, undoubtedly, because the Democrats in the electorate so greatly outnumbered the Republicans. The most obvious explanation for President Johnson's failure to follow suit in 1964 is that he hoped to capitalize on the opportunity to win Republican support that postconvention divisions in the opposition's ranks gave him. He may also have felt, however, that a nonpartisan appeal was less risky than a partisan appeal would have been. Early in the campaign Senator Goldwater seemed likely to attract the support of a number of Democrats, possibly a large number, by his civil rights stand. Such

[45] *New York Times,* Oct. 31, 1964.
[46] *New York Times,* Sept. 6, 1964.
[47] David (ed.), *The Presidential Election and Transition 1960-1961,* p. 65.

backlash losses might therefore have to be recouped in "frontlash" gains.[48]

If the Democrats did not try to make the voter choose between parties, they did try to make him choose between policies and between men. President Johnson characterized the administration's program as "prudent" and "progressive." He expressed concern for the interests of group after group, observing that "by strengthening each group, we strengthen the nation." [49] He promised to preserve the nation's military might, and to support "every realistic measure that will bring the world closer to peace." [50] He expressed the hope that he could lead the nation to a "greatness almost within its grasp." [51] No one would count these and other statements of purpose as memorable, and they were probably not intended to be. The Democrats wanted voters to see that the Johnson program involved familiar goals and familiar methods, and it was described, therefore, in familiar words.

The opposition's program was attacked by the Democrats as a rejection of the nation's future, of its past, and, perhaps most important, of concrete benefits enjoyed by its citizens in the present. The President denounced Senator Goldwater's supporters for talking as if nuclear war were inevitable and as if a nuclear bomb "were merely another weapon." [52] Johnson and Humphrey charged that the "factions" supporting Goldwater were against minimum wages, aid to education, farm subsidies, the recently passed tax reduction bill,

---

[48] President Johnson told members of the Democratic National Committee that votes of dissident Republicans would more than compensate for any backlash losses. In reporting his remarks, the *Washington Post* observed: "Mr. Johnson's message to the Party leaders was clear: Don't panic over the backlash talk. Republicans have worse problems. Get to work and scoop up those anti-Goldwater votes." *Washington Post,* Aug. 29, 1964.

[49] *New York Times,* Sept. 8, 1964.

[50] *Ibid.*

[51] *New York Times,* Nov. 1, 1964.

[52] *New York Times,* Oct. 22, 1964.

the fight against poverty, the Tennessee Valley Authority, Social Security, and the test ban treaty. In one summary statement, Johnson called his opposition "contemptuous toward the will of majorities, callous toward the plight of minorities, arrogant toward allies, belligerent toward adversaries, careless toward peace." [53]

Another summation of the case against the Goldwater program was given in television advertising. The Democrats decided, according to one reporter, "to hammer away at the following points: Nuclear responsibility, Social Security . . . and anti-Goldwater Republicanism." [54] One television announcement showed hands tearing a Social Security card in two as a voice explained, "Goldwater has said he would change the system. Even his running mate admits that the voluntary plan would wreck your Social Security." In another spot announcement a little girl plucked petals from a daisy, a voice intoned the countdown for an atomic test, and the picture suddenly dissolved into a shot of a rising mushroom cloud. Then, as "Vote for President Johnson on November 3" appeared on screens, voters were told, "The stakes are too high for you to stay at home."

The Democrats' treatment of Senator Goldwater as a person reinforced their attempt to define the voter's choice as one between policies of an extremist fringe and policies of the bipartisan center. Democratic spokesmen portrayed Goldwater, or a vaguely indicated "opponent," as dangerously impulsive—"reckless," having "more guts than brains," thinking that arguments are to be settled "with a quick draw and a shot from the hip." [55] The Senator was represented as an isolated figure, "one of a few lonely voices." [56] And he was treated, not as the leader of the

[53] *New York Times,* Sept. 11, 1964.
[54] Pete Hamill, "When the Client is a Candidate," *New York Times Magazine,* Oct. 25, 1964, p. 128.
[55] *New York Times,* Oct. 13, 1964.
[56] *New York Times,* Oct. 16, 1964.

Republican party, but as the head of an extremist faction that had captured the Republican party—"the temporary spokesman of a fraction of a faction of reaction." [57]

The attitude that President Johnson took with respect to his opponent merits special comment, because it served so many of the President's purposes so well. In an early discussion of his campaign plans, the President told reporters that he did not intend to deal "in personalities." [58] From that point on, he all but ignored Goldwater, rarely if ever mentioning him by name or even referring to him as "my opponent." The tactic was not original—Presidents Roosevelt and Eisenhower had treated opponents similarly. An announced policy against dealing in personalities, however, permitted Johnson to win whatever sympathy goes to a candidate who does not run his opponent down; to justify virtual silence on issues raised about his own conduct; and to appear all the more convincingly as a "builder" interested in policies and programs. Also, not mentioning names allowed the President to suggest that Senator Goldwater was unworthy of notice, and to say, in what many took to be references to Goldwater, things that might have seemed grossly unfair if said explicitly about the Senator. [59]

The Democrats took steps to minimize the effect of two charges that they rightly expected to face. One was that the Kennedy-Johnson administration had been overly solicitous

[57] *Washington Post,* Oct. 29, 1964.

[58] *New York Times,* Sept. 13, 1964.

[59] For example, in one speech the President issued a vague warning against "a raving, ranting demagogue." It seems likely that a direct statement attacking Senator Goldwater in these terms would have earned the President some editorial demerits. As it was, however, the *New York Times* (Sept. 23, 1964) featured the epithet in the lead sentence of its report, said there was speculation about "how sharply aimed" the words had been, and observed that the President might have worried that his phrase would be "too widely interpreted as an indirect reference to Mr. Goldwater." Thus, while President Johnson made the shoe, he didn't have to suggest whom it might fit: the *New York Times* did that.

of the interests of Negroes. The other was that the President and members of his staff had been engaged in influence-peddling.

The defensive posture assumed on the first of these issues had several features. The President repeatedly identified himself with his fellow southerners: "I know the burdens the South has borne. I know the ordeals that have tried the South all these years." [60] He appealed to feelings that it would be good to have the fight on civil rights over and done with: "Our first work must be to bind our wounds and heal our history—and make this nation whole." [61] He made "the Klan and the Birch Society and those others who preach hate" the villains of the civil rights drama.[62] And he indicated his concern for the preservation of law and order: "No person, whatever his grievances, can be allowed to attack the right of every American to be secure in his home, his shop, and in his streets. . . . Where help is needed, or Federal law is violated, we will be there." [63]

One tactic of the Democratic response to the corruption-in-government issue has been noted already—for the most part the issue was ignored. The President also asked an accounting firm to audit his and his family's holdings, and he put himself on record as backing thorough investigations by Congress and the Federal Bureau of Investigation of the scandal involving Robert G. (Bobby) Baker. In one campaign telecast in which the President answered the questions of a panel of youthful supporters, he made one of his rare public comments on the Bobby Baker case: Baker, he said, had been "a very faithful and dedicated and competent employee" of the Senate majority, and "the matter will be presented to the proper authorities and in our own American

[60] *New York Times,* Oct. 27, 1964.
[61] *New York Times,* Oct. 10, 1964.
[62] *New York Times,* Oct. 13, 1964.
[63] *New York Times,* Aug. 13, 1964.

way—with the sense of justice that we all have—Mr. Baker will be called to account. . . ." [64]

Just as the Democrats showed sensitivity to the special circumstances of 1964 in their principal propaganda themes, so they did also (although less obviously) in choosing the geographical foci of their campaign activities. Over 60 percent of President Johnson's scheduled time went to ten states —New York, California, Illinois, Florida, Ohio, Texas, Louisiana, Tennessee, Michigan and Indiana.[65] He put nearly a third of his time into three of these—New York, California, and Illinois. Senator Humphrey's scheduled time was divided among the states in a similar manner. He devoted just under 30 percent of his time to California, New York, and Illinois; and seven of the ten states that took the greatest amounts of his time were among the ten states that took the greatest amounts of the President's time.

According to Theodore H. White, the Democrats realized immediately after Goldwater's nomination that President Johnson could "design a victory to his own taste," and consequently changed their initial plans to send him to the usual vote-hunting grounds of liberal Democratic presidential candidates.[66] Analysis of Johnson's schedule, however, seems to indicate that the Democratic strategists were both more wary of risks and less bound by precedents set in previous Democratic campaigns than one might suppose from White's account of the matter. The value of campaigning in any given state in any given year is primarily a function of the state's electoral vote and the closeness of the race there,[67] and both these factors should therefore be strongly reflected in any rational allocation of a presidential candidate's time.

<hr />

[64] *New York Times,* Oct. 25, 1964.

[65] The states are listed in rank order. Together they have 229 electoral votes.

[66] White, *op. cit.,* p. 353.

[67] Assuming, that is, that the object of campaigning in presidential elections is to maximize the expected yield of electoral votes.

Both were thus reflected in the scheduling of Johnson's campaign tours. When an index of the expected value of campaigning is constructed to give equal weight to the electoral votes of states and the closeness of the race in each, differences in the amount of Johnson's time allotted to each of the fifty states show a correlation of .8 with interstate variations in the index.[68] Thus, if President Johnson did believe a victory could be designed to taste, his tastes led him, in the main, where prudence and calculation would have taken him also.

Other considerations support the same conclusion. Johnson spent less time in the northeastern states than Kennedy had four years earlier (see Table 2.1). The downgrading of that region by the strategists of the Goldwater campaign would in some measure justify its downgrading by the Democrats also. The President spent more time in the South than Kennedy did, and less time in the Midwest. Johnson was probably at his best as a campaigner before southern audiences—that had been his primary assignment in 1960— and Hubert Humphrey could serve as an effective substitute for him in the midwestern states.[69]

---

[68] The index of the expected utility of campaigning used here was obtained by subtracting from 100 the difference between the vote received by the two presidential candidates in each state (the vote for each expressed as a percentage of the two-party vote) and multiplying the result by the state's electoral vote total.

The .8 correlation between state-by-state differences in this index, on the one hand, and differences in the amount of President Johnson's time assigned to each state, on the other, is significant at the .01 level of confidence.

The correlation between variations in the amount of Senator Goldwater's time allocated to each of the states and variations in state index values was .84, significant at the .01 level of confidence.

[69] Particularly in Minnesota and Wisconsin, both of which received sizable amounts of Senator Humphrey's time. President Johnson spent little time in Wisconsin and none in his running mate's home state of Minnesota.

Table 2.1. Percentage Distribution of Total Campaign Time Scheduled for Democratic Presidential and Vice-Presidential Candidates, 1960 and 1964, by Region [a]

Region	1960		1964	
	Kennedy	Johnson	Johnson	Humphrey
Northeast	36.0	21.0	29.9	19.9
Midwest	33.0	19.5	24.6	38.6
South	15.0	43.4	27.5	21.7
West	16.0	16.1	18.0	19.7
	100.0	100.0	100.0	100.0

Note: Details may not add to totals because of rounding.

[a] Regions are as defined in Paul T. David, Ralph M. Goldman, and Richard C. Bain, *The Politics of National Party Conventions* (Brookings Institution, 1960), App. A, Table 10.

The Course of the Campaign

The initial strategy of a political campaign may be usefully regarded as an investment plan in which the level of investment in the several undertakings is set in accordance with estimates of the likely return in votes from each. Strategists may revise these estimates in the course of a campaign, as reports come in from pollsters and as events work for or against the success of particular ventures. The strategists of the side that is losing are particularly likely to take a second look at their initial decisions and to alter them; thus, a campaign may change its character considerably even while it is in progress. The 1964 Republican presidential campaign is a case in point.

In July and August conditions became—or at least seemed to become—increasingly favorable to the success of the southern-backlash strategy. On July 19 Governor George Wallace of Alabama, apparently under strong pressure from his backers, abandoned his candidacy for the Presidency. By doing so he greatly increased Senator Goldwater's chance to become the political beneficiary of the feeling that the Negro revolution was proceeding too fast and going too far. That feeling was given added force by riots in the Negro ghettos of Harlem, the Bedford-Stuyvesant section of Brooklyn, and Rochester in late July, and in Jersey City, Elizabeth, Paterson, the Chicago suburb of Dixmoor, and North Philadelphia in the month of August. When the Democratic convention opened on August 24, Democratic uneasiness about the possibility of extensive white backlash was probably at its height. In an article entitled "White 'Backlash' Scares Democrats," Robert C. Albright reported on August 30 that one Democratic tactician had said, "Some days I am convinced we are going to win big—I mean by a historic landslide. Then something goes wrong and I cross my fingers. We could be so wrong." [70]

Both the administration and the leaders of the civil rights movement took steps to minimize backlash, and what they did removed some of the tension and attention from relations between Negroes and whites in later stages of the campaign. On July 21, three days after the rioting in Harlem began, President Johnson dispatched two hundred FBI agents to New York City with orders to investigate the causes of the riots there; he took the occasion to state his belief that "American citizens have a right to protection of life and limb—whether driving along a highway in Georgia, a road in Mississippi or a street in New York City." [71] And the President's efforts to tame the civil rights movement for campaign purposes did not stop there. According to Theodore White, "Every form of pressure—political, financial, investigative, and persuasive—was quietly applied to the problem [minimizing white backlash] in maneuvers directed from the White House." [72] The object of these maneuvers

[70] *Washington Post*, Aug. 30, 1964.
[71] *New York Times*, July 22, 1964.
[72] White, *op. cit.*, p. 237.

was to get civil rights groups to abandon "hell-raising" in favor of registration drives.[73] On July 29 four prominent leaders of the civil rights movement did ask for a "broad curtailment, if not total moratorium" of demonstrations until after election day,[74] and a substantial decline in the numbers of organized demonstrations followed in apparent response to their plea.[75] There were also substantial increases in Negro registrations.[76]

The failure of southern Democratic leaders to defect from the Johnson cause in large numbers was a further blow to the southern-backlash strategy. A few maintained silence, a few declared themselves neutral, and others did little to help the national ticket, but there were few outright bolters. On August 16 the *New York Times* had reported that Governors Orville Faubus of Arkansas, George Wallace of Alabama, and Paul Johnson of Mississippi would support Senator Goldwater. Wallace and Johnson did so, but Faubus finally came out for the President, as did six other southern governors. The only bolters in the entire southern congressional delegation were Senator Strom Thurmond of South Carolina, Representative Albert Watson of the same state, and Representative John Bell Williams of Mississippi.

As the President's relations with dissident southerners improved, Senator Goldwater's relations with moderate Republican leaders went from bad to worse. On July 17, two days after the Goldwater nomination, former President Eisenhower declared himself unable to give active support to his party's nominee until Goldwater had explained his (Goldwater's) views on extremism, and the former President was

[73] *Ibid.*

[74] *New York Times,* July 30, 1964.

[75] The *Washington Post* reported that there were not more than 25 organized civil rights demonstrations in the period July 29-October 29, while there had been about 100 in the three-month period immediately preceding; Oct. 29, 1964.

[76] See *Washington Post,* Aug. 3, 1964, and *New York Times,* Oct. 11, 1964.

joined in his decision to "wait and see" by many other prominent Republicans. The Senator and his aides then moved to conciliate the Republican moderates. On July 23 National Chairman Dean Burch sent a letter to Republican state chairmen, soliciting their advice on the conduct of the campaign, and assuring them that they would be consulted on appointments of the state chairmen of the Citizens for Goldwater-Miller organizations. In early August Senator Goldwater, in a letter to Richard Nixon, paraphrased the statement regarding extremism in his acceptance speech, and Nixon expressed satisfaction with the thought in its new form.[77] At a conference of party leaders in Hershey, Pennsylvania, on August 12, which had been arranged at Goldwater's request, the Senator declared the Eisenhower-Dulles foreign policy to be his own, promised to support the United Nations and North Atlantic Treaty Organization, pledged conscientious administration of the Civil Rights Act of 1964, said that he favored strengthening the Social Security system, repudiated the support of extremists, and denied any desire to read anyone out of the Republican party. This speech persuaded General Eisenhower to endorse Goldwater but little seemed to come of it otherwise.

In September and October, more and more Republican leaders took steps to disassociate themselves from the Goldwater candidacy. Those who at first refused to give their endorsement remained adamant,[78] and those who declared their support made it increasingly clear that such support was nominal. Governor Rockefeller was seen pocketing Goldwater buttons offered him, and Governor Scranton,

[77] For Senator Goldwater's original statement, see above, p. 35. In his letter to Nixon he wrote, "If I were to paraphrase the two sentences in question [the last two] . . . I would do it by saying that wholehearted devotion to liberty is unassailable and that half-hearted devotion to justice is indefensible." See *New York Times,* Aug. 11, 1964.

[78] Senator J. Glenn Beall of Maryland was an exception to this rule. He first said that he might find it impossible to endorse Senator Goldwater's candidacy, then came out in support of it on Aug. 1.

who earlier had made several speeches on Goldwater's be-
half, in late October introduced the Senator at a rally not, as
tradition would have it, as "the next President of the United
States," but as "the Republican candidate for President."
Near the end of the campaign even many conservative
Republican candidates for office went it alone.[79]

Republican hopes were buoyed up very briefly by the disclosure on October 14 that Walter Jenkins, President Johnson's chief assistant and an associate of the President's for
many years, had been arrested for indecent acts. The incident both drew attention to and seemed to confirm Senator
Goldwater's charges that the administration was infected by
corruption in the highest circles. Chairman Dean Burch said
that the incident raised grave questions of national security,
while bumper stickers issued by the Republican National
Committee declared, "No Wonder They Turned the Lights
Off at the White House." Chalmers Roberts, writing in the
Washington Post on October 16, described the Johnson staff
as "deeply worried" about the political consequences of the
Jenkins case.

The sudden fall from power of the Soviet Union's Premier Nikita Khrushchev on October 15 and the detonation
of a nuclear device by the Red Chinese one day later, however, relegated the Jenkins story to the inside pages of
newspapers and turned the attention of voters to foreign policy. President Johnson spoke to the nation on the meaning
of these developments and restated, in a nonpartisan context,
one of the basic themes of his campaign: "We must be ready
to defend the national interest and to negotiate the common
interest. . . . Those who test our courage will find it strong,
and those who seek our friendship will find it honorable." [80]

---

[79] See particularly the discussion of the attitude toward the Goldwater
candidacy taken by Republican candidates in the mountain states, *Washington Post,* Sept. 11, 1964.
[80] *New York Times,* Oct. 19, 1964.

A survey taken by the Louis Harris organization after the Jenkins incident, Krushchev's removal, and the Red Chinese nuclear test, showed 60 percent of the voters favoring President Johnson, 34 percent Senator Goldwater, and 6 percent undecided. Only 5 percent of those who told Harris' interviewers that they intended to vote for Johnson said that the revelations about Walter Jenkins had made them think less well of the President.[81]

The Republicans seem to have chosen mid-October, or shortly before, to reassess their strategy. That the possibility of a Goldwater victory had by this time almost evaporated must have been clear from polls commissioned by the Republican National Committee.[82] These showed defeatism to be widespread among Goldwater supporters—only 37 percent of those stating an intention to vote for the Republican candidate thought he would win.[83] In a list of eighteen issues there was but one that voters thought would be better handled by Senator Goldwater than by President Johnson— the Bobby Baker case—and even so, relatively few believed the case incriminated the President in any way.[84] A significant number of voters saw Goldwater as a radical; few saw Johnson as such. Over one-third of the public believed the Senator to be opposed to Social Security, despite his many

[81] *Washington Post,* Oct. 23, 1964.

[82] Stephen Shadegg has written, "For all his faults . . . Goldwater is a perceptive politician. It is difficult for anyone who has known and worked with the Senator to believe that he was unaware of impending defeat. Indeed, in many of his speeches following October 10 he appeared to be rationalizing not only the conduct of his own campaign, but the anticipated action of the voters." *What Happened to Goldwater?* p. 241.

[83] Thomas W. Benham, "Polling for a Presidential Candidate: Some Observations on the 1964 Election," *Public Opinion Quarterly,* Vol. 29 (Summer 1965), p. 193.

[84] "Public Opinion Trends . . . Their Meaning for the Republican Party," exhibits 18 and 19.

protestations to the contrary.[85] Voters thought a nuclear war more likely under Goldwater than under Johnson, and by a margin of about 5 to 1.[86] Extensive white backlash had failed to materialize. Opposition to the civil rights movement had increased after the riots of July and August, but most voters did not blame the administration for the unrest, nor did they see Goldwater and the Republicans as better equipped to resolve racial tensions.[87] And as demonstrations became fewer and rioting ceased, concern with the civil rights issue also declined. By October the international situation—not civil rights—was the problem most frequently cited as the nation's most serious one.[88]

Whether or not the Republicans consciously made minimizing defeat the goal of their campaigning in late October, they acted as if they had. In the campaign's final three weeks Senator Goldwater for the first time visited Nebraska, South Dakota, Nevada, Wyoming, Colorado, and Washington—all states which had originally been counted on by the Republicans for hard-core support. He also gave substantial amounts of time to Arizona, Wisconsin, and Iowa in this period, while downgrading (relative to the proportion of his time given them in the campaign as a whole) New York, Illinois, New Jersey, and Michigan. In his speeches after October 15, Goldwater devoted himself to a narrower range of issues than he had earlier. He spent very little time outlining the choice he offered voters in welfare and economic policy. Instead, he denounced "forced integration," attacked the Kennedy-Johnson administration for its alleged foreign

[85] Benham, *op. cit.*, pp. 191-92.
[86] "Public Opinion Trends . . . Their Meaning for the Republican Party," exhibit 14.
[87] See *ibid.* and the Harris Survey, *Washington Post*, Sept. 29, 1964.
[88] AIPO press release, Oct. 10, 1964.

policy blunders, hit hard at corruption in government, and pronounced Lyndon Johnson incapable of providing the kind of moral leadership the nation required.[89]

The Democrats, as the campaign came to an end, seem to have decided that they could enlarge upon a victory already within their grasp. In the last three weeks before election day, President Johnson spent a considerable amount of time in states that, for the most part, would have to be considered quite marginal to any winning strategy. It was then that he visited Delaware, Kansas, and South Carolina for the first time. He gave an inordinate amount—about one-third—of his time to New York in this period. He also devoted sizable amounts of time to Florida, South Carolina, Georgia, and Missouri. Toward the end of the campaign, reporters noted a slight change in the President's speaking style—as Richard Rovere put it, "He moved from a defense of past Democratic administrations to evangelistic and almost utopian views of the future. . . ." [90] Illustrative of this change of tone were speeches in Pittsburgh and New York. In the former city the President heralded the advent of the Great Society. In New York he made a prediction:

. . . this Administration has passed more legislation, made more progress and fulfilled more promises than any Administration since the New Deal of Franklin Roosevelt.
And we've just begun.[91]

---

[89] On October 14 Earl Mazo reported that "Senator Barry Goldwater's strategy board decided at private meetings in Washington Saturday and Sunday that the Republican campaign should now concentrate on political morality, violence in the streets, international Communism and President Johnson's alleged failure as a national and world leader. The Republican candidate's political inner circle agreed that there had been too much 'scatter gun' talk about issues so far." *New York Times,* Oct. 14, 1964.

[90] Richard H. Rovere, *The Goldwater Caper* (Harcourt, Brace and World, 1965), p. 166.

[91] *New York Times,* Nov. 1, 1964.

Concluding Observations

At this point it will be useful to compare the strategy adopted by Senator Goldwater and his staff with those which have shaped other recent Republican presidential campaigns. The comparison makes more evident both the degree to which, and the ways in which, the 1964 Republican campaign broke with the past.

The strategy of the Goldwater campaign was not distinctive in the value it assigned to get-out-the-vote efforts. The strategists of the Nixon and Eisenhower campaigns had also regarded such efforts as of great importance.[92]

The personal attack on President Johnson in 1964 had no counterpart in the Republican campaigns of 1960 or 1956, but this did not make it unusual either. In the 1952 campaign against Adlai Stevenson, moderate Republicans had charged President Truman with the same kind of misconduct that was attributed to Johnson. In 1964 Goldwater's leading rival for the nomination, Governor William Scranton of Pennsylvania, was ready to make the campaign against Johnson "a very personal one." [93]

The attitude taken by Senator Goldwater toward parties and partisanship in 1964 differed only marginally from that adopted by Eisenhower in 1956 and Nixon in 1960. The speeches of the three Republican leaders contained few positive references to the Republican party and were almost en-

[92] See David (ed.), *The Presidential Election and Transition 1960-1961*, p. 64.

[93] In February Governor Scranton, according to Joseph Alsop, told an Indiana Republican group, "It [the 1964 presidential campaign] would have to be a pretty personal campaign. Most Americans at the moment are reasonably well off and reasonably contented . . . And I must say President Johnson has handled himself skillfully so far. But I don't think the United States wants a wheeler-dealer in the White House, and the campaign would have to be keyed to that. In fact, it would have to be a personal campaign, because it would have to turn on personalities." *Washington Post*, Feb. 3, 1964.

tirely devoid of negative references to the Democratic party. Goldwater began his campaign by opposing *administration* policies and the record of the *administration* to *Republican* policies, and to the *Republican* record in the White House and in Congress, but he did not persist in doing so. He identified himself with his party more frequently than Nixon did in 1960, but no more often than had Eisenhower in 1956.

The strategies of the Republican presidential campaigns of 1964 and 1960 also differed only marginally in the states selected as the foci of the most intensive campaigning. Nixon and Goldwater did allocate their scheduled time among regions in a somewhat different way (see Table 2.2). Goldwater gave less time to the Northeast and more to the South than Nixon had. The list of the ten states where Nixon was scheduled to campaign longest, however (and to which as a group he devoted about 63 percent of his time), includes seven of the ten states that appear in a similar Goldwater list. (Since a willingness to engage the Democrats in a battle for the industrial states has been regarded by some as a hallmark of the moderate Republican way, it is noteworthy that Kennedy and Goldwater lists of this sort include eight of the same states.) [94]

Senator Goldwater's foreign policy position—in substance —was very like that of the two men who had preceded him

---

[94] The ten states to which Nixon, Kennedy and Goldwater gave the largest amounts of their scheduled time were (in rank order) as follows:

Nixon	*Kennedy*	*Goldwater*
New York	New York	California
California	Pennsylvania	Texas
Illinois	California	Ohio
Pennsylvania	Ohio	Illinois
Ohio	Illinois	Pennsylvania
Michigan	Michigan	New York
Wisconsin	Texas	New Jersey
Iowa	New Jersey	Arizona
New Jersey	Indiana	Wisconsin
Missouri	Kentucky	Indiana

Table 2.2. Percentage Distribution of Total Campaign Time Scheduled for Republican Presidential and Vice-Presidential Candidates, 1960 and 1964, by Region [a]

Region	1960		1964	
	Nixon	Lodge	Goldwater	Miller
Northeast	30.9	47.0	20.0	22.7
Midwest	35.1	24.0	32.4	36.0
South	14.2	21.0	22.3	15.0
West	19.8	8.0	25.2	26.2
	100.0	100.0	100.0	100.0

Note: Details may not add to totals because of rounding.
[a] Regions are as defined in David and others, *The Politics of National Party Conventions,* App. A, Table 10.

at the head of the Republican ticket, although it differed considerably in tone. Like Eisenhower in 1952, he criticized the administration's policy toward the "captive nations" of eastern Europe and the foreign policy "blunders" of the Democrats. Like Nixon, the Senator was for peace through preparedness, and firmness in dealing with Communist nations. He put much less emphasis than either Eisenhower or Nixon, however, on negotiation as an instrument for attaining his foreign policy objectives; and he did not, as Nixon had, ascribe virtue to refusing to "trade insults" with the Russians.

It was Senator Goldwater's stand on domestic issues that made his campaign differ in a fundamental way from the Eisenhower and Nixon campaigns. The difference was not primarily ideological. Goldwater's attack on "the regimented society," "handouts," "unwarranted intervention in our private economic lives," and on "centralized power" [95] paralleled attacks by President Eisenhower on "big government,"

[95] RNC press release, transcript of speech at Prescott, Ariz., Sept. 3, 1964.

"paternalistic direction by Washington bureaucrats," and "socialized medicine." [96] Goldwater's expressions of faith in "private property, free competition, hard work" [97] echoed Eisenhower's. But General Eisenhower took pains in 1952 to assure voters that a vote for him was *not* a vote to repeal the New Deal.[98] In 1964 Senator Goldwater gave no such assurances. Eisenhower in 1956 and Nixon in 1960 favored measures that implied an important role for the federal government in the solution of domestic problems, while Senator Goldwater had hardly any suggestions for action on the home front.

Insofar as its basic strategy was concerned, then, the case for considering the 1964 Republican presidential campaign as precedent-breaking rests on fairly narrow grounds. Senator Goldwater chose to appeal for the votes of southern whites on a basis almost certain to alienate northern Negroes. He failed to couple attacks on big government, bureaucracy, and spending with assurances that, were he elected, something very like the status quo would obtain with respect to federal welfare programs and economic and foreign policy. For the rest, his campaign, particularly in its final weeks, was not very different from the kind of campaign one would have expected on behalf of a moderate Republican leader.

What lessons can be learned from what happened?

Many observers have been quick to link as cause and effect the conservatism of Senator Goldwater's positions on issues of public policy and the one-sidedness of the outcome of the election; Goldwater's conservatism, in this view,

---

[96] RNC press release, transcript of speech in Cleveland, Ohio, Oct. 1, 1956.

[97] RNC press release, transcript of speech at Prescott, Ariz., Sept. 3, 1964.

[98] See Stanley Kelley, Jr., *Professional Public Relations and Political Power* (Johns Hopkins, 1956), p. 173.

alienated many voters who otherwise would have voted Republican, while it failed to win him the support of any sizable group of previous nonvoters. Walter Lippmann, for instance, wrote soon after the election that "the returns prove the falsity of the claim . . . that there is a great, silent latent majority of 'conservative' Republicans who will emerge as soon as the Republican Party turns its back on 'metooism' and offers them a 'choice.' The Johnson majority is indisputable proof that the voters are in the center." [99] Tom Wicker of the *New York Times* agreed, and went on to argue that Republicans in the present era can win only as a "me-too" party.[100]

This popular view of the meaning of the presidential election of 1964 has won an easier acceptance than it deserves on the basis of the evidence thus far advanced in support of it. The election returns, in and of themselves, proved very little—certainly not that conservatism or any other particular feature of the Goldwater campaign was the cause of the Republicans' overwhelming defeat. The prospects were poor for a close race by any Republican candidate in 1964 because any Republican candidate was fated to run against a popular incumbent President of the majority party in a time of relative peace and prosperity. Moreover, Senator Goldwater was a far from ideal standard-bearer for the conservative Republican cause. Before he ever began to campaign against President Johnson, Goldwater had put himself on record as holding opinions far more extreme than any he expressed in the campaign itself; that he had done so helped the Democrats in their efforts to get voters to see him as an extremist and a radical.[101] The Senator's campaign, finally,

[99] *Washington Post,* Nov. 5, 1964.

[100] Faber (ed.), *The Road to the White House,* p. ix.

[101] Statements which lent the color of truth to the charge that Senator Goldwater was "against" the Social Security system, for instance, were made *before* his nomination, not during the campaign.

was marked by several blunders.[102] To the extent that these facts had anything to do with the one-sidedness of the election's outcome, the severity of Senator Goldwater's defeat cannot be properly attributed solely to the character of the program he offered the electorate.

The strategy adopted by the Senator and his advisers may have contributed to the Republican defeat, but it may also have saved the Republicans from a defeat more disastrous than that which they actually sustained. Angus Campbell, reporting the preliminary findings of the Survey Research Center's study of the 1964 election, suggests that probably Goldwater's stand on civil rights lost votes for him in the North but won votes for him in the South. A moderate Republican candidate might have minimized these northern losses but there is little reason to think he could have matched Goldwater's gains in the southern states, since there is no reason to believe that Governor Wallace would have abandoned his presidential candidacy if the Republicans had nominated a moderate. Campbell suggests also that the broad issue of governmental responsibility raised by Senator Goldwater was "not a major contributor to movements of the vote from normal party positions." [103] It is possible that this issue had an indirect impact on the vote not detected by the Survey Research Center's study that was disadvantageous to Goldwater; this could be the case, for example, if voters who did not react negatively to the Senator's position on domestic policy nevertheless took their cues for voting from those who did. It is also possible, however, that Goldwater's

[102] For example, vice-presidential candidate Miller's warning that the elimination of discriminatory immigration quotas would "open the floodgates" to unwanted immigrants was out of order in a campaign in which special efforts were being made to win the votes of Polish-Americans. Similarly, Senator Goldwater's attack on clergymen for supporting the President would be hard to justify as practical politics. The attack most probably served only to alert voters that not all those concerned about the nation's morals were siding with the Senator.

[103] See below, p. 273.

conservatism won him votes indirectly, because it stimulated a great deal of grass-roots activity in his behalf. Whatever the effect of the Republican drive to get out the vote, the Senator's candidacy apparently did inspire considerably more activity by Republicans at the grass-roots level than was in evidence in 1960 and before; [104] and it is reasonable to relate this fact to the strength of his ideological appeal.[105] One can justifiably conclude that the Republican strategy in the 1964 campaign was a losing one and perhaps that it was a desperate one; but, even given what we know now, it can hardly be considered an irrational response to the situation in which the Republicans found themselves.

The campaign and its outcome did show the difficulties of the Goldwater strategy, however, if not its folly. Both Goldwater's stand on civil rights and his statements regarding domestic policies were intended to bring a realignment of forces in party politics. To a certain extent they succeeded in doing so, at least temporarily. One of the more impressive facts about the campaign of 1964, however, was the scarcity of bolters in the top leadership ranks of the southern Democrats. This fact is not so difficult to understand. President Johnson was an odds-on favorite to be reelected. Southern Democratic leaders had a great deal to lose in defecting from his cause—certainly the favor of the President and

[104] According to Dr. George Gallup, the Democrats were more active than the Republicans at the local level in 1960, whereas the reverse was true in 1964. (See AIPO press release, Oct. 6, 1964).

[105] Richard Rovere's comment on Goldwater's prenomination campaign is to the point: "Goldwater's victories thus far have not been in doctrinal combat, but it is doctrine that has made a combatant out of him. He represents a small state, and, unless his friends in the party are to be regarded as a power unit in themselves, he controls no important piece of political machinery. He has few favors to grant and few to withhold. . . . He commands only volunteers. Those who toil in the vineyard for Goldwater do so because they like the message he brings. . . . In numbers, the volunteers may not constitute a very impressive force, but they are an indispensable one, and to them doctrine is just about everything." *Op. cit.*, p. 36.

possibly their congressional seniority rights. Under the circumstances, Senator Goldwater and his staff found that the leaders of the moderate Republicans could be alienated from his candidacy much more easily than southern Democratic leaders could be won to it. Rats desert a sinking ship, one anonymous observer of the 1964 campaign has observed, but they rarely jump off a floating one.

In another respect, Senator Goldwater's campaign efforts must have been even more disappointing to him. He failed to stimulate that debate of "fundamentals" he seems to have expected. Neither the President nor his running mate seriously discussed any of Goldwater's favorite themes. The Senator contended that private enterprise, and not governmental action, could most effectively insure full employment; that states and localities should have a larger share of responsibility for providing public services; that public action against de facto segregation violated the right to free association; and that the Supreme Court's reapportionment decision constituted "judicial legislation." Johnson and Humphrey never attempted to refute any of these contentions. Argument about the points Goldwater raised would have both advertised and lent respectability to them, and the President had little reason to give this kind of aid and comfort to his Republican opponent.[106] As a result, there was certainly no greater, and probably a smaller, element of debate in the 1964 campaign than there had been in earlier ones.[107]

[106] The same motive was most probably back of the President's refusal to take notice of Goldwater's challenges to debate before the television cameras.

[107] Certainly in 1960 the two presidential candidates commented directly on each other's statements far more often than in 1964.

3

Strategic Considerations

NELSON W. POLSBY

The presidential election of 1964 was an important event for students of American politics primarily because it broke some of the rules that politicians had lived by for a generation, and that had been codified in the texts and analytical writings of political scientists. Nevertheless, in the end this election confirmed more of the conventional wisdom than it undermined, and thus it preserved relatively unscathed the principal explanatory paradigm of political science in the field of American electoral politics.

The main assumption in the conventional theory is that politicians like to win and that they want to win the Presidency most of all. From this and from findings about the behavior of voters, one could deduce a series of propositions that would describe with tolerable accuracy the tactical moves of Democrats and Republicans, of the party in power and the party out of power, in a normal election year. Merely to review a few of these propositions in the light of the strategies the parties actually adopted in 1964, and of the results, will show how this election was both exceptional and—what is even more unusual—an exception which reinforced the rules of the game as they had come to be understood.[1]

[1] See Nelson W. Polsby and Aaron B. Wildavsky, *Presidential Elections: Strategies of American Electoral Politics* (Scribner, 1964), for an attempt to spell out the rules of the game in some detail, and to show how they were related to the strategies adopted by the parties in presidential elections prior to the election of 1964.

The Republican Strategy

For Republicans involved in presidential nominating politics the most important fact of life is that their party is without question the minority party in the United States. What is more, the Republican minority seems to have shrunk steadily over the last twenty-five years, if we can judge from the party identifications Americans have been reporting to the Gallup surveys: [2]

Year	Republican	Democratic	Other
1940	38%	42%	20%
1950	33	45	22
1960	30	47	23
1964	25	53	22

The Survey Research Center at the University of Michigan has found repeatedly that about three-quarters of those in their samples eligible to vote claimed a party identification; of these, three-fifths were Democrats.[3] In presidential elections in which considerations of party are foremost, and allowing for the greater propensity of Republicans to turn out and vote, it has been plausibly argued that the Democrats could expect to win with about 53 percent or 54 percent of the vote.[4] This is close enough justifiably to kindle hope in Republican breasts; despite the clear Democratic majority in this country, it must be assumed that either major party can win a presidential election. But over the last thirty years it has generally been necessary for the Republicans to devise a strategy that could not only win, but win from behind.

[2] American Institute of Public Opinion (AIPO), news release, Nov. 8, 1964.

[3] See below, Chap. 8, Table 8.11, p. 278.

[4] See Philip E. Converse, Angus Campbell, Warren E. Miller and Donald E. Stokes, "Stability and Change in 1960: A Reinstating Election," *American Political Science Review*, Vol. 55 (June 1961), pp. 269-80, esp. p. 274.

With the handwriting so plainly upon the wall, the strategic alternatives available to Republicans can hardly be regarded as secret. They can be boiled down to three possibilities. First, Republicans can attempt to deemphasize the impact of party habit as a component of electoral choice by capitalizing upon a more compelling cue to action. The nomination of General Dwight D. Eisenhower, the most popular hero of the Second World War, overrode party considerations and is a clear example of the efficacy of this strategy.[5] Efforts to play upon popular dissatisfaction in a variety of issue-areas also exemplify this strategy—but these dissatisfactions must preexist in the population, and must be widespread and intense before they will produce the desired effect. When issues do come to the fore in a compelling way, the payoff to the advantaged party is sometimes enormous because these are the circumstances under which new party loyalties can be created.

Another possible Republican strategy, similar in some ways to the first, also seeks to depress the saliency of party in the minds of voters by blurring the differences between the parties, by seeking to efface certain of the stigmata that have attached to the party over the years as stereotypes having general currency (for example, "party of the rich").[6] This strategy gives full recognition to the arithmetic of Democratic superiority, and also to the unit rule of the electoral college, which allots disproportionate weight to votes cast in the large states that so often contain the heaviest concentra-

---

[5] See Angus Campbell, Philip E. Converse, Warren E. Miller and Donald E. Stokes, *The American Voter* (Wiley, 1960), pp. 537-38; and Herbert H. Hyman and Paul B. Sheatsley, "The Political Appeal of President Eisenhower," *Public Opinion Quarterly*, Vol. 19 (Winter 1955-56), pp. 26-39.

[6] For indications that this strategy is feasible despite the existence of general stereotypes, see Campbell and others, *American Voter*, pp. 44-59, 179-87. See also AIPO news releases, Feb. 6, 1963, Oct. 9, 1964, Oct. 25, 1964.

tions of traditional allies of the Democratic party.[7] Although it has been used often, by Republican nominees such as Wendell Willkie, Thomas E. Dewey, and Richard Nixon, with results that always fell short—sometimes barely short —of victory, this "me-too" strategy has over the years become increasingly controversial among Republicans. The fact that no Republican candidate has actually been able to win with it has created doubts about its efficacy.[8] The me-too strategy may entail the advocacy of policies generally favored by most American voters, but this approach apparently does not correctly mirror the political sentiments of Republican activists.[9] Critics of the me-too approach have argued that this strategy merely alienates potential Republican voters while failing to attract sufficient Democrats. Alienated Republicans, so goes this argument, seeing no difference between the policies espoused by the major parties, withdraw from politics into apathy.[10]

Thus a third strategy, whose claim of victory is based upon the presupposition of a hidden Republican vote, can be

[7] For a striking demonstration of this concentration, see Ithiel de Sola Pool, Robert P. Abelson, and Samuel L. Popkin, *Candidates, Issues, and Strategies* (M.I.T. Press, 1964), pp. 117-18. These authors argue, on the basis of a computer analysis of voting patterns, that in 1960 the religious issue cost John F. Kennedy one and a half million popular votes, but because of the geographic distribution of Democratic voters he actually gained twenty-two votes in the electoral college on this issue.

[8] Recall Senator Dirksen's famous castigation of Thomas E. Dewey at the Republican convention of 1952: "We followed you before, and you took us down the path to defeat."

[9] For indications that this is so, see in particular Herbert McClosky, Paul J. Hoffman, and Rosemary O'Hara, "Issue Conflict and Consensus Among Party Leaders and Followers," *American Political Science Review*, Vol. 54 (June 1960), pp. 406-27.

[10] Good accounts of debates over strategy among Republicans can be found in such sources as Charles O. Jones, *The Republican Party in American Politics* (Macmillan Co., Government in the Modern World Series, 1965); Robert Donovan, *The Future of the Republican Party* (New American Library, 1964); Malcolm C. Moos, *The Republicans: A History of Their Party* (Random House, 1956); Robert Novak, *The Agony of the G.O.P. 1964* (Macmillan, 1965); and Conrad Joyner, *The Republican Dilemma: Conservatism or Progressivism?* (University of Arizona Press, 1963).

identified. This was the strategy pursued by the Goldwater forces in 1964. It has as its main characteristic the attempt to sharpen rather than blur party lines on matters of substantive policy.

As readers of the newspapers are well aware, this third strategy was not first settled upon unanimously by Republicans who then looked around for a candidate to carry it out. Rather, the strategy was adopted from the beginning by those within the party who first decided to advance the Goldwater candidacy. Indeed, even the slogan Goldwater used, "A choice not an echo," contained an implied rebuke to the "me-too" approach. In selecting Senator Barry Goldwater at the national convention, the Republican party chose a strategy of sharp and general opposition to the incumbent Democratic administration on such matters as government intervention in the economy, the extension of government-sponsored welfare and medical benefits, and the use of the powers of the federal government to further the cause of civil rights.

The change in direction that this represented for presidential Republicans was not accomplished without cost. Many Negro delegates to the Republican national convention expressed dismay at the turn of events; so did party leaders and candidates from the urban Northeast, who were beaten back in attempts to strengthen the civil rights plank of the platform and to insert a plank criticizing "extremism."

Senator Goldwater, throughout the platform battle and thereafter, adhered to an uncompromising line with impressive fidelity. He and his allies withstood all attempts to amend the platform from the floor. For his running mate Goldwater "balanced" his ticket by choosing a man almost as conservative as he is, Representative William E. Miller of New York. And when the time came to bind up his party's wounds and unite them for action against the Democrats—which is one traditional function of the acceptance speech—

Goldwater seemed to be addressing these words to his fellow Republicans:

Anyone who joins us in all sincerity we welcome. Those, those who do not care for our cause, we don't expect to join our ranks in any case. And let our Republicanism so focused and so dedicated not be made fuzzy. . . .

Immediately thereafter came his famous allusion to the platform battle:

I would remind you that extremism in the defense of liberty is no vice.
And let me remind you also that moderation in the defense of justice is no virtue.[11]

Throughout the campaign, the Goldwater-Miller ticket continued to differentiate itself sharply even from Democratic policies likely to be favored by audiences the candidates were addressing. On Labor Day, Representative Miller criticized liberalized immigration policies in South Bend, Indiana, an industrial community heavily populated with immigrants and their children. Before the American Political Science Association on September 11, Senator Goldwater criticized the United States Supreme Court as, among the three branches of the government, "least faithful to the constitutional tradition of limited government, and to the principle of legitimacy in the exercise of power." On September 16, in Knoxville, Tennessee, Senator Goldwater said, "I know that you know, and most of you share my faith in private initiative and private enterprise. . . . Now what I said with respect to TVA is within the general framework of that philosophy and I stand by it." Two days later, in the economically depressed Appalachian region, he attacked the administration's poverty program as "phony," "cynical," and "irresponsible," and called for free enterprise to combat pov-

[11] Shortly after the convention, in a meeting at Hershey, Pennsylvania, Goldwater made a half-hearted attempt (and his only attempt) to unify the party behind him.

erty. At the National Plowing Contest in North Dakota, Goldwater said that "a gradual decline [in farm price supports] would be good for you." [12]

Another feature of the Goldwater strategy was his unequivocal bid for support from the South and his forthright sacrifice of Negro votes. Whereas Vice President Nixon did his best in 1960 to appeal to both southerners and Negroes,[13] Goldwater's campaign was marked by attacks upon the Supreme Court; by reminders that he had voted against the Civil Rights Act of 1964 because he believed sections of the bill were unconstitutional; and by promises that a Goldwater Presidency would restore "law and order" in the streets and would not tolerate civil disobedience and demonstrations of a kind associated by many of his listeners with the civil rights movement.[14]

In all of these particulars, the Senator's campaign represented a sharp departure from Republican tactics of the recent past.

The Hidden Vote Hypothesis

The overwhelming magnitude of Senator Goldwater's defeat and the disastrous accompanying consequences for the Republican party at the congressional and state levels [15] in-

[12] Contrast this last statement with a more conventional Republican campaign: General Eisenhower's pledge at this same gathering during the 1952 campaign to work for farm price supports at 100 percent of parity. *New York Times*, Sept. 7, 1952.

[13] See the discussion of this in Theodore H. White, *The Making of the President 1960* (New York: Atheneum, 1961), pp. 203-04, 315, and in Polsby and Wildavsky, *Presidential Elections*, pp. 128-29.

[14] See Goldwater statements on Sept. 3, 10, and 15, summarized in *Congressional Quarterly Weekly Report,* Oct. 2, 1964, pp. 2323-24.

[15] *Congressional Quarterly Weekly Report,* Nov. 20, 1964, p. 2709, estimated that Republicans had lost more than 500 seats in state legislatures. Republicans gained one governor (for a total of 17), lost two U.S. Senators (reducing their senatorial representation to 32), and sustained a net loss in the House of Representatives of 38 seats (reducing their strength to 140 members, the lowest since the Roosevelt landslide of 1936).

vite the exercise of hindsight. But, for once, hindsight merely confirms foresight. It was apparent before the election as well as afterward that the factual grounds supporting the notion that there is a "hidden" Republican vote, waiting to be tapped by an unequivocally conservative candidate, are weak indeed.

Let us examine the evidence. First, where can the Republican vote be hidden that this strategy seeks to tap? Presumably not among Democrats, at least outside the South, since this approach relies so heavily upon sharpening the cleavage between the two parties. Nor can there be much of a hidden vote among disaffected conservative Republicans who fail to turn out, since the best knowledge we have of Republicans is that they do turn out and vote Republican.[16] The only other location for the hidden vote is among those who profess to no regular party affiliation—roughly 25 percent of the potential electorate. What is known about these people that would lead to the conclusion that they can be moved to vote Republican by a highly ideological appeal based on conservative and right-wing doctrines?

There is, in fact, no reason at all to suspect that these people can be reached in this way. All the available information on party neutrals indicates that they are much less interested, less informed, less likely to seek information about politics, and much less likely to vote than are regular partisans. Non-affiliates are relatively unconcerned about issues and are only dimly aware of political events.[17] Efforts to reach this population, to attract their attention, are likely to fail. Attempts to outline issue-positions to them, to engage their support in behalf of any self-consistent philosophical

[16] See, for example, Jones, *op. cit.,* pp. 66-71.

[17] This point has been confirmed as often as any in the entire literature of voting behavior. See Bernard Berelson, Paul F. Lazarsfeld, and William McPhee, *Voting* (University of Chicago Press, 1954), pp. 333-47, for example, propositions 39, 50, 51, 66, 68, 69, 70, 71, 78, 79; Campbell and others, *American Voter,* pp. 142-45.

and political position, seem as futile as the famous campaign to sell refrigerators to Eskimos.

There is a well-known suspicion, voiced from time to time by imaginative writers, that conservative elements of the population are in fact alienated from politics and sit in the wings, frustrated, immobilized, and without party loyalties, until someone pursuing a Goldwater-like strategy gives them the "choice" they are looking for. This is probably a canard. What fragments of evidence exist point to the probability that dedicated conservatives and right-wing ideologues who are sufficiently interested in politics to hold strong opinions about public policy do in fact belong to political parties and participate actively in them. Outside the South, it seems certain, these people are almost all Republicans. Thus the "hidden vote" that Goldwater hoped to attract was probably hidden inside the vote Richard Nixon received in 1960.[18]

Another assumption underlying the Goldwater strategy was that it would be possible to attract this mythical hidden vote in substantial numbers without losing the allegiance of large numbers of more moderate people who supported the

[18] The study of right-wing ideologues and their supporters is more speculative than empirical. Nevertheless, there are a few straws in the wind, and all blow in the same direction. In 1962, Raymond E. Wolfinger and his associates administered a questionnaire to 308 "students" at an anti-communism school conducted by Dr. Fred Schwarz's "Christian Anti-Communism Crusade" in Oakland, California. Among the findings of this study were that 278 of the 302 persons in this sample who voted in 1960 (or 92 percent of those who voted) had voted for Nixon, and that 58 percent of those who answered the question chose Goldwater over Nixon for 1964. At about this time, a nationwide Gallup poll showed Goldwater the choice of only 13 percent of Republicans. Raymond E. Wolfinger, Barbara Kaye Wolfinger, Kenneth Prewitt, and Sheilah Rosenhack, "America's Radical Right: Politics and Ideology," in David Apter (ed.), *Ideology and Discontent* (Free Press of Glencoe, 1964), pp. 267-69. Analysis of various election returns and of a 1954 Gallup poll suggest that support for the late Senator Joseph McCarthy was importantly determined by party affiliation, with Republicans far exceeding Democrats or independents in the ranks of his supporters; Nelson W. Polsby, "Towards an Explanation of McCarthyism," *Political Studies*, Vol. 8 (October 1960), pp. 250-71.

almost successful candidacy of Richard Nixon in 1960. In the event, this proved impossible to accomplish. An enormous number—probably about 20 percent—of Nixon's 1960 supporters voted for Lyndon Johnson in 1964.[19] But this outcome might have been extrapolated from poll and primary election data in the preconvention period which showed that even among Republican voters Goldwater enjoyed far from overwhelming support.[20]

In addition, Goldwater aroused great antipathy in the general population. According to the Gallup poll in mid-September, 38.3 percent of their respondents expressed definite hostility to Goldwater (including 14.7 percent ex-

[19] AIPO news releases of Sept. 6, 1964, and Oct. 16, 1964, suggested that Republican defections would run as high as 30 percent, but their release of Dec. 11 indicated that a 20 percent defection is more accurate. This compares with defections by Republican voters of 5 percent, 4 percent, and 8 percent in the three previous elections. Democratic defections in the 1964 election were also high—13 percent of those calling themselves Democrats voted for Goldwater—but these were confined mostly to the southern states.

[20] In early July, the Gallup poll showed the following preferences among Republican voters: Goldwater 22 percent; Lodge 21 percent; Scranton 20 percent; Rockefeller 6 percent. Just before the Republican convention, the figures among Republicans were: Scranton 60 percent; Goldwater 34 percent; Undecided 6 percent. AIPO news release, Nov. 11, 1964.

Goldwater received 23 percent of the vote in the New Hampshire primary; 18 percent in Oregon; 8 percent in Pennsylvania (fourth in a field of five write-ins); 10.5 percent in Massachusetts; 71 percent in Indiana, where Harold Stassen received the remainder; only 49 percent in Nebraska, where his name alone was on the ballot; 51.6 percent in California; 76 percent in Texas, running in a trial heat only with Rockefeller; 31.9 percent in South Dakota; and a bit better than 60 percent in Illinois, where he was opposed on the ballot only by Margaret Chase Smith and where there is no law requiring election officials to tabulate write-in votes.

Gallup trial heats before the Republican convention showed Goldwater running a poorer race against President Johnson than either Scranton or Nixon, for example:

Goldwater 18%	Scranton 26%	Nixon 27%
Johnson 77	Johnson 69	Johnson 70
Undecided 5	Undecided 5	Undecided 3

AIPO news release, July 1, 1964.

pressing the most extreme hostility on an eleven-point scale), while only 8.1 percent expressed any antipathy at all toward President Johnson.[21] Likewise, on a number of issues, Louis Harris surveys found that sizable majorities in the general population defined themselves as opposed to positions they believed Senator Goldwater held.[22]

Reasons for Goldwater's Nomination

If the Goldwater strategy for victory was transparently implausible and his showing in the public opinion polls and in presidential preference primaries indifferent, how did the Republican party come to nominate him? This question is difficult to answer fully, but it is of great importance, because it is Senator Goldwater's nomination more than any other event in this election year which challenges the textbook explanations of American electoral politics.

My explanation—which I regard as partial and plausible rather than definitive or scientifically established—has several main points.

First, there is the weakness of Goldwater's opposition within the Republican party. There was a fatal flaw, for ex-

---

[21] AIPO news release, Sept. 13, 1964.

[22] Louis Harris survey news releases, July 13, 1964, and Sept. 14, 1964. Some of the Harris survey findings on foreign affairs were:

Issue		Position Ascribed to Goldwater		Voters' Own Position	
		July	Sept.	July	Sept.
Go to war over Cuba	For	78%	71%	29%	29%
	Against	22	29	71	71
Use A-bombs in Asia	For	72	58	18	18
	Against	28	42	82	82
United Nations	For	42	50	82	83
	Against	58	50	18	17

ample, in the candidacy of Nelson A. Rockefeller. As each new incident unfolded in Governor Rockefeller's private life —his divorce, his remarriage, and the birth of Nelson A. Rockefeller, Jr., just days before the California primary—his presidential candidacy became less and less tenable.[23] Yet Rockefeller was the only Republican willing to contest the primaries openly with Goldwater.

Henry Cabot Lodge, who won the early-bird New Hampshire primary as a write-in candidate with 35 percent of the vote and who showed write-in strength in the Massachusetts, Texas, Illinois, and Nebraska primaries, refused to resign his ambassadorship to Vietnam in order to come home to campaign. This may have cost him the Oregon primary, which he lost narrowly to Rockefeller. Lodge's strategy could be defended on the grounds that he is an indifferent campaigner and hence was less likely to damage his candidacy by his absence. On the other hand, it cast grave doubts upon the seriousness of Lodge's interest in the nomination. For party professionals, these doubts seem to have reinforced preexisting antipathies toward certain of Lodge's personal mannerisms, and many in addition still nursed resentment over Lodge's active role in securing the Eisenhower nomination of 1952.

The attractive, though inexperienced, William Scranton adopted a Stevensonian posture of reluctance. But unlike Stevenson, who was the designated successor of President Truman in 1952, Scranton could never manage to win more than qualified encouragement from General Eisenhower. No doubt the Scranton campaign was delayed not only by the hesitancy of the candidate, but also by the hope that Rocke-

---

[23] Here, and in the following paragraphs, I rely upon contemporary newspaper coverage in the *New York Times, Wall Street Journal, Washington Post* and *Evening Star* (Washington), upon accounts in *Congressional Quarterly Weekly Reports*, and also upon a manuscript account being prepared for publication by John Kessel, tentatively titled *The Goldwater Coalition*.

feller and Goldwater would effectively cancel one another out in the primaries. This hope was dashed by the unexpected Rockefeller defeat in California. By the time the Scranton campaign got started, too many people had been otherwise committed. Only a *force majeure,* such as the Eisenhower blessing, could have shaken the situation loose—but instead, Eisenhower's main impact was to delay Scranton's entry into the race until after the crucial Governors' Conference in early June—giving him less than a month to campaign before the convention began.

Finally, Richard Nixon's candidacy seems to have been hampered to a remarkable degree by his own activities following his narrow loss of the Presidency in 1960. In 1962 he ran for governor of California and lost, creating some skepticism in the minds of party leaders about his continued popularity with voters. Nixon compounded his problem, moreover, by his immediate reaction to this defeat. His bitter, recriminatory (and also somewhat disconnected and emotional) remarks about press coverage of the campaign were given wide publicity, including on-the-spot radio and television, and handed a potent weapon to his future opponents. Shortly after this debacle, Mr. Nixon gave up his titular leadership of the California Republican party and moved to New York City, where he entered the private practice of law. But unlike Thomas E. Dewey, in whose steps he seemed to be following, Mr. Nixon retained a sufficient interest in public office to embark upon a low-key campaign for the Presidency, which consisted—in the absence of any more tangible resources—of statements reminding Republicans of his broad ideological acceptability to all wings of the party and of his general abilities as an experienced campaigner and public servant. These statements were understandably received with something less than enthusiasm by party leaders who had made commitments to other candidates; but even among the dwindling uncommitted (for example, at the

Governors' Conference), Nixon seems to have created a negative impression by efforts in his own behalf that could not be energetically seconded by some identifiable bloc of troops at the national convention.[24]

In addition to the various flaws in the candidacies of Goldwater's potential opponents, the Republican party in 1964 was somewhat more loosely organized than usual in many states. Normally, state party organizations are unified by incumbent governors. Without the centralizing forces of state patronage and coherent party leadership embodied by a man in the governor's chair, state parties tend to fragment into local satrapies and territorial jurisdictions which can be played off one against another by astute aspirants for the presidential nomination. The lack of strong leadership at the state level also means that a set of presidential preferences and a strategy for pursuing them is less likely to be worked out in advance and agreed upon by all elements of the state party. Decentralized state parties thus become happy hunting grounds for early starters in the presidential sweepstakes. They can move into a vacuum, make alliances and receive commitments, and build delegate strength from the ground up. In 1964 the Republican party held only sixteen governorships. The advantages to Goldwater's early candidacy are obvious.

Another factor in the nomination of Senator Goldwater, besides the weakness of the Republican party, was the corresponding strength of the Democratic party. In 1964, reasonable Republicans might well have asked themselves whether the nomination of their party was worth fighting for. Less than a year before a Democratic President had been slain. John F. Kennedy's hairline margin of victory in 1960 sud-

[24] See Rowland Evans and Robert Novak, "The Unmaking of a President," *Esquire*, Vol. 62 (November 1964), p. 91, and J. F. Ter Horst, "Nixon Hopes as GOP Unifier Clouded by June Maneuvers," *Evening Star* (Washington), Dec. 2, 1964.

denly was replaced as a point of reference by a massive bipartisan wave of sympathy, remorse, and retrospective popularity following his assassination.[25] His chosen successor, Lyndon Johnson, had had only eight months on the job, and by astute management had prolonged his honeymoon with Congress, the press, and the people.[26] These factors had to be added to the normal advantages which accrue to Democrats by virtue of their majority of supporters and to incumbent Presidents because of their access to publicity, their command of the resources of the entire government for political purposes, and the various emotional linkages of the populace with them—feelings of dependency, demands for "security," and so on—all of which were no doubt magnified by the Kennedy assassination.

As a third element, Goldwater's own strength among Republican party professionals should not be neglected in explaining his nomination. He had been building a base of support at the Republican grass roots for some time. He was chairman of the Republican Senatorial Campaign Committee for the elections of 1956, 1960, and 1962. After the 1960 election, while Nixon was pinned down in California and Governor Rockefeller was engrossed in domestic problems, Goldwater became the most active party leader on the national banquet circuit, helping to raise money for local candidates and parties, and (not incidentally) widening still further his acquaintance with state and local party leaders. Furthermore, there is no doubt that he struck a responsive chord with many of these leaders not only because he was personally charming and likable, but also because he expressed many of their own views on public policy. Slowly

[25] See Bradley S. Greenberg and Edwin B. Parker (eds.), *The Kennedy Assassination and the American Public: Social Communication in Crisis* (Stanford University Press, 1965).

[26] Before the nominating conventions, pro-Johnson sentiment in national sample surveys was expressed by well over 70 percent of the voting public. See summary in the *Washington Post*, Nov. 2, 1964.

the image of politicians as cynical manipulators devoid of interest in public policy is giving way to a more complicated description in which practicality and patronage are mixed with idealism and issue orientation.[27] In an era of economic prosperity and great opportunities in the private sector, recruitment into political involvement and leadership is bound to include more issue orientation than when the government is a major source of direct income through the distribution of jobs and favors.[28] In fact, a high degree of interest in party politics usually is associated with a high level of political information and strong policy preferences. Among Republican political activists—even allowing for diversity of opinion—these preferences can be characterized as definitely conservative, and in general as more conservative than the views of ordinary citizens who classify themselves as habitual Republican voters, as well as of Democratic activists.[29]

In short, it seems to me plausible to argue that Goldwater won the nomination because his opponents were weak, because the chances of winning seemed sufficiently remote to discourage much competitive effort by candidates who might otherwise have contested the nomination more effectively, because the state party organizations were particularly susceptible to preconvention campaigning, and because he reflected the policy preferences of many party activists and leaders.

This explanation does not account fully for what some saw at the Republican National Convention: a kind of ama-

---

[27] For a good example of this sort of description at the state level, see James D. Barber, *The Lawmakers* (Yale University Press, 1965).

[28] See James Q. Wilson, *The Amateur Democrat* (University of Chicago Press, 1962); and Fred I. Greenstein, "The Changing Pattern of Urban Party Politics," *Annals*, Vol. 353 (May 1964), pp. 1-13.

[29] See McClosky and others, in *American Political Science Review*, pp. 406-27. This article compares the responses on a long self-administered mail questionnaire of three populations: 1788 delegates to the Democratic National Convention of 1956, 1232 delegates to the 1956 Republican Convention, and 1484 persons in two successive waves of AIPO national cross-section surveys in January 1958.

teur take-over of the Republican party. The journalist Murray Kempton commented at the time:

> The Goldwater forces seem in fact to have captured a number of state conventions with the device of mass amateur influx which Dewey and Henry Cabot Lodge used to seize so many southern states from Taft in 1952. A mountain state Republican senator, who had assumed that he would be his delegation's favorite son, was shocked to find that his state convention had elected a Goldwater delegate slate. "There were people at the convention," he said, "that I've never seen before." [30]

One assumption underlying this idea seems to be that professional politicians would never, if left to their own devices, have supported a candidate who promised to be as weak as Goldwater. Even if they entertained small hope of winning the Presidency, these politicians had a stake in the preservation of party competition further down on the ballot, where the right candidate for the Presidency could at least attenuate the effects of the Johnson coattail. Such considerations, it is suggested, are bound to be less salient to amateurs, who are more likely to value ideological purity above all other considerations.

There can be little doubt that in addition to his unimpeachably conservative voting record in Congress, Goldwater made a general appeal based on ideological considerations, laying particular emphasis upon issues of morality and rightness "in your heart" and on vague complaints about unidentifiable malaise in American society. These sorts of appeals can be contrasted with the identification of specific issues, the making of promises about the content of policies, and the suggestion of concrete steps to be taken. This latter approach can be used when there is a specific coalition of inter-

---

[30] "GOP Disestablishment," *The New Republic*, Vol. 151 (July 11, 1964), p. 6.

est groups to be put together. But Senator Goldwater took a novel public posture with respect to interest groups: "If I had to cater to every special interest in the country to get elected, I wouldn't want the job." [31]

This seems to have struck a note of responsiveness among a great many of the delegates to the 1964 Republican Convention. Interviews with 150 Goldwater delegates at San Francisco brought responses such as the following:

"The delegates are for Goldwater because they agree with his philosophy of government. That's what you people will never understand—we're committed to his whole approach." . . . "He is straightforward." "He does not compromise." "He doesn't pander to the public; he's against expediency." "He is frank." "He has courage." "He stands up for what he believes." . . . "He votes his convictions when he knows he's right." "He doesn't go along with the crowd." . . .

One colloquy went as follows:

Interviewer: What qualities should a presidential candidate have?
Delegate: Moral integrity.
I.: Should he be able to win the election?
D.: No; principles are more important. I would rather be one against 20,000 and believe I was right. That's what I admire about Goldwater. He's like that.[32]

Thus it is plausible to argue that Goldwater may have appealed to professionals—despite the misgivings of many of them that he could not win—on the ground that he repre-

[31] Speech at Madison Square Garden, New York City, Oct. 26, 1964. Contrast this with General Eisenhower's final TV appearance, Nov. 4, 1952.

[32] Aaron Wildavsky, "The Goldwater Phenomenon: Purists, Politicians, and the Two-Party System," *Review of Politics,* Vol. 27 (July 1965), pp. 393-94. Note also the finding of the Michigan Survey Research Center, reported by Angus Campbell below (p. 261), indicating that, in a national sample of voters, the quality of Goldwater's that received the most favorable response was his "integrity."

sented their predominantly conservative views of public policy.[33] To amateurs, his appeal seems to have been general, and not tied to any particular issues. The general stance was negative, vague, and highly charged emotionally.

We are accustomed to reading about new faces at national conventions. Each election year, so it seems, some leading politician well-known to members of the press is irked to discover that his delegation has been taken over by strangers. Indeed, at both the Republican conventions of 1952 and 1956—one a hard-fought contest among factions of the out-party, the other a love-feast dedicated to the renomination of an incumbent—large numbers of regular delegates had not served at the previous convention.[34] Nevertheless, the Republican convention of 1964 was extraordinary: 74.3 percent of the delegates had not been at *either* of the two pre-

[33] In mid-June, one group of professionals, consisting of 54 Republican congressmen, jointly released an endorsement of Goldwater, in which they claimed he would help the Republican ticket in their area; 17 of them were beaten in the election; of 5 others who retired voluntarily, 3 were replaced by Democrats.

[34] Paul T. David, Ralph M. Goldman, and Richard C. Bain, *The Politics of National Party Conventions* (Brookings Institution, 1960), pp. 349, 350, shows that, in 1952, 60.7 percent of the Republican delegates were new to national conventions. In 1956, 28.6 percent had been at the preceding convention; no figures are given for convention veterans who appeared in 1956 but had skipped 1952.

These turnover figures raise an interesting question as to the proper inferences one can make from the McClosky data discussed above on party leaders who attended the 1956 convention. Clearly, a substantial number of delegates to the 1964 convention did not attend the convention of 1956. (As a matter of fact, 153 of 1308 delegates to the 1964 convention were delegates or alternates at the 1956 convention according to my own comparison of the two convention rosters.) Therefore, we would have to take the McClosky findings as indicative rather than demonstrative of attitudes of a much larger—and somewhat different—group of party activists. Because the 1956 Republican nominations were a foregone conclusion, enlivened in the event only by the brief candidacy of one "Joe Smith" for Vice President, the number of party insurgents at this convention must have been unusually low. This gives a greater plausibility to the use of responses from delegates to this convention as in some sense accurately representative of regular Republican activist sentiment.

ceding conventions. Thus the proportion of new faces was extraordinarily high, and so also, we may surmise, was the number of amateurs, of persons moved by passionate conviction and relatively insensitive to demands for compromise or the necessities of team play with copartisans whose general orientation to politics, or whose policy preferences, differed from their own.

In short, it appears that while Goldwater failed to bring out a hidden vote in November, he may well have changed —at least temporarily—the composition of the activist core of the Republican party.

The Democratic Strategy

If Senator Goldwater's nomination was unexpected and his campaign strategy unorthodox, according to the best available knowledge of presidential elections, the Democratic strategy was a model of orthodoxy and scarcely needs either description or explanation.

Most of the resources available to President Johnson have already been mentioned: incumbency, the halo effect resulting from the trauma of his predecessor's assassination, which undoubtedly prolonged his honeymoon with the press and with Congress, and his leadership of what, after all, is the majority party.

Mr. Johnson's main problem, standing in his way when he sought the nomination in 1960, was the fact that he was from the South. Indeed, labor and civil rights groups had opposed even his nomination for the Vice-Presidency in that year.[35] But the passage of the Civil Rights Act of 1964 with vigorous support from the President served, as no honeyed words alone could possibly have served, to underscore to lib-

[35] See Philip Potter, "How LBJ Got the Nomination," *The Reporter,* Vol. 30 (June 18, 1964).

eral Democrats that Johnson understood the necessities of the times as they understood them, and demonstrated that he was ready, like President Truman and Adlai Stevenson before him, to sacrifice the demands of the South where they conflicted with the demands of the rest of the Democratic coalition.

The Democratic convention of 1964 seated representatives of the predominantly Negro Freedom Democratic Party of Mississippi in a compromise approved by the White House. Television viewers whose memories ran back four years remembered Joseph Rauh, a prominent leader of the liberal Americans for Democratic Action and delegate from the District of Columbia. When the word went out that Senator John Kennedy wanted Lyndon Johnson for his running mate, Rauh seized the nearest microphone and pleaded over nationwide TV, "Don't do it, Jack." In 1964, appearing as counsel for the Freedom Democrats, Rauh flayed the regular Mississippi delegation for repudiating the leadership of "our great President Johnson." Thus far had Johnson come in allaying the fears and winning the support of his party's liberal activists. The choice of Senator Hubert Humphrey as his vice-presidential candidate sealed the bargain.

In this way, before the campaign began, President Johnson solved his major problem—to unite the Democratic party behind him. Once the campaign was fairly started, it rapidly became apparent that Mr. Johnson had no further problems. To win he needed only to refrain from rocking the boat. On the Democratic side, the campaign was unexciting. A comprehensive statement of the President's views in a book published for the campaign was justly hailed by critics as comparable only to the prose of Warren G. Harding in unexceptionable blandness.[36] The President sensibly refused

[36] Lyndon B. Johnson, *My Hope for America* (Random House, 1964). See, for example, the review by Murray Kempton, "The People's Choice," *New York Review*, Vol. 3 (Nov. 5, 1964), pp. 3-4.

to debate with his challenger on nationwide television. He shook thousands of hands and exuded hospitality and sympathy for disaffected Republicans—some of whom turned out to be prominent businessmen and former members of the Eisenhower administration who endorsed him publicly. For once, the Democratic party had less difficulty than its opponent in financing the campaign.

As the campaign wore on, the message of the polls, now suitably chastened by the debacle of 1948 and hence especially cautious in the face of overwhelming evidence of a Johnson landslide, became unmistakable. The outcome could hardly be regarded as a surprise.

Picking Up the Pieces

Despite the size of Johnson's victory, Goldwater supporters were saying after it was all over that the 26 million people who voted for their man constituted an endorsement of right-wing Republicanism, although the figure represented a decline of over seven million from the vote for the 1960 Republican candidate, and was a stunning 16 million fewer than voted for the winner. Such a reaction would not surprise students of messianic movements and of other organizations heavily dependent upon faith rather than rational calculation as a method of achieving internal cohesion.[37] But political parties in the United States cannot long survive solely as vehicles for drastically unpopular doctrines, no matter how passionately these doctrines are upheld by the minority of activists who believe in them. Indeed, a clamor among Republicans for a "new image" was not long in coming. A month after the election, the Republican governors met for two days in Denver and issued a statement

[37] See Leon Festinger, Henry Riecken, and Stanley Schachter, *When Prophecy Fails* (Minneapolis: University of Minnesota Press, 1956).

endorsing civil rights and condemning radicalism "whether of the right or left."

Writing in the January 1965 issue of *Fortune,* Republican Representative Gerald R. Ford of Michigan suggested that his party in the House abandon its attempts to coordinate with leaders of the southern Democrats.[38] In spite of the misgivings of some of his colleagues about the import of this article, Ford, running on a "new image" platform, successfully displaced Charles Halleck of Indiana as Republican leader of the House at the start of the Eighty-ninth Congress. At the same time, Barry Goldwater's handpicked chairman of the Republican National Committee, Dean Burch, was forced out of office. His successor was Ray Bliss of Ohio, preeminently a rationally calculating organization politician, used to testing his personal preferences against political realities. According to reports, "Though a staunch conservative in his own thinking, Bliss was fearful of the effect of a Goldwater candidacy in '64. He arranged to tie up the Ohio delegation behind the favorite-son candidacy of Governor James A. Rhodes." [39] "Associates say Mr. Bliss is basically rather conservative and that his personal beliefs probably closely paralleled those of former Senator Barry Goldwater. But he also believes that Republicans, as a minority party, need to draw moderate voters to win, and he tends to shy away from extreme candidates." [40]

To an outside observer, the lesson of this election for Republicans seems remarkably clear; as always, a question remains as to who within the Republican party will be charged with interpreting that lesson. Normally, this task falls to officeholders of the defeated party. No one can believe, on the record of their past performance and prefer-

[38] "What Can Save the G.O.P.?" *Fortune,* Vol. 71 (January 1965), p. 140.

[39] *Evening Star* (Washington), Jan. 13, 1965.

[40] *New York Times,* Jan 13, 1965.

ences, that the elevation to leadership of Mr. Ford and Mr. Bliss heralds a drastic leftward turn in the policies espoused by the leaders of the Republican party. Rather, both men recognize the need to strike a bargain with reality. Whether merely giving ground before popular sentiment will be enough to transform the Republican party from a minority to a majority party may be doubted. But there is less doubt that such a leadership is capable of attracting a larger share of the voting population than are unyielding candidates and leaders.

It may be that some pro-Goldwater Republicans recognized that their chances of winning the election were slim, but believed that even a debacle in 1964 would enhance their long-run chances of controlling the Republican party and in possibly pushing political dialogue in this country to the right. Judging from the activity of the Eighty-ninth Congress, and from the tendency of political parties to cohere around elected officeholders rather than defeated candidates, this seems to have been a gross miscalculation.

Conclusions and Speculations

A cliché of American politics holds that Republicans cannot get themselves elected, and Democrats cannot govern. If the Republicans had their moment of truth for this generation when they finally tested the hidden vote hypothesis in a Presidential election, a similar period of illumination took place for the Democrats as they discovered during the first session of the Eighty-ninth Congress whether a vigorous President and overwhelming majorities in both houses of Congress would suffice to allow them to put their program into effect. It is a rare election which provides even a partial test of popularly held notions about parties or the party system. This one helped us understand something about the problems of the Republican party in winning elections. And it also was instructive about Democrats.

No estimate of the net effect of the election on the Eighty-ninth Congress can fail to note an increase in the floor strength of the Democratic majority in both houses. That is to say, on most matters brought to a vote, and especially on matters of high priority to the Johnson administration, the Democrats had more than enough votes to win. With its loose rules of germaneness, the Senate provides few obstacles to floor action, since any bill bottled up in committee can be attached as a floor amendment to any other bill by any Senator.[41] But in the House, bringing bills to a vote has over the years been more difficult. The intricate and strict parliamentary rules of the House, the rigidities of its internal structure, and the conservatism of Democratic leaders of key committees have in the past effectively kept bills off the floor—including some bills the Democratic leadership wanted to pass and were confident they had the votes to pass. In the Eighty-ninth Congress this bottleneck was broken. At its first session, the rules of the House were changed so as to facilitate floor action; the Speaker is now allowed at his discretion to call up bills for floor action after they have been reported by a committee (favorably or unfavorably) and at least 21 days have elapsed; bills may be sent to conference by majority vote instead of by unanimous consent or, failing that, through the sometimes intransigent Rules Committee; and the petty twenty-four-hour harassment of the demand for an engrossed copy of an amended bill is abolished. Thus the liberal majority in the Democratic caucus made it procedurally possible for the Eighty-ninth Congress to govern according to the rule of the majority party to an extent greater

[41] The major obstacle in the path of Senate action is thus the filibuster, an effective weapon, but one that cannot be used with success in all situations. For a brief summary of conditions under which filibusters are likely to succeed, see Nelson W. Polsby, *Congress and the Presidency* (Englewood Cliffs, N.J.: Prentice-Hall, 1964), pp. 77-78.

than in any Congress since the overthrow of Speaker Cannon in 1910. Party ratios on committees were changed to reflect the Democratic majority; and an ambitious legislative program was enacted.

It is difficult to assess the net effect of this election on the party system. Despite what appear to be prompt and meaningful measures within the Republican party to mend the damage caused it by Senator Goldwater's candidacy, the effort may be insufficient to prevent an effective shift in this country to a one-and-one-half party system, a shift that has been in the making for some time.[42] This is not necessarily a deplorable development, even to staunch defenders of a vigorous two-party system. For it may be that ultimately the health of a two-party system depends upon the capacity of the two parties to agree on most issues and at the margins offer alternatives attractive to slightly different components of the population. This makes for disagreement on live issues, not on issues already settled and part of an overriding national consensus. There seems to be no reason, other than empty piety toward the abstract idea of two-party competition, to reward with public office an out-party that fails to seek out new opportunities to appeal to the preferences of voters.

The question is not whether enough Republicans are ready to adapt to these preferences, for it is apparent that they are. A more serious problem for Republicans to face is whether the opportunity will soon arise for them to capture the loyalties of enough voters to return them to power for any lengthy period of time. I am speaking now not of a momentary aberration but of the creation of long-term party loyalties. The great historic opportunities for the creation of

[42] There is some indication, for example, that the number of noncompetitive Democratic congressional seats has increased over the years. See Charles O. Jones, "Inter-Party Competition for Congressional Seats," *Western Political Quarterly*, Vol. 17 (September 1964), pp. 461-76.

party loyalty seem to have been associated to a certain extent with domestic disasters, but even more, it seems to me, with the entry into suffrage of great numbers of people similarly situated. The prospects for civil war seem dim; we are now growing accustomed to the role of the government in putting a floor on many aspects of the economy which heretofore were capable of combining and producing drastic depressions. And so the Republican chances to create on account of domestic crisis lasting adherents among those who now vote Democratic must be rated as slim. What is worse, from a Republican standpoint, the Goldwater candidacy seems to have solidified a trend, visible since the New Deal, away from the Republican party of the last great bloc of voters to enter American political life: the Negro voters. Once Negroes everywhere vote, the long march toward universal suffrage in America will have ended. Even allowing for the past instability of the Negro vote, the loyalties of the Negro seem likely to be predominantly Democratic. Looked at in this light, and projected into the medium-range future, the Goldwater candidacy was a disastrous bargain for the Republican party. It is much easier for a political party to win new friends than to convert old antagonists. The decision of Senator Goldwater and his advisers to lock the Negro out of his historic home may have had a greater impact on the Republican party's future fortunes than any other strategic choice of 1964.

Finally, what conclusions can we draw from the experience of 1964 about the political institutions engaged in the process of choice? One conclusion from this election year would be that national conventions are possibly overrated as decision-making bodies.[43] They are not now taken seriously as decision-making instruments of the party of an incumbent

[43] Cf. William Carleton, "The Revolution in the Presidential Nominating Convention," *Political Science Quarterly*, Vol. 72 (June 1957), pp. 224-40.

President. Looking at the high turnover of delegates, and at the success both of Senator Kennedy in 1960 and of Senator Goldwater in 1964, it could be plausibly argued that increasingly commitments to candidates are being made earlier and earlier in the nominating process, even when the nomination of the out-party is being contested among several factions.

The number of first-ballot nominations since 1928 suggests that important things are happening even in the out-party before the convention meets (see Table 3.1). Over this time-span each party has nominated ten presidential candidates, eight of whom have been nominated on the first ballot. All seven incumbents seeking renomination have received first-ballot nominations; and so have nine nonincumbents. Nationwide television coverage of the primaries gives early-bird candidates a head start on the free publicity of the election year. Private polls (as well as those published in the newspapers) put more information about the comparative popularity of candidates in the hands of party leaders earlier

Table 3.1. *Number of Ballots for Presidential Candidates in National Party Conventions, 1928-1964*

Year	Democratic	Republican
1928	1	1
1932	4	1[a]
1936	1[a]	1
1940	1[a]	6
1944	1[a]	1
1948	1[a]	3
1952	3	1
1956	1	1[a]
1960	1	1
1964	1[a]	1
Total nominations	10	10
First-ballot nominations	8	8

a Renomination of an incumbent President.

than before. Thus the pressures upon state party leaders to decide what they want to do seem to be urging them to make decisions earlier in the election year—before national publicity creates a rush of sentiment in one direction or another that takes matters wholly out of their hands. When one or a few party leaders come to feel the need for early decisions, soon the others must follow suit or lose their own room for maneuver. These early decisions must, perforce, take place at widely separated places on the map, thus enhancing the bargaining power of candidates, who can deal with party leaders piecemeal under these circumstances, rather than having to face them *en masse* at a convention, where they can wheel and deal with one another.

If this tendency is correctly identified—and I should argue that it is a tendency for which only scattered and inconclusive evidence can presently be assembled—it leads to the further conclusion that over the long run, as mass communications media continue or possibly increase their saturation coverage of early events in the election year, successful candidates (at least of the out-party) increasingly will have to have access to large sums of money apart from the funds generally available to the party, a large personal organization, and an extra measure of skill and attractiveness on the hustings and over television. In these circumstances, other resources—such as the high regard of party leaders—would come to be less important.

It seems to me that most of these qualities I have named —early candidacy, opulent private financing, and strong personal organizations—characterized both the Kennedy and Goldwater preconvention campaigns; and both these out-party candidates overcame strong misgivings on the part of leaders of their own party whose main concern was winning the election. Time will tell whether candidates of the out-party in future years read the signs similarly and plan their campaigns accordingly.

4

Mass Media Performance

CHARLES A. H. THOMSON

In the presidential nominations and elections of 1964, the most important development from the standpoint of media was the new collaboration achieved between television and the printed press. Prompted by competitive urges and cost considerations, television inaugurated a comprehensive and accurate Network Election Service for the reporting of returns, and, building on the experience of 1962, launched services of prediction and analysis of returns (such as the Columbia Broadcasting System's Vote Profile Analysis) that vastly improved television's capability to do its job of immediate reporting and commentary. Both these services were put at the disposal of the nation's major news agencies and newspapers (with appropriate contractual arrangements and provision of financial support), much to the improvement of their natural functions of reporting in depth and providing an enduring record of event, analysis, and evaluation. The book and pamphlet also achieved unusual prominence in 1964, playing a more than ordinary role in this day of electronic media, in reinforcing loyalties if not in the shaping of perceptions of preferences, issues, and candidate images in both parties. But television, although audiences for particular events ran far smaller than those for the conventions and debates of 1960, played a major role both in the immediate electoral process, and in contributing to public understanding of the anatomy, the personalities, and the dynamisms of that process.

Television did not produce a repetition of the "debates" of 1960, although the issues of such confrontations, their preferred format, and their contributions to the democratic process were carefully examined during 1964. They foundered on the preferences of the President, as ways could have been found—had the will been there—to obviate the difficulties posed by the failure of Congress to relax the provisions of the Communications Act as it did in 1960. Hopefully, given different competitors or a different legal situation, future candidates will explore ways of avoiding the dangers of such confrontations while capitalizing on their apparently unique capability of providing more nearly balanced exposure of the candidates and arguments to partisans of both parties for whatever values might be served thereby. Even more critical to the future of presidential debates, however, will be the calculations by each party of whether it stands to win or lose by engaging in debate under the special circumstances of the election.

By failing to relax the Communications Act, Congress not only complicated the problem of setting up confrontations between the major candidates; it also failed to bring any closer to solution the manifold problems of control of political broadcasting at the presidential level. Not until the campaign was well over were fresh new solutions proposed that might facilitate debate, reduce costs to the parties, put new responsibilities on parties as such rather than on candidates, or establish shorter campaigns.

The Federal Communications Commission tightened its interpretation of what constitutes a political broadcast by deciding that the presidential press conference was political within the meaning of the Act, and hence would generate a basis for demands for equal time for all qualified candidates. The Commission broke no new ground in its decision, upheld by a tie vote of the Court of Appeals, that the President's broadcast on worsened world affairs on Ocober 18, 1964, was not "political." The problem and the issue were aired again, but to no great purpose. From the standpoint of access to the major medium, the advantages of being President to a candidate for that office were demonstrated again.

Problems of equal access to radio also came into prominence. Stations committed to broadcasting the position of the radical right, for instance, came under belated challenge for their failure to give equal time or to apply the fairness doctrine to broadcasts sponsored by those with a less extreme point of view.

The printed press distinguished itself by giving more support to the Democratic candidate than ever before. It came under sharp attack, less from the Republican candidate than from some of his more extreme supporters, for alleged distortion of Goldwater positions, in particular with respect to control of nuclear war, Social Security, and the TVA. (Early in the New Hampshire campaign, headlines announced that Goldwater wanted to protect himself from the press—in particular from its invasions of informal *kaffee-klatsches* and other efforts to meet people quietly. Although he said that the preponderance of the press was Republican, and that the press was "generally fair," he did complain that the GOP suffered at the hands of the news media.) [1]

Some observers have commented that in 1964 the press as a whole—and in particular television's reporters and commentators—expanded their role as newsmakers rather than mere reporters. Faced with dull stretches at the conventions, reporters may have brought into undue prominence activities that perhaps affected party and candidate image, if not the

[1] *Washington Post*, April 12, 1964.

outcome of the conventions' labors. And faced with the requirement for immediate interpretation and comment, they may have shaped unduly the public's perception of the events themselves.

The Preconvention Period

In early 1964, President Johnson enjoyed the usual advantages possessed by any incumbent President for access to news media. He also had the inestimable advantages of his own performance in taking over the reins of government from the assassinated President, and the intensive news coverage of all his acts of asserting firm governance at a time of national mourning, loss, and uncertainty as to the future. His nearly flawless performance in moving government forward, and in forging legislation that had previously eluded passage under Kennedy, established not only his stature as President, and his unexampled capability in congressional relations, but also his driving energy and common touch in carrying out the ceremonial as well as the substantive tasks of his office. Many uncertainties remained, particularly as they touched on probable performance in the field of foreign relations. But the media had recorded tremendous achievement.

Goldwater, however, started his national campaign from no such eminence. In the preceding years, his major work had been done with organizations; his appeal was exercised for the most part on small and particular audiences, with only occasional more public events, or opportunities to recall his performance as candidate and campaigner in earlier years.

During the preconvention period, then, the President could fashion his image by his very acts of being President. He did not have to stave off any challenge for the nomina-

tion; it was his for the taking, and there was little doubt that
he would take it, despite his occasional references to the fact
that the nominating convention had yet to act. Goldwater
had to fashion much of his national image, and in the process meet competition from a determined Rockefeller, a distant Lodge, a reluctant Scranton, and an ever-hopeful Nixon.

Goldwater moved from his tactic of engaging improvisa-
tions on many major issues, as he had refreshingly done in
preceding years and months, until the bitter rebuff of the
New Hampshire campaign signaled that this tactic, however
frank and honest, was politically costly. What might be
quite appropriate over teacups was disquieting to voters
when voiced over statewide or nationwide networks. He
startled and dismayed many voters by offhand references to
such topics as nuclear war, the future of the United Nations,
and the sale of TVA, when such views were expressed not
only with full publicity, but before audiences not all of
whom were predisposed to favor him, or such views, or such
cavalier ways of talking about fundamental issues.[2] He modified his tactics, striving for maximum personal exposure at
large and enthusiastic gatherings, where he made no statement at all on controversial issues, or restricted himself to
pronouncements carefully prepared in advance. (One notable exception was his offhand remark to a large and enthusiastic California audience about the possibility of using nuclear weapons for defoliation in Vietnam.) He did not risk
much so far as the nomination was concerned by his decision
to deal cautiously with his TV audiences. Even when challenged on his wariness by Governor Scranton in the Governor's initial TV appearance after he had decided to seek the
nomination,[3] Goldwater held firm. Scranton was able by his

[2] See Joseph Alsop, *Washington Post*, July 6, 1964.
[3] *New York Times*, June 29, 1964.

belated TV appearances to prompt rank-and-file Republicans to flood convention delegates with telegrams and mail in support of his candidacy. But the delegates were not to be budged, either by this classic form of expression of political choice, or by Scranton's televised pleas. Goldwater's strength lay in delegates, not in rank-and-file Republicans.[4]

Some of the other Republican candidates may have suffered as well as gained from press activities in the preconvention period. Rockefeller, although making sharp short-term gains from his dominance of press attention and his victory in the Oregon primary, nevertheless had to shoulder the political burdens of nationwide coverage of the pregnancy of his wife—a pregnancy that came to its term at a bad time indeed for the Governor's late-dwindling chances in the vital California primary. Scranton suffered, too—especially at the point prior to the National Governors' Conference when he appeared briefly (so ran the main press interpretations) as Eisenhower's favorite candidate, only to be told by the former President two hours before a nationwide television appearance on Sunday, June 7, that Eisenhower did not want to be part of any cabal to unseat Goldwater. Scranton's discomfiture and weak retreat into "principle" was documented for the country. At this and at other points, the major moderate candidates gave all too visible evidence of failure to agree on the candidate and the tactics that might have successfully upheld the moderate position, even at that late date in the campaign as a whole. Given the possibilities offered by the former President's ambiguities, the press could not necessarily be criticized for putting Scranton into a false position. Even less could it be criticized for reporting the weakness and political ineptitudes of the Republican center.

---

[4] The Gallup Poll reported on July 11 that 60 percent of the GOP rank-and-file (with 6 percent undecided) favored Scranton. *Washington Post*, July 12, 1964.

In the months immediately following his accession to office, President Johnson dealt with the press informally and sporadically, calling impromptu conferences and giving important statements to particular reporters. In short, he handled the press with less system, respect, and attention than they had been accustomed to during the Kennedy regime, and to a degree, during the Eisenhower period. Reluctant, so speculated some well-placed observers, to compete with his predecessor as master of a full-dress press conference, the President let almost five months go by before he essayed that role.[5] Heartened by the favorable reactions he received, the President proceeded to hold many press conferences, some coming almost daily. He would seek out a television studio to make an important announcement if in his judgment the matter would not keep until equipment could be set up in the White House. He marshaled the political notables in his entourage as an effective supporting cast in many nationwide events receiving nationwide coverage. Later, after the Federal Communications Commission had determined that the presidential press conference in a campaign was political, he willingly abandoned it. At the same time he continued to make impressive appearances on news shows and in news coverage that would not generate valid claims for equal Goldwater time because they were news events exempted from the equal time requirement, under the terms of the 1959 amendments to the Communications Act.[6] In May, by agreement with the three major networks, President Johnson approved the permanent installation of TV equipment in the White House, to be manned and ready fifty-four hours per week, so the President could go to the

[5] In the *New York Times*, March 1, 1964, James Reston commented on Johnson's initial effort: "President Johnson achieved his major objective in his first live televised news conference today: He survived."

[6] See Charles A. H. Thomson, "Mass Media Activities and Influence," in Paul T. David (ed.), *The Presidential Election and Transition 1960-1961* (Brookings Institution, 1961), pp. 90-91.

people with an important statement on a moment's notice.
The advantages of such media arrangements, not only to the
networks and stations, but also to an incumbent presidential
candidate, are apparent.[7]

Television at the Conventions

Television coverage of the 1964 conventions did not begin
and end with the banging of a gavel: programs about the
conventions began well in advance of each, and postmortem
shows were also scheduled summarizing the highlights as
television's commentators judged them. This decision to provide extended coverage had much to recommend it, since it
was clear that the earliest hard public evidence of Goldwater's hold on the Republican delegates would come in the
preliminary meetings of the platform and rules committees,
as his opponents would seek to test strength by proposing
amendments. It was also likely that major news of Democratic developments would be made by the outcome of
efforts of Negro delegations to be seated. At both conventions, political picketing and rumbling from left and right
would surely provide political color if not evidence of factional strength and candidates' and delegates' responses.

The networks knew that in both conventions they would
face a tremendous task in providing good fare during the
sometimes extended periods when the actions of the conventions themselves did not reveal the most important developments in the total event. Television reporters, along with the
rest of the press, probed insistently and widely for stories
behind the often tedious proceedings in the convention committees or on the floor. During convention sessions TV and

[7] The installation and arrangements were described by Laurence Laurent in the *Washington Post*, May 8, 1964. Dr. Frank Stanton, president
of the Columbia Broadcasting System and a close friend of Mr. Johnson,
was instrumental in this important innovation.

radio reporters of all the networks chased hidden clues (that may, like the black cat in the black room, not have been there at all), and interrogated participants off the floor, rather than exposing their audiences to the overt unfolding of events on it.

Comment and corridor pursuits more often than not obscured the stark reality of the proceedings, however dull. The observer interested in following the reading of the platform in the Republican convention (done in full as a means of postponing a probable party fight until poor viewing hours) would have had a hard time on any of the networks. Perceptive television critics complained of the overcoverage and overreportage.[8] Party candidates and convention managers were freed from the incentive, however slight, to produce platforms that would not only accommodate the conflicts and tensions of party factions, but compel attention if not consent from the national audience.

The Republican convention did produce some interesting moments. Goldwater's decision not to make himself freely available to the media gave Governor Scranton an unexpected media windfall, as time reserved for confrontations between the candidates fell completely to Scranton. Although the Senator did not risk any perceptible short-run loss of loyalty or dependability of the delegates already firmly committed to him, he did give to a probably formidable future opponent the opportunity to recoup the minor disaster of the preceding June 7, and become a national figure in very short order—and in the bargain, to give favorable press attention to Scranton's politically sophisticated and skillful as well as personally attractive wife.

An apparent even if not equally matched competition for delegates seems to have increased audiences slightly for the

[8] Laurence Laurent, *Washington Post*, July 16, 1964; Alfred Friendly, *Washington Post*, July 27, 1964; Jack Gould, *New York Times*, July 26, 1964.

Republicans in 1964 over 1960. Nielsen's figures indicate that somewhat more viewers looked considerably longer at the 1964 proceedings. In 1960, 82 percent of United States TV homes were tuned in for an average of 7 hours and 32 minutes; in 1964, 83 percent of TV homes were tuned in for an average of 8 hours and 22 minutes. In 1964, the Republicans received 36 hours of convention coverage, as compared to 17 in 1960.

Audience size for particular events was not markedly different from 1960. In 1964, the most watched event was Milton Eisenhower's nomination of Governor Scranton, seen by nearly 17 million homes. Goldwater's acceptance speech amassed an audience of 15.1 million homes, while Senator Dirksen's nomination of Goldwater, coming at 6:23 p.m. Eastern Daylight Time, gathered less than 10 million. Other events that would normally have excited major audience interest were similarly underexposed. Nelson Rockefeller's dramatic effort to speak sense to the convention, despite the turmoil of the impatient and the impolite, coming between 11 p.m. and midnight EDT, had an audience of slightly over 12 million homes. The critical vote on the civil rights amendments to the platform, coming at 2 a.m., was watched by less than 10 percent of TV homes (about 5 million).[9]

Probably the greatest damage to political image was suffered not by a candidate, present or potential, but by the Republican party. Television unavoidably pictured the spectacle of the pro-Goldwater mob. Far from the dignity, decorum, and smooth procedure characteristic of most Republican conventions, here was a spectacle of impatience, ill-breeding, unwillingness to accord the courtesy of a fair hearing to opponents who had no chance whatsoever either of the nomination or of palpable influence on the platform. The savaging of Stassen in 1956 was muted and pale in

[9] Laurence Laurent, *Washington Post*, Aug. 19, 1964.

comparison, and—more important—done behind the scenes. Almost inevitably TV reportage of events in the hall failed to picture the efforts of the Goldwater organization to restore order in the galleries.

The 1964 convention threw into sharp contrast the dignity and patience of a Rockefeller speaking out for moderation, or the intellectual quality and persuasiveness of a Milton Eisenhower nominating Governor Scranton, against the unreasoning angry Goldwater delegates and galleries. Goldwater, at the moment of his nomination, failed to make the move toward party unity that might have offended some of his supporters for the moment, but that would have done much to improve Republican chances in November. This omission, which television covered with cold clarity, contrasted sharply with Goldwater's charitable and wise words to Rockefeller in his statement after the California primary.[10] Television brought a full share of human interest; chief here was its coverage of the Scranton family as the inexorable vote count went on and the tears flowed. Possibly the wriest turn was casting President Eisenhower as the reluctant commentator. The American Broadcasting Company may have risked mixing political influence with media commentary, but the risk was not large, and the former President's hesitancy was predictable.

The Democratic convention faced something like the same problem the Republicans faced in 1956 (and to some degree in 1960)—how to maintain an effective and compelling show despite the lack of uncertainty about who would be its nominee for President. The Democrats, just as the Republicans in 1956, had to go to considerable lengths to contrive arrivals and departures and to manipulate other convention

---

[10] "To Gov. Rockefeller, who waged a tenacious campaign, I extend my best wishes, and I express the hope that he will join with me in resolving to make every effort to unseat the Democrats in November." *Washington Post*, June 4, 1964.

events in order to maximize attention and present favorable images. President Johnson—admittedly in full charge not only of the grand design but also the details of the convention—maintained suspense over his choice for running mate almost until his arrival at the convention. He engineered a skillful compromise concerning the claims of the contested delegations to be seated. He postponed the powerful emotional impact (and potentially disruptive effects) of the memorial to President Kennedy until a point in the proceedings when it could not possibly challenge his personal dominance over the convention, and more important, when it would have maximum favorable effect in solidifying sentiment and heartening Democratic delegates and supporters both in the hall and across the country. The Kennedy image, so prominent in 1960 whether borne by John or by another of the family, was present but well modulated in the 1964 convention. There was, at the end, no doubt as to who and what entourage was in charge in 1964.

The Campaign

Despite the relatively minor *contretemps* suffered by Goldwater in using television in New Hampshire and California, the Republican strategists made clear early that they intended to use the medium on a large scale. Of an early national committee budget of $13 million, Goldwater estimated that $4.5 million would go for television, saying he would rely on the medium "more than we have ever relied on it before." [11] It was also announced that the strategy of the campaign would not duplicate Nixon's heroic travels into all fifty states in 1960; Burch had already declared that Goldwater's campaign exposure would be limited to "meaningful experiences." What he had in mind was the last week

[11] *Washington Post*, Aug. 19, 1964.

of the California primary, with stress on "big crowds, big TV, big issues." [12] Goldwater would rely on set-piece performances before chosen audiences; he would continue to eschew large-scale press conferences. As the candidate expressed it later in his campaign, he would be "just pooping around."

The Senator's programs were planned to look that informal, but were not quite so casually prepared. His first major appearance on TV took place on September 18, as a $150,000 thirty-minute television show replaced Twilight Zone (9:30 to 10:00 p.m. EDT) on a 200-station lineup, the first of a series of half-hour presentations to appear weekly until election day. This first show dealt with peace and preparedness; others were planned for exploitation of the Bobby Baker scandal and the evils of Big Government.[13] The first full-dress show capitalized on themes already trumpeted in earlier filmed Republican commercial broadcasts: Johnson's failure to mention communism in his acceptance speech at Atlantic City; responsibility of the Democrats for the Berlin Wall, the mess in Vietnam, and Castro's Cuba. The show also commenced defensive efforts to picture Goldwater as a believer in peace through military preparedness, and far from "trigger-happy." [14]

As the campaign progressed, two problems emerged from the welter of Republican campaigning: how to defend Goldwater from the charge of being cavalier and "trigger-happy" (and the related problem of establishing his ability to project a firm and stable policy position on several controversial issues); and how to take best advantage of opportunities to saddle Johnson and the Democrats with responsibility for the nation's moral shortcomings. The Republicans' major set-piece effort to deal with the first was a conference be-

[12] *Washington Post*, Aug. 10, 1964.
[13] *Washington Post*, Sept. 18, 1964.
[14] Laurence Laurent, *Washington Post*, Sept. 19, 1964.

tween Goldwater and Eisenhower, telecast on September 22, an attempt to guarantee Goldwater's military judgment and *bona fides* by approval from the General-President. In the event this turned out a pallid, unconvincing journey to the Eisenhower farm. The Democrats proceeded unimpeded to picture Goldwater's several stands on the several issues.

Despite the windfall of the Jenkins affair, the Republicans were similarly unable to make headway with the issue of Democratic responsibility for immorality. Not that they did not turn increasingly to this issue as the campaign progressed; both the commercials and the statements of the candidates and their most prominent spokesmen talked increasingly on the point as the campaign neared its end. But the Republicans ran into a major problem of media use in their film "Choice." Their handling of this problem not only revealed Goldwater as a good deal more decent and less ruthless than some of his supporters and technical aides, but also underlined some of the seamier side of the Republican coalition. The problem encompassed not only content—beer cans, speeding black limousines, topless bathing suits, pornographic books, and flaming, twisting youth—but also sponsorship. The ostensible immediate sponsor was Mothers for a Moral America, a new division of the Citizens for Goldwater-Miller organization, organized in September at a meeting in Nashville, Tennessee, allegedly active in thirty-seven states, but possessing no formal organization, no officers, no membership, and no dues. (The film "Choice" was apparently paid for by Citizens for Goldwater.) It did have several "project directors" and "coordinators," including a former national president of the General Federation of Women's Clubs, a former United States Treasurer, and a prominent newspaper columnist.[15]

As for content, the planned film (not shown nationwide, but previewed for the press by courtesy of an undercover

[15] Elsie Carper, *Washington Post*, Oct. 26, 1964.

man for the Democratic National Committee) was designed to contrast two Americas—the immoral America associated with the Johnson administration in time if not in causal sequence; and the America of the Declaration of Independence, the Bill of Rights, and Senator Barry Goldwater. The film was made by the Citizens for Goldwater-Miller apparently after a disagreement on campaign strategy and policy —whether to provide homey, bland TV fare, as proposed by the National Committee's advertising agency, or whether to provide "hard-hitting" TV with a punch, as proposed by militants in the Citizens' Committee.[16] As to intent, Laurence Stern of the *Washington Post* obtained a transcript of an interview held on September 22 with the public relations director of the Citizens for Goldwater-Miller, quoting him in part:

> The purpose of this film then is to portray and remind the people of something they already know exists, and that is the moral crisis in America, the rising crime rate, rising juvenile delinquency, narcotics, pornography, filthy magazines . . . We want to just make them mad, make their stomachs turn. . . .
>
> This is what we are going to have to do in this movie: take this latent anger and concern which now exists, build it up, and subtly turn and focus it on the man who drives 90 miles an hour with a beer can in his hands, pulls the ears of beagles, and leave them charged up to the point where they will want to go out and do something about it. They will see all this on television, and there is only one way they can go, and that is with Goldwater. . . .[17]

The film was scheduled for nationwide showing over NBC at 2 p.m. EDT, Thursday, October 22. As of October 21, National Chairman Dean Burch said he had not seen the film. NBC's department of standards and practices still had the film "under review," but the network agreed to run it

---

[16] Rowland Evans and Robert Novak, *Washington Post*, Nov. 8, 1964.
[17] Laurence Stern, *Washington Post*, Oct. 20, 1964.

only after the film's producers agreed to delete certain passages NBC thought were "unduly suggestive." The Republican National Committee's advertising agency repudiated the film and disassociated themselves from it on professional grounds. The publicity director for Citizens for Goldwater admitted that the film was "shocking," but insisted that "we believe what is happening today in America is shocking." [18] Senator Goldwater decided, and it was announced in October 22 newspapers, to withdraw the film temporarily.[19] On the morning of October 23 he publicly repudiated the production, saying, "It's nothing but a racist film." [20] He almost lost the services of the Citizens' publicity director,[21] while he gained credits in the editorials of the moderate to liberal press. Although he himself, other candidates, and in particular the campaigners from the radical right were to continue to use the themes set forth in the film, this particular distillation was no longer available to be taken whole and neat. At least one other "shocker" was shot down by Goldwater at the same time: a film called "Ballot Box 13," an effort to depict alleged irregularities in President Johnson's 87-vote victory in his race for the Senate in 1948.[22] As the campaign wore on, the Republicans began to deal with the morality

[18] Laurence Stern, *Washington Post*, Oct. 21 and 23, 1964.

[19] Nan Robertson, *New York Times*, Oct. 22, 1964. The article quoted G. Frederick Mullen, Director of the News Bureau of the Citizens for Goldwater-Miller, as saying, "Naturally we are acceding to the request of the Senator and are now proceeding to make minor changes in the film to take account of new developments. The changes have nothing to do with Mr. Bailey's charges. The film will be shown as soon as possible." Two hundred unexpurgated copies of the film had already been distributed by the Mothers for a Moral America.

[20] John H. Averill, *Los Angeles Times*, Oct. 24, 1964.

[21] See Chalmers Roberts, *Washington Post*, Oct. 24, 1964; Rowland Evans and Robert Novak, *Washington Post*, Nov. 8, 1964. Also Don Irwin, *Los Angeles Times*, Oct. 22, 1964. Irwin quoted Paul Wagner, the candidate's press secretary, thus: "The senator 'does not believe it is appropriate for a political campaign in its present form.'" Dean Burch issued the following statement: "At the request of Senator Goldwater, the Citizens for Goldwater film entitled 'Choice' has been withdrawn."

[22] Evans and Novak, *Washington Post*, Nov. 8, 1964.

issue by emphasizing the positive values exemplified by the Goldwater and Miller families.

Meanwhile, although President Johnson continued to dispense folksiness at a frenzied pace throughout the campaign, the Democratic efforts at commercialized political campaigning did their part to lower the tone of the campaign as a whole, in particular by commercial shorts insinuating that Goldwater would be erratic and irresponsible in dealing with questions of nuclear war, and would willingly disregard the interests and safety of innocent women and children in the process. Two of these commercials were withdrawn after only one airing each (although they were shown after the campaign in various roundups and analyses of political campaigning). One was known as the "Daisy Girl Spot"—an effort to dramatize the danger from nuclear warfare. The other highlighted dangers from strontium 90 allegedly heightened by Barry Goldwater's opposition to the Test Ban Treaty.

Choice Without Debate

Although one candidate strove to clarify a political choice while the other clamped his control on the political center, the campaign was characterized neither by debate in the general sense of a dialogue about issues, nor by debate in the special sense signaled by the television debates of 1960. President Kennedy had said he would engage in such debates in 1964. The Congress in 1963, before his death, passed legislation that would have paved the way for such confrontations, although the House and Senate versions differed as to the length of time Section 315 of the Communications Act should be relaxed. When Johnson became President, conferees had not yet been appointed. They were eventually named in February of 1964, but Johnson was disinclined to commit himself on whether to debate and no meeting of the conferees was scheduled. The Republicans wanted debates, and wanted the way cleared for them. In April, Republican National Chairman William Miller prodded Senator Warren Magnuson and Representative Oren Harris, chairmen of the House and Senate Commerce Committees, to bring the bill out of conference. Neither chairman, possibly mindful of President Johnson's public reluctance, promised action.[23] Representative Harris a few days later evinced his unwillingness to proceed with the bill, because "nobody directly involved has asked me about it." The nobody, it seems reasonably certain, was the President, although not all observers agreed it was. Harris added that he did not think it was "good business" for an incumbent candidate to debate; he had to be "responsible," while the other party need not; he might have to conceal facts not known to the nonincumbent; and it wasn't "good policy" to relax the provision for the office of President only.[24]

The networks made very clear their hope that the bill would be passed, and that debates would take place. On May 5 Frank Stanton, president of CBS, announced results of a Gallup poll taken for CBS indicating that 71 percent of the American people favored debates; 9 percent expressed no opinion; 20 percent disapproved of them.[25]

On May 7, the conference committee finally met and agreed on a version of the bill based on the Senate 60-day provision; thus the legislation could be called up at any time

[23] *Washington Post*, April 21, 1964. President Johnson had said at a February 29 news conference that he would cross the bridge of deciding whether to debate when he came to it. The House version of the bill called for a 75-day suspension of the equal-time requirement for presidential candidates immediately preceding November 3; the Senate version, 60 days.

[24] Richard L. Lyons, *Washington Post*, April 26, 1964. See also editorial, *Washington Post*, April 30, 1964.

[25] *Washington Post*, May 6, 1964.

in either house. Passage was adjudged "assured," once the bill came up.[26]

However Goldwater may have felt about the desirability of debates at the presidential level, on June 14 he refused offers to debate his principal opponents for the nomination, implying he wanted no part of helping them to get public attention. The Columbia Broadcasting System had proposed a two-hour debate among Goldwater, Rockefeller, and Scranton. The latter two accepted, but with Goldwater's refusal, no program was planned.[27]

On July 12, a panel established by the American Political Science Association issued virtually the only comprehensive report to appear in 1964 on the issues raised by proposals for debates between the major candidates.[28] This report not only discussed the issues raised, but also arrived at conclusions, made recommendations, and appended a summary of letters received from members of Congress, governors, and party chairmen. The APSA Commission, noting the contribution to the improvement of political discussion made by the debates of 1960, and noting also the differences of opinion concerning the overall value of such confrontations, considered two major questions: 1) are there circumstances under which such debates should not be held at all? and 2) what procedures and format offered the best promise of contributing most to political education and to effective political participation?

As to the first point, the Commission noted that the situation is markedly different depending on whether one of the

---

[26] Cabell Phillips, *New York Times*, May 8, 1964. Richard Lyons reported in the *Washington Post* that Harris had convened the conference committee because he had not heard from the President, and he was tired of taking the heat for Congress's failure to act.

[27] *Washington Post*, June 15, 1964.

[28] The American Political Science Association, *Report of the Commission on Presidential Campaign Debates, 1964* (Washington, D. C., 1964).

candidates is an incumbent. If neither is, the Commission was convinced "that television debates, properly conducted, are a desirable extension of traditional campaigning. . . ." However, if one were an incumbent, the matter would be less certain.

Extraordinary situations may be created by the exigencies of the world situation and the international position of the United States. In *some* of these situations it may be contrary to our national interest for the President to engage in debates. The Cuban invasion and the missile crisis are recent examples.

Referring to opinions received from two congressmen to the effect that an incumbent President should not debate, the Commission noted that "the argument for caution is compelling," although many respondents expressed no concern. The Commission stressed that a presidential candidate who was also President should consider fully the duties and responsibilities of his office before engaging in campaign debates; the decision was not only his, but properly his.[29]

In closing its short discussion, the Commission pointed out that debates were not the only important innovation in the use of modern means of communication for political purposes; that improvement in the use of the press conference by the President and by opposing candidates could be made; that better means could be found to intensify the interaction of the President with his national constituency.

The development of new methods and new techniques for informing the electorate should be a matter of concern to all who are actively interested in political life and in the maintenance of a vital democratic system. In perfecting various campaign devices, we must remain keenly aware of what it is we are attempting to accomplish: The promotion of the most reasonable basis for choice among candidates best qualified on all

[29] *Ibid.*, pp. 2-3.

counts for public office. The choice of Presidential candidates must not be limited to those who are masters of appearance on television. If the trend seems to be toward such a limitation on our choices, then emphasis must be placed on strengthening methods of campaigning that enable citizens to make judgments on other bases.[30]

The Commission concluded with fourteen judgments and recommendations. Mindful of the preceding caveats, it suggested carefully structured debates and similar discussions and other presentations; called for attention to representatives of minor parties; pointed to the need for research to test the effects and effectiveness of such meetings; recommended appropriate action to deal with Section 315 of the Communications Act to remove obstacles to such confrontations; hoped for wide public discussion of the problems; and mentioned that the broadcasting companies, in carrying out broadcasts of this nature, would be rendering the kind of public service on which their licenses are based under American law. Such encounters, said the Commission, could provide an effective means of presenting candidates and issues to an ever larger electorate; they could also serve candidates for our country's highest office, assisting them in acquainting the electorate with their views on important issues of public policy. "Thus, they can inform, invigorate, and strengthen a vital aspect of the nation's political life."[31]

Not unexpectedly, this nudge from the pundits did nothing to alter the trend of events. On July 24 President Johnson told a press conference that he hadn't come to the bridge yet. Four days later Goldwater told seventy House Republicans that he wanted to debate the President, under "sensible ground rules."[32]

---

[30] *Ibid.*, p. 4.
[31] *Ibid.*, p. 10.
[32] Laurence Stern, *Washington Post*, July 29, 1964.

On August 1, the *New York Times* published a letter from President Frank Stanton of CBS, reviewing the state of affairs, and indicating that "as a practical matter, broadcasters cannot carry such debates under the present law." Stanton referred to an offer made the preceding November, predicated on passage of relaxation of Section 315, of "prime time for an extended series of joint appearances of the major parties' Presidential candidates and of their Vice Presidential candidates during the eight-week period from Labor Day to Election Day." [33]

On August 4, Senator Dirksen signaled that the Republicans wanted to bring up the measure for action, although on the fifteenth Dean Burch doubted that debates would take place. Referring to President Johnson, Burch said, "I don't think he's about to get suckered into that. Let's say he's the complete politician. He's not going to take any undue risks." [34]

The Senate voted on August 18 to kill the bill, tabling, by a 44-41 vote, the conference report. Twelve Democrats joined twenty-nine Republicans in voting against the motion to table, as Republican Senator Hugh Scott of Pennsylvania and Democratic Senator John Pastore of Rhode Island— both of whom voted against tabling—had a shouting debate over whether the Democrats were "chicken." [35]

The Republicans assailed Johnson on the death of the bill, while reporters recalled that as late as the preceding February Mr. Goldwater had said, "I don't think a President

[33] *New York Times*, Aug. 1, 1964. President Stanton expressed his preference for direct dialogues between the candidates without the intervention of a panel; he noted the possibility of debates on single issues such as civil rights, defense policies, etc. He suggested the value of initial and concluding joint appearances in which the candidates would discuss their overall approach to the sum of the problems facing the nation. He emphasized also that time would be available for joint appearances of the major-party candidates for the Vice Presidency.

[34] *Washington Post*, Aug. 5, 1964; Joseph A. Loftus, *New York Times*, Aug. 16, 1964.

[35] *Washington Post*, Aug. 19, 1964.

of the United States should debate anybody. He could very well disclose secrets only he knows." And it was recalled that when Mr. Johnson was a senator, he had not opposed debates.[36] A *Washington Post* editorial concluded that the Senate had made a serious mistake; the bill would have permitted debates but not required them; what was more important was to improve the possibilities for effective political discussion on TV.

> The case against requiring equal time on the air for the major national candidates and the candidates of obscure fringe parties, if they demand it, grows stronger every year. We think the provision should be not merely set aside in presidential campaigns but repealed outright as to all political contests.[37]

Other papers did not go quite so far, but the *Post* editorial pointed clearly to a problem that had been obscured by the issue of the debates themselves: the times and terms on which major candidates could be brought to the nation's viewers without risk of undue claims not only on the broadcasters (assuming they were willing to run such risks) but also on the interest and tolerance of the public. The *New York Times* regretted editorially that in 1964 of all years, there would be no opportunity to develop a coherent and responsive dialogue between the two candidates via televised debates. "They could have been especially useful this year in view of the Republican candidate's apparent determination to avoid press conferences and his propensity for repudiating or reinterpreting his previous remarks." [38]

Immediately after the Senate rejected the bill, Robert Sarnoff, chairman of the board of NBC, invited both candidates to meet in a series of six hour-long programs in the format of "Meet the Press" (NBC's regularly scheduled,

[36] Joseph A. Loftus, *New York Times,* Aug. 20, 1964.
[37] *Washington Post,* Aug. 20, 1964.
[38] *New York Times,* Aug. 20, 1964.

bona fide news interview program, under the network's control, and thus qualifying for exemption from the requirement to offer equal time to fringe candidates). Such programs, he suggested, could take place on Sundays between 6 and 7 p.m. EDT.[39] The Republican response was prompt: they accepted provided they could choose half the interviewing panelists. They would, moreover, be willing to pay half the costs of such programs, and if the Democrats were unwilling or unable to pay for the remainder, the Republicans stood willing to pay the whole cost. The White House said it had "no comment." It was recalled that Mr. Johnson, not yet officially the candidate, had said he would face the issues of a debate only after the Democratic convention.[40] The proposal foundered on the Democrats' failure to accept.

For the balance of the campaign, the Republicans occasionally jabbed at the President for his unwillingness to debate. But with the Senate's action, the issue was effectively closed for 1964.

Neither party, it may be concluded, inaugurated any creative new uses for television during the campaign. Both underused the medium, but the responsibility for underuse must rest chiefly with the Democrats. Despite *post facto* judgments by some observers that it would not have been possible to have a serious debate on the genuine issues facing the country, especially between the protagonists of 1964, it must nevertheless be noted that the candidates did not take

[39] Val Adams, *New York Times*, Aug. 20, 1964. The Sarnoff proposal was imaginative and flexible. He suggested that the candidates could be interviewed for the full hour by a panel of impartial newsmen, or that the hour could be broken into half hours, so each candidate would appear separately. Four of the programs could be for the presidential candidates, and two for the vice-presidential candidates, and each program could range over a wide gamut of issues, or if the candidates preferred, they could agree in advance to explore more restricted areas.

[40] Charles Mohr, *New York Times*, Aug. 21, 1964.

advantage of debates or the Sarnoff proposal to deal with issues in a format that itself would conduce toward a more serious and balanced treatment of the issues.

The Goldwater entourage, by its decision to cut back on nationwide television during the latter weeks of the campaign, when it had become almost decisively apparent that the Goldwater cause was lost, demonstrated a failure either to use television as a short-run means of redressing the balance, or as a powerful instrument to create long-run effects that would favor the cause of the conservatives, whether within or without the Republican party. Given the unimaginative use of the medium in the short run, and the limited vision of television's technical and media specialists helping the Republicans in the world of advertising and public relations, the decision to cut back is hardly surprising. What more could they do? In the campaign's last days, balancing the National Committee budget was more important in their view than all-out use of a vital medium, whether for short-run or long-run purposes.

As for budget-balancing, Republican television use in the 1964 campaign provided a pleasant surprise. The Republican tactic of combining political appeals with personality appeals (the use of movie stars, in particular), and both of them with appeals for television funds, put very substantial amounts of money into the Republican treasury during the last weeks of the campaign and helped with the image of a balanced budget if it did not indicate support from anyone who was not yet converted. Prominent among these appeals were the pleas of Ronald Reagan, coming at the end of various Goldwater telecasts. The total amount raised by the Republicans via television was estimated at $2 million, most of it in contributions of less than $100—and a good deal of that in dollars and half-dollars.[41] TV appeals do not seem to

[41] Rowland Evans and Robert Novak, *Washington Post*, Nov. 11, 1964; *Washington Post*, Jan. 10, 1965.

have provided similar leverage in the Democrats' programs for fundraising.

Election eve television produced no surprises in either party: family, country, party unity in the usual formats. Election night broadcasting did demonstrate a new development portending an order-of-magnitude improvement in its quality and probable educational effectiveness, resting on the new perceptiveness made possible by such analytic techniques as Vote Profile Analysis. The prospects are damped somewhat by the related prospect that an authoritative announcement early in the evening of the outcome will send many viewers away from their sets. This will be discussed in more detail below.

Newspaper Coverage of the Campaign

Most informed analysts would have predicted before the campaign that press coverage, on balance, would favor the Democrats if for no other reasons than the leverage a President exercises on press attention and the generally attributed preference of much of the working press for the Democrats over Republicans. Some of the more astute analysts might have noticed the onset of an antipress syndrome on the part of the Republicans—as evinced by Richard Nixon's imputation of his loss in 1960 to the manner in which the press had handled him, by his unprecedented public outburst against the press after his defeat for the governorship of California in 1962, and by the savage outburst from the galleries at the 1964 Republican convention when President Eisenhower (adding his testimony to the judgments of other Republicans) said the commentators did not care about the welfare of the Republican party and never had. But none of these kinds of observations prepared anyone for the unprecedented massive swing in editorial endorsements from Republican to Democratic.

On September 27, *Editor and Publisher* reported the results of a poll of 828 daily newspapers throughout the country: 31.2 percent supported Goldwater and 29.3 percent supported Johnson, with a full 40.5 percent remaining independent or uncommitted. In terms of readership, however, the President had a clear advantage. The 250 daily papers which favored Goldwater had a circulation of 5,268,691, while the 243 dailies endorsing Johnson had a total circulation of 12,618,721, representing 42.3 percent of the total circulation of all papers polled.[42] Earlier ten Hearst newspapers had announced their editorial support of the Johnson-Humphrey ticket—the first time since 1932 that the Hearst papers had supported a Democrat for President. The *Los Angeles Times* after much internal turmoil announced for Goldwater, but in an editorial so hedged that it was clear it retained much sentiment of another persuasion, reflecting its choice of Rockefeller over Goldwater in the California primary. The *New York Herald Tribune,* Republican before there was a Republican party, announced for Johnson, thus supporting a Democratic nominee for the first time in 124 years.[43] By the end of September, many of the staunchest supporters of the Republican cause had come out for Johnson. Only two other major newspapers, the *Chicago Tribune* and the *Cincinnati Enquirer,* joined the *Los Angeles Times* in keeping the Republican faith.

As early as the California primary, James Reston had summarized the dilemma created for reporters and editors by the Goldwater candidacy as it moved from the inconsequential expressions of a chairman of the Republican Senatorial Campaign Committee to the pronouncements of a serious candidate for the Presidency. Reporters who spent much of

[42] *Congressional Quarterly Weekly Report,* Sept. 25, 1964, p. 2218.
[43] Charles Rabb, *Washington Post,* Oct. 4, 1964.

their time with the Senator watched him half the time with personal affection and half the time with dismay, not knowing whether to explain him or to quote him. Editors remained troubled by Goldwater's stance on foreign policy, fearing that the Republican party might be captured by his more militant supporters.[44] These doubts remained throughout the campaign. The Republican candidates enjoyed less press support than at any time before. Meanwhile, editorials and news stories across the nation reflected to some degree the extent to which Johnson had been able in his campaigning and in his conduct of office to win vital support from members of the business establishment who would normally be found squarely in the Republican camp.

The Battle of the Books

Although it cannot be said in retrospect that anything serious was achieved, or any vital outcome changed, it must be noted that the book played an uncommonly prominent part in the 1964 campaign. Although there was little to do on the Democratic side, the Republican convention choice may have been swayed slightly, or reinforced, by Phyllis Schlafly's *A Choice Not an Echo*—a special writing of Republican history designed to discredit the machinations of an alleged Eastern Establishment, and to capture the nomination for a representative of true conservatism. Once the campaign had been joined, however, the hate and exposé books jostled those aimed at creating a favorable image for a candidate. Both parties produced their examples of each kind, although each party abjured responsibility for the more extreme ones. And each national committee complained of the unfairness of books circulated on behalf of the opponent.

[44] James Reston, *New York Times*, May 31, 1964.

Prominent among the anti-Johnson books were J. Evetts Haley's *A Texan Looks at Lyndon* and John Stormer's *None Dare Call It Treason*. Anti-Goldwaterism found less than respectable statement in Ed Reid and Ovid Demaris's *The Green Felt Jungle,* in which the authors attempted to link Goldwater with the Nevada gambling interests. Favorable statements included the pro-Johnson *The Professional,* by William S. White, and Edwin McDowell's *Barry Goldwater: Portrait of an Arizonan.* Less virulent statements were Frank Kluckhohn's *Lyndon's Legacy,* and Fred Cook's *Barry Goldwater: Extremist of the Right.* Conservative columnist John Chamberlain assessed the honors as even, and pointed as the one constructive use of bookmanship to the Republican National Committee's advice to its clients to make good use of Eugene Lyons's biography, *Herbert Hoover.*[45]

Although the national committees did not approve the hate books, the Republicans did make grandiose plans for the purchase and distribution of Barry Goldwater's *Where I Stand,* plans that failed of effective execution owing to inexperience with the logistical problems of buying, storing, distributing, and selling books in wholesale quantities. There is some question whether a success in distribution would have meant political gains for the Republicans, in view of the contribution this book made to the image of Goldwater's uncertainty in dealing with fundamental issues, when contrasted with his earlier publications and his other campaign speeches.[46]

The campaign period saw the appearance of the usual collection of books on how to understand politics, how to con-

[45] John Chamberlain, *Washington Post,* Oct. 21, 1964.

[46] On the plans for purchase and distribution, see Rowland Evans and Robert Novak, *Washington Post,* Jan. 21, 1965. On the problem of consistent utterance, see, for example, Richard Rovere, "The Minds of Barry Goldwater," in *Harper's Magazine,* Vol. 229 (September 1964), pp. 37 ff. See also Arthur Frommer, *Goldwater from A to Z* (Pocket Books, 1964).

duct political activities, facts and figures bearing on the current campaign, and the like. Strange fellow in this company was the surprisingly frank how-to book by Goldwater's colleague Stephen C. Shadegg, *How to Win an Election,* with its unabashed advice to follow the principle (attributed to Mao Tse-Tung) of penetrating opposing political organizations by cells manned by persons each one of whom was made to feel that an opposition victory would be a threat to him personally.[47] At lower levels, party organizations or affiliated groups used books as fundraisers, but fundraising as such was not always the main object. One organization, American Bookracks, Inc., riding the conservative wave, sold a "bookrack" of paper books by or about Goldwater for $50 per collection. Their initial selection included Jack Bell's *Barry Goldwater: Mr. Conservative.* Customer reaction to the inclusion in that book of even a few anti-Goldwater comments was so severe that the book was promptly replaced by something not so blemished.[48]

Moneymaking, concluded Geoffrey Vincent, was a prime object for some who helped provide and distribute the millions of paperbacks that made the 1964 campaign reminiscent of the political pamphleteering of the eighteenth and nineteenth centuries. Characteristic of this wave of books, rising in the spring with the early primary results, cresting in the later stages of the campaign, and subsiding with little trace after the election, was publication by unknown publishers, or by houses set up by the authors themselves. Whether for money or political influence, the books amassing the greatest publication figures were Haley's *A Texan Looks at Lyndon*—some 6 million copies published and distributed; Stormer's *None Dare Call It Treason,* published by his own company, the Liberty Bell Press of Florissant, Missouri, for which a Chicago firm printed 7 million copies,

[47] Marquis Childs, *Washington Post,* Aug. 10, 1964.
[48] *Washington Post,* April 26, 1964.

with 6 million finding their way into the hands of readers; and Mrs. Schlafly's *A Choice Not an Echo,* of which some 2 million were printed and an admittedly large proportion distributed.[49]

Not all of the political pamphlets were published by fly-by-nights; Cook's book was published by Grove Press, and McDowell's by Regnery. Random House published the President's late-appearing *My Hope for America.* Vincent's informal survey of the big paperback publishers indicated that they were not interested in getting into what looked like a remunerative if sporadic market. They did not wish to risk reputations for balanced professional editing by publishing books attractive to extremists; there are the hazards of libel actions that might completely demolish an established company. While they might publish occasional titles dealing with a controversial issue like civil rights from a single point of view, they expressed no interest in vilifications and sweeping charges.

Among the best-sellers of 1964, the *New York Times Book Review* section listed not only Goldwater's *Conscience of a Conservative,* published first in 1960, but also John F. Kennedy's *Profiles in Courage,* a repeater from the 1963 list, published first in 1957. It also listed Reid and Demaris's *The Green Felt Jungle.*[50]

Although comprehensive evidence is lacking, it may be plausibly speculated that the campaign book played a useful role in energizing the already dedicated partisans at many points and times throughout the campaign. As for more lasting legacies, it may also be speculated that Barry Goldwater's *Conscience of a Conservative* will have a more lasting effect in shaping the American concept of what the conservative choice may be than any other work. And it may be

[49] Geoffrey Vincent, "New Pamphleteers," *New York Times Book Review,* Jan 10, 1965.
[50] "The Year's Best Sellers," *ibid.*

speculated that it will have more of an impact on American political thought than Lyndon Johnson's *My Hope for America*. For, as Murray Kempton said in a perceptive review of the latter book:

> There is hardly a sentence Mr. Johnson prints which is not routine, lusterless, and worn thin from usage by other men. . . . And yet how many conceptions of national purpose that were disputed as visionary come now to rest comfortably in the wardrobes of Mr. Johnson's stall. . . . We begin to be grateful to Mr. Johnson just for the tone and the style which impels the recognition of their kinship.[51]

Johnson's utterance is of thoughts that have arrived, and enjoy current political usefulness and approval. Goldwater's is of a world that is past, or may never have been; but it etches a picture of a world for which some still hanker, and which continues to create tension in our political life.

Election Returns

Since the days of radio, election night has presented increasingly favorable opportunities for the electronic press to contribute to the political education of the public as well as to provide it with the latest information about the count and the outcome. With the onset of television and the ability to add important visual aids to the process of reporting and analysis—totaling boards, political maps, and so forth—the electronic press moved into a new dimension of usefulness and responsibility.

But in 1964, two interrelated developments promised an order-of-magnitude increase not only in the role and effectiveness of the electronic press, but a linked improvement in

---

[51] "The People's Choice," *New York Review of Books,* Vol. 3 (Nov. 5, 1964), p. 4.

the effectiveness of the printed press as well. The first of these was a joint arrangement among the networks and some of the press to provide for a rapid and common count of the vote as it came in. The other, symbolized by its most developed example, Vote Profile Analysis, was a vastly increased capability not only to predict the probable outcome, but simultaneously to explore and report the reasons for it.

Prompted by the costs of reporting the primaries in New Hampshire and California, plus the confusion about election reporting and election predicting that nearly caused acute embarrassment, the three networks, the Associated Press, and the United Press International agreed to set up a Network Election Service (NES). The networks in effect agreed to abandon their efforts to amass larger audiences by spending increasing amounts of money on hordes of special reporters in the field to provide them with the latest and most comprehensive counts; they were forced to the abandonment by sheer costs. The press associations, unable to keep up with the networks in the raw vote count process simply because they had not been able to hire the necessary reporters in the field, happily joined a pooled arrangement whereby NES would put 150,000 workers into 130,000 of the nation's 177,000 precincts to make quick counts on the most important races and report the results to tabulation centers in each state. (The rest of the precincts were covered by county and town reporters.) The estimated cost was $1.7 million, to be split among the five participants, and met half in cash and half in personnel.[52]

This innovation worked beautifully in providing a quick count, and may well be used in later years and extended to include more balloting than that for the major races. By reducing confusion on election night, keeping costs within manageable limits, and providing a quick and authoritative

[52] Susanna McBee, "Vote-Counting Barrier Broken," *Washington Post,* Nov. 1, 1964.

basis for newscasting and newswriting, the operation represented all gains and no foreseeable drawbacks.

The matter was not so simple with respect to Vote Profile Analysis. This was a joint product of the Louis Harris organization, International Business Machines, and the Columbia Broadcasting System. It stemmed from experience in advising the Kennedy campaign in 1960, and built on successful limited applications in 1962. It is a tool for the most rapid prediction of the outcome of an election, based on quick reporting of the behavior of precincts chosen so as to simulate the behavior of the larger system in which those precincts are found. It rests on the assumption that "people tend to vote in patterns by groups," that precincts can be found to represent political components, and that a "recipe" can be constructed to reflect the overall mix of voting groups within a state.[53] By the fastest reporting of the behavior of the representative precincts and application of the correct recipe, and by computer comparison of differences between current and previous behavior plus projection and summary of the results, the system can state with great accuracy the probable outcome of the election—providing nothing has happened (such as the purchase of a precinct) to disturb the relation between the component precincts and the overall model and thus interfere with the representation in the total electorate of the behavior of the group, class, or interest it was chosen to represent.

In 1962, VPA had proved itself in thirteen races in eight states. It picked George Romney over John Swainson in the Michigan gubernatorial race three hours before raw returns showed that Swainson's lead of 75,000 at the time of the prediction would not hold up. It predicted the winner of a Kentucky race one minute after the last polls closed, by relying on reports received from selected precincts in the eastern

[53] Carroll Kilpatrick, "New Tool Speeds Voting Results," *Washington Post*, Nov. 1, 1964.

half of the state. In the Maryland primary in 1964, VPA not only predicted within twenty-seven minutes after poll closing that Senator Daniel Brewster would receive some 50 percent of the vote and defeat Wallace, but it permitted observations on the structure of the vote: that Negro voters had supplied the margin of victory, that low-income white workers voted more heavily for Wallace than any other population group, and that the suburbs of Baltimore and Washington had split sharply.[54]

During the course of the 1964 campaign, VPA's spokesmen learned not only when to predict, but when not to—at least after their scare in the California primary in which they had predicted a Goldwater victory before they had heard from all of their own sample precincts. What had looked like a comfortable 6 percent margin at the point of prediction dwindled to a narrow 1.5 percent when all sample reports had been received.[55] On election night, VPA refrained from making any predictions about the outcome of the tight race for Ohio's senatorship.

The political community was not long in sensing the impact and some of the consequences for politics and policy of a really dependable means of fast prediction—especially if the results were announced before the formal balloting had ceased. On the heels of the California primary, Republican Representative Oliver Bolton of Ohio called on the networks to hold off announcing a winner in the November contest until polls had closed all over the country, and suggested he would take the matter to the FCC if the networks did not

[54] Laurence Stern, "VPA's a Mind Reading Machine," *Washington Post*, May 24, 1964.

[55] Jack Gould, *New York Times*, June 4, 1964; *Washington Post*, June 4, 1964. Applying probable error to the 50.8 percent prediction that had resulted for Goldwater, VPA would have had a lower limit value well below 50 percent. By the time CBS realized how tenuous its basis was, Harris made a reassuring calculation: the raw votes then in showed Rockefeller would have to take 58 percent of the remaining count, and most of it was going to come in from Goldwater territory.

work out such a policy on their own. President LeRoy Collins of the National Association of Broadcasters said the NAB would resist any such action, on the somewhat dubious ground that "you cannot tell a good reporter a fact and not expect it to be reported. As long as the people understand that such projections are mechanically estimated, there can be no harm in that." Representative Durward Hall (Republican from Missouri) simultaneously called for a congressional investigation of polls and pollsters, on the ground that they seemed to seek to influence elections, not merely predict them.[56]

NBC's Robert Sarnoff opposed any such controls over newscasting in a speech on July 24, in which he said it was "the obligation of radio and television, in common with all news media, to present significant information to the public as soon as it is available, using all of the best tools at their command." [57] Two weeks later CBS President Frank Stanton spoke in similar vein:

There is no necessity for any such radical embargo on news of election results. There is no support for charges that the early reporting of results in one part of the country has an effect on the outcome in other sections—by way of creating a bandwagon stampede for the leader, an underdog sympathy for the lagger or a reluctance to vote at all.

The fact is that a competent reporting organization today can reliably determine the outcome of elections long before the total vote is in.

At the point on election day when that determination is made, it immediately becomes news. And the job of any news organization worth its salt is to report it.

An embargo on reporting such news would involve a "banning of news, in no way involving national security, for a period of up to six hours." [58]

[56] *Washington Post*, June 8, 1964.
[57] *New York Times*, July 25, 1964.
[58] *New York Times*, Aug. 8, 1964.

Governor Grant Sawyer of Nevada, chairman of the National Governors' Conference, appointed a nine-man committee of governors to look into the intentions of television networks to declare election winners before the polls close. He declared that he fully supported the public's right to know and the broadcaster's right to broadcast a properly labeled prediction, but said:

But that was no prediction which CBS made on TV at 7:22 the night of June 2. Their announcer flatly stated, "Goldwater has won the California primary." This was a rude shock for voters on their way to the polls in some areas of northern California. I'm confident it had an effect.[59]

One proposal appeared that was reportedly acceptable to the network heads. Senator Jacob Javits (Republican from New York) on August 14 introduced legislation requiring that all polling places in the nation should close at the same (real) time. But the beast would not down. Senator Karl Mundt (Republican, South Dakota) proposed prohibiting radio and television from nationally reporting early returns before the polls had closed in all states. And Senator Winston Prouty (Republican, Vermont) introduced a bill to bar publication or release of national election results until the last vote had been cast.[60]

On August 31, news media executives met with Governor Sawyer's committee of governors. In a communiqué worthy of the Department of State, Sawyer announced:

The broadcasting media shared the concern of the Nation's governors that premature declarations of election victories might influence the election results in those areas where the polls have not closed. . . .

[59] Hal Humphrey, *Washington Post*, Aug. 15, 1964.

[60] *Washington Post*, Aug. 15, 1964. The Javits plan called for the polls to close in the East at 11 p.m. EST, at 6 p.m. Alaska-Hawaii Standard Time, and 5 p.m. Bering Standard Time. This would curtail voting by only two hours in Alaska and one hour in Nevada; polls would remain open up to three hours longer in the East.

There was general agreement that studies are inconclusive on whether or not the reporting of election results affects an elector's decision to vote.[61]

Senator Javits made public on September 18 a letter to the chairman of the Senate Rules Committee urging action before the election to establish a uniform closing time for all polls. Javits said his bill was supported by Frank Stanton, who had written him a letter saying:

I am persuaded that your bill represents an important step forward in remedying one of the central problems and that it does so without violating fundamental concepts of journalistic enterprise and freedom. We believe that yours is the sound and appropriate approach.[62]

Congress took no legislative action before the election. The networks, having asserted their proper journalistic independence, heeded the substance of what their critics had been saying. Election night reporting was a model of correct labeling. On that night, VPA produced two important results: one, in the judgment of qualified observers, it permitted an easy and relaxed treatment of the unfolding of the electoral results, well after the highly predictable outcome had been adumbrated; two, it demonstrated remarkable accuracy in assessing state returns, not only for the presidential race, but for other key races as well.[63]

Probably more important than an improvement in the demeanor and ease of the news commentator is the prospect

---

[61] *Washington Post*, Sept. 1, 1964.

[62] *Washington Post*, Sept. 19, 1964.

[63] VPA made its prediction of the presidential outcome at 9:07 p.m. EST, when no more than a quarter of the actual vote was in. VPA projected that 61.3 percent of the two-party vote would go for the President. The Democrats' share of the actual vote for all parties, as reported later, was 61.0 percent; *Congressional Quarterly Weekly Report*, Dec. 11, 1964, p. 2791. Across the board, VPA rarely varied by more than 1.5 percent from tabulations reported hours later; see Laurence Stern, *Washington Post*, Nov. 5, 1964.

that VPA will improve the quality of his contribution to political education by helping him to fulfill the task of immediate comment that is imposed on him by the nature of the medium. There is both temptation and pressure on the newscaster to be immediately knowledgeable. His comment, especially since TV has assumed major importance as a medium for political reporting, becomes part of the event. Anything that makes his comment more relevant, impartial, and objective, can produce both immediate and long-run benefits.

Jack Gould, the *New York Times* specialist on television, reported that Tuesday night, November 3, was a turning point, a revolution for the Fourth Estate. Figures were compiled much more quickly than before. More important, "the viewer was informed almost instantly on the nature of the vote, the demographic make-up of President Johnson's landslide. It was TV . . . which was the originating source of the major bulk of election night material. . . . The complementary character of broadcasting and the Fourth Estate seldom was so strikingly illustrated." CBS, he opined, by making full use of VPA, recaptured pride of place from the NBC team of Chet Huntley and David Brinkley that had taken honors in 1956 and in 1960. CBS displayed not only boards to total the raw results as reported by NES; it also had separate boards to record the outcomes as estimated by VPA. The other networks had only a single set of panels, showing the tabulated results for each contest, but experienced difficulty in combining reporting of the results, analysis, and predictions. Yet NBC was the more correct, announcing at 8:47 p.m. EST: "Our projection is that President Johnson is the projected winner. . . ." CBS at 9:04 plumped: "Johnson Elected." [64]

---

[64] Jack Gould, "Taking the Wait Out of Election Night," *New York Times*, Nov. 8, 1964.

As an example of the quickness of newspaper reporting based on VPA, the *Washington Post's* Julius Duscha and Carroll Kilpatrick coauthored an article appearing on November 5, that asserted as fact:

On Election Day, [Mr. Johnson] was accepted by rich and poor, city and suburb, town and country, black and white, Catholic, Protestant and Jew. Only in the racially troubled Deep South was he rejected.

They found profound changes in the American electorate and in the prominence of issues. For the first time in recent elections foreign policy eclipsed domestic policy; the Democrats had shed the image of war party; new splits appeared in a new, industrialized South united only by tragic racial conflict but exhibiting political behavior similar to that of border states, and showing it was unwilling to penalize a politician for favoring civil rights, except in the Deep South. They noted that straight party voting was still on the decline, as ticket-splitting showed itself more popular in both parties. They underlined the unprecedentedly high Negro majorities for Democrats (90 percent or better), large Democratic majorities in formerly Republican New England, and the swing in the suburbs to the Democrats from the Republicans. They drew on the wealth of polling that underlay VPA to comment on many other developments signaled by the election, pointing to the apparent polarization of choice around candidates rather than issues, while Mr. Johnson's campaign against poverty and his slogan of a Great Society had failed to catch on.[65]

TV and Turnout

Earlier estimates of TV's probable political effectiveness have emphasized its possible effect on turnout, and the judg-

[65] *Washington Post*, Nov. 5, 1964.

ment usually is that TV tends to increase it. Although enough data are not at hand to permit a categorical judgment, the experience of 1964 suggests on the surface that TV played its expected role in this respect. Although down somewhat from 1960, turnout was high, about 62.0 percent according to early analyses; the total of 70.6 millions who voted was the largest yet.[66] TV might even be credited with creating enough voter interest to amass that good a record in an election in which the outcome was so consistently predicted from the time the two contenders were chosen. Issues and personalities involved in the election were such as to create interest and to activate formerly and usually apathetic voters, but there is no evidence that TV did more than any other medium to bring this home. Given the ambiguity of the available data, it is difficult for the analyst to sort out the relative influence of media or of organization.

Problems of the Future

The 1964 campaign left important work undone. The failure to hold debates or something like them bequeathed to later elections the problems inherent in this device for improving political communication. The discussion and argument of 1964 were not conclusive. The experience of the future will turn, in large part, on the estimates made by each party about the relative advantages of use or non-use of debates or similar confrontations. It remains to be seen whether candidates, parties, broadcasters, and scholars can work out devices to circumvent the difficulties of debates when one candidate is the incumbent—as may frequently be the case. Slightly delayed broadcasts should circumvent most of the difficulties of accidental disclosures of security information by an incumbent. An opponent seeking to demon-

[66] *Congressional Quarterly Weekly Report*, Dec. 11, 1964, p. 2791.

strate his qualifications of responsibility as a requirement for the highest office ought to avoid irresponsible claims or charges—if such charges in fact are politically potent. The chief value of debates remains the benefit from a confrontation available to a broader spectrum of the electorate, disciplined by the prospect of immediate challenge and immediate reply.

The issue of Section 315 is no closer to solution than ever; the limits of the problem have been plumbed; it remains for more courageous politicians to arrange the relaxations that would assure, at least for the presidential race, a better chance of genuine confrontation and adequate exposure. Nothing the minor parties did in 1964 indicates any need to give them and their candidates more protection than they would enjoy under the fairness doctrine and the broadcaster's competitive drive to play a full role in reporting the newsworthy among political candidates, ideas, and movements. The failure of the minor parties in 1964 was not to win enough television time; it was to dramatize fresh issues in the fashion that has always been proper to minor parties in American political experience. Governor Wallace gave three northern states a chance to express their pique at the regimes enjoying office; he failed to raise any new banner to serve the political requirements of a nation faced with challenges on both the domestic and international fronts. The parties of the radical left did no more than warm over ancient Socialist dogmas.

The decision of the FCC that the presidential press conference is a "political" use within the meaning of Section 315 of the Communications Act illustrates the complexities and absurdity of some of the consequences of the law as now drafted and applied. It also points to the necessity of clarifying the language of the Act, if that is not done by amendments allowing full use of radio and television during the presidential campaign. It cannot be stated with much confidence that the nation was visibly the poorer in political awareness because the press conference was canceled by the October 1 decision.[67] But it also cannot be argued that a regulatory body's controversial decision should deprive the nation of a virtually institutionalized news practice, in which the President's announcement of news is subject to the discipline of reporters' questions.

A lesser illustration of the sort of problem arising under Section 315 was the refusal by the United States Court of Appeals to grant Barry Goldwater free time to answer a broadcast of October 18, when the President addressed the nation on Premier Khrushchev's dismissal and the nuclear explosion accomplished by the Chinese Communists. In a 3-3 vote, without any accompanying decision, the court issued an unsigned order that left in force the decision of the FCC denying equal time. Whatever the merits, a favorable decision would have created the basis for equal time demands by candidates of six splinter parties; it was estimated that the cost to the three networks of nineteen minutes of equal time for a Republican reply would have approximated $500,000. And if the networks had granted the time under

---

[67] *Washington Post*, Oct. 2, 1964. The decision was made by a 4-3 vote, Commissioners Kenneth Cox, Robert E. Lee, and Robert T. Bartley joining Chairman E. William Henry in the majority, and Commissioners Rosel Hyde, Frederick Ford, and Lee Loevinger in the minority. The latter issued sharp dissents. Loevinger pointed to the Commission's 1962 ruling that a governor's radio news conference was exempt, and asserted the decision was contrary to common sense. Ford, a former FCC chairman, complained of the majority's narrow legalistic approach, and said the decision was "completely contrary to congressional intent." He called for an investigation by all interested groups. The majority had held that the presidential press conference was neither a "bona fide interview" nor "on-the-spot coverage of a bona fide news event," hence it could not escape under the 1959 amendments.

the fairness doctrine, they would have risked similar demands by the other candidates.[68]

The issues of public policy involved in the broadcasters' assertion of their untrammeled newsman's right to report "facts" as soon as they found them, and the efforts of legislators or regulatory authorities to control them, were outlined but not settled. Uniform closing of polls would provide a neat solution to the broadcasters' immediate problem, provided they would agree to a code of ethics as to labeling and the time of authoritative prediction. For it cannot be ignored that the effectiveness of VPA as such—and of similar predictive and analytic devices generated by other broadcasters, political analysts, and computer manufacturers—will translate a carefully labeled "projection" into an announcement. It is not enough for the broadcasters to say that there is no evidence yet of the effect of such predictions on the vote when the vote is not yet completed. It is quite probable that such effects, if present, would be either small or politically ineffective in a national election. If the margin were so narrow that a prediction might affect the outcome, it is also probable that the revealed basis for a forecast would be so uncertain that a responsible analyst or broadcaster would not take the risk. There remains the case in which an irresponsible actor might make the prediction in the hope of achieving the marginal effect; and it cannot be denied that small margins at election time have sometimes led to important turning points in national political trends. There is the more puzzling case in which the operations of the electoral college might render marginal a decision that actually was not marginal in terms of national voter preference.

The issue of preference if not policy is clear; the broadcasters should be left free journalist's rein; they should also apply rules of common sense to the statement of predictions

---

[68] *Washington Post*, Oct. 28, 1964. The court at least acted promptly; the Republican suit had been filed on October 21.

as facts, and carefully scan their action under circumstances in which their predictions might be politically decisive. The promise of VPA for the voter at large is less as a predictive instrument and a tool for competition in producing scoops than it is as a means to political enlightenment.

The broadcast media issued gentle hints that in later elections they might enlarge their role to include making political endorsements.[69] It is possible but not likely that movements in this direction will be strong or swift. And the odds are that such movements will be made only after those responsible for broadcast editorials and political endorsements have canvassed not only the effect on politics, but also on the competitive position of their station.

Although the format and occasions for use of television did not reveal any important innovations from previous practice and the audiences amassed did not begin to approximate the huge ones assembled for the 1960 debates, television did well in 1964. Its notable improvements in the analysis and reporting of the vote, and its establishment of new complementary relationships with the printed press, signaled great progress and greater prospects for the future.

Could the press legitimately be criticized, as Senator Strom Thurmond (Republican of South Carolina) claimed, for robbing Goldwater of the election by persistently slanting its reportage of the Senator's positions on issues? Or is it fair to conclude that the press, possibly with relish in some quarters, only reported and allowed to resonate through its channels the well-documented instances in which the Senator

[69] Note the action of R. Peter Straus, president of WMCA in New York City, whose station was the first to endorse a political candidate when he favored Kennedy in 1960. He broke new ground, but no one followed. Frank Stanton had told Columbia University's National Broadcast Editorial Conference on July 7, 1964, that CBS-owned TV stations might endorse candidates for governor or for congressman during 1966. He also urged his audience of some seventy-five broadcasters to use their editorial right to support the Civil Rights Act. *New York Times,* July 8, 1964.

had talked on more than one side of an issue, and had to spend a good deal of time trying to rectify an image to which he had contributed by his utterances? [70]

The disappointments of the campaign, at least as they were assessed by Walter Lippmann, could not be laid to any of the media. They would have to be charged to the chief participants. Lippmann himself would not hold them seriously at fault, beyond pointing out that in his opinion it was impossible for anyone to conduct a dialogue with Senator Goldwater. The real problem lay in the magnitude of the issues and the incapacity of any of the politicians of the day to lay them fully bare, and to cope with them. For these issues in his view turned on such imponderables as the level of anxiety in our affluent society; the reasons why crime is increasing at such an alarming rate among the young; or how the United States should adjust its military and economic strength to the impressive new power of Europe and to the rising expectations of a host of new nations.[71]

There is no reason to suppose, at the present writing, that the nation's media of mass communication cannot be used in the future as in the past to contribute to the tasks of political discussion, enlightenment, and formation of consensus on these and many other issues of public policy. These media are themselves rooted in the center of the nation's life, its

[70] The *Columbia Journalism Review* editorialized, in its Fall 1964 issue, that attacks on news media campaign coverage were "unfair" and "irresponsible." Based on a survey of news coverage of Goldwater activities during the week of August 24-30, the *Review* concluded "there was no significant difference in frequency of coverage in the papers that have declared editorial support of Senator Goldwater, those that have come out for President Johnson, and those that were not committed as of October 5." (Quoted in the *Los Angeles Times,* Oct. 23, 1964.) Although these findings and this judgment might have been more telling had they been based on news activity later in the campaign, when more newspapers had declared and the developments of the campaign itself had become more controversial, they nevertheless point to a reassuring judgment about the performance of the press.

[71] Walter Lippmann, *Washington Post,* Oct. 8, 1964.

economics, its politics, its concept of its role and of its interest. However, the media provide for experimentation and agitation on the fringes of consensus. They provide the opportunities for those who seek clear choice to state the issues and to uphold their views. As the nation moves, so will they.

5

Financing the Parties and Campaigns

HERBERT E. ALEXANDER

The financing of the presidential campaigns of 1964 contrasted sharply with the voting patterns: the victory of Lyndon Baines Johnson was built on a narrow financial base but a broad electoral base; the Barry Goldwater candidacy had a broad financial but a narrow electoral base.

The total spending for election contests at all levels of government in 1964 was approximately $200 million, undoubtedly making it the most expensive election year in history. This represents an increase from estimated totals of $175 million in 1960, $155 million in 1956, and $140 million in 1952,[1] but seems realistic in view of such factors as: increases in the national-level totals; increases in political broadcasting, literature, and mailing costs; the Republican presidential prenomination costs, far exceeding those of the Democrats in 1960; special efforts in many states to gain command of legislatures in order to control

[1] In this chapter most data comparisons with other years are derived from Alexander Heard, *The Costs of Democracy* (University of North Carolina Press, 1960); Herbert E. Alexander, *Financing the 1960 Election* (Citizens' Research Foundation, 1962); and *1956 General Election Campaigns*, Report to the Senate Committee on Rules and Administration, 85 Cong. 1 Sess. (1957).

reapportionment; the general price rise of about 5 percent since 1960. Offsetting reductions in expenditures are hard to find.

The various committees operating at the national level reported spending $34.8 million in 1964, as shown in Table 5.1. This is more than twice the $17.2 million spent in 1956—only eight years before—and a 39 percent increase from the $25 million spent in 1960. Major party national campaign costs in 1964 were $29.2 million ($17.2 million for Republicans, $12 million for Democrats), compared with $21.9 million in 1960, or 41 cents per voter for the 70,642,496 votes cast in the 1964 presidential election. Labor and miscellaneous committees spent an additional $5.6 million.

Table 5.1. Summary of Political Spending at the National Level, 1964

(In thousands of dollars)

Committees[a]	Gross Reported Disbursements[b]	Known Debt	Total Campaign Costs	Transfers to Candidates and Committees	Direct Expenditures[c]
18 Republican[d].......	$17,187	$ —	$17,187	$1,163	$16,026
32 Democratic[e].......	10,973	1,000	11,973	3,216	8,757
31 Labor.............	3,665	—	3,665	2,940	725
26 Miscellaneous......	1,963	—	1,963	889	1,074
Total (107).......	$33,788	$1,000	$34,788	$8,208	$26,582

    [a] The number of national-level committees increased from 70 in 1960, but the same criteria were used in identifying them.
    [b] Data derived from reports filed with the Clerk of the United States House of Representatives.
    [c] Details on all categories of expenditures were not obtained from the campaign fund reports. Hence direct expenditures were determined by subtracting from total campaign costs all transfers of funds out. Though the totals in this column may be subject to error, enough evidence is available to indicate that the totals represent fair approximations.
    [d] For further information, see Table 5.3.
    [e] For further information, see Table 5.2.

Exact figures for political campaign costs are almost impossible to determine, and those that are available lack the exactitude and detail one would wish for. The data used in this chapter are largely limited to national-level sources, particularly the reports of national political committees required to be filed with the Clerk of the House of Representatives, but the federal law on the subject allows many exceptions. Furthermore, committees and nonfederal candidates who make expenditures only in a single state are not required to make such reports. Consequently, the figures in Table 5.1 omit state and local expenses on behalf of the national tickets. Other costs are also omitted: campaigns for congressional candidates, except for transfers from national level committees; presidential and congressional nominating campaigns, as well as campaigns for state, county, and other offices; and the national nominating conventions. Responsible estimates of some of these items have been obtained and will be reported.[2]

Along with dollar increases went increases in the number of national-level committees—from 70 in 1960 to 107 in 1964—reporting as required by federal law with the Clerk of the House of Representatives. In 1960 the Democrats operated with 13 committees, though some of these subsumed various divisions; in 1964, each division was organized separately, making a total of 32 committees. The number of Republican committees increased by only one. There was an increase of 10 reporting labor committees, perhaps because of widespread labor opposition to Senator Barry Goldwater. Miscellaneous committees increased from 19 to 26, reflecting the growth of independent committees to support congressional candidates.

---

[2] In all cases, attempts were made to verify findings through interviews with finance managers and others.

During the period of Democratic ascendancy from 1932 to 1952, the Republicans consistently spent more money in presidential campaigns than the Democrats, and the pattern continued during the Eisenhower campaigns. In 1960, the Democrats went deeply into debt to spend as much as the Republicans, though the GOP also incurred a small deficit. In 1964, the Republicans surged ahead again and finished with a surplus; the Democrats went into debt though they raised more than ever before. The Republicans at the national level were able to maintain financial support from many of their usual sources, and they also broadened their appeal dramatically through massive direct mail drives and effective television appeals for funds, which yielded some 650,000 contributions of less than $100 each. Some normally Republican sources of funds were closed to Goldwater, and some actually aided the Johnson campaign, but total Republican receipts were $18.5 million.

The Democrats in 1964 probably spent about half as much as the Republicans for prenomination and general election expenses. Given their control of the Presidency and other advantages, they did not need to spend more. Instead of operating without a deficit, however, they chose to increase spending for registration and congressional campaigns in order to extend the predicted Johnson landslide to other offices; the national campaign ended with a deficit of $1 million or more. Despite the seeming Republican advantage in spending, the Democrats have never in recent times conducted such a well-financed national campaign as in 1964. Spurred by the President's Club, which throughout the country had about 4,000 members contributing at least $1,000 each, they raised over $11 million, attracting funds far in excess of those for the Truman, Stevenson, and Kennedy candidacies.

The Preconvention Campaigns

Federal law does not require that the expenses of nominating campaigns for federal office be disclosed, and not all states holding primaries require comprehensive disclosure of expenses in presidential nominating campaigns. Some data have been obtained from responsible participants for the campaigns of all major Republican candidates, and in several of the Democratic nomination campaigns entered by Governor George Wallace of Alabama.

The Republicans

Admitted expenses of campaigns for candidates seeking the Republican presidential nomination totaled almost $10 million, not including considerable amounts raised and spent at the state and local level. This total also excludes the payroll and personal expenses of Governor Nelson Rockefeller, and probably some Nixon expenditures.

For Senator Goldwater's candidacy the early Draft Goldwater for President Committee and allied committees raised a combined total of $3.5 million. An additional $2 million was raised separately, chiefly in California for the primary in that state. Further amounts were raised by other groups. Funds were estimated to have come from more than 300,000 contributors; the flow was uneven and money was scarce at times.[3] Many were one-dollar contributions, accompanying a petition for the Senator's nomination. These

---

[3] One writer states there were three financial crises in this period; Robert G. Spivack, "Men Behind Goldwater," *Look*, Vol. 28 (November 3, 1964), p. 48. See also Robert D. Novak, *The Agony of the G.O.P. 1964* (Macmillan, 1965), p. 287.

contributors were part of a mass army of volunteers who worked at the grass-roots level and contributed services of incalculable value.

Known transfers from national Goldwater funds for the New Hampshire primary campaign were $88,210. The Oregon primary cost national and state Goldwater committees at least $109,000. As noted, the California primary cost at least $2,000,000.

Most of the funds for Governor Nelson Rockefeller's campaign were supplied by the candidate and his family personally. Rockefeller sources admit that less than $100,000 was raised outside of the family.

Estimates of Rockefeller expenditures range from $3.5 million to $5 million and more. According to close associates, admitted out-of-pocket Rockefeller expenditures were as follows: New Hampshire—a little under $100,000;[4] New England—another $100,000, in connection with the New Hampshire primary (New Hampshire places a legal limitation of $100,000 on the amount that can be spent within the state); West Virginia—$80,000; Oregon—$477,135;[5] California—a little over $2,000,000; New York office—$100,000 (having a bearing on primary campaigns); and the Republican Convention—$70,000. This totals $2,927,135.

For the one-month campaign of Governor William Scranton of Pennsylvania, nine major committees accounted for the receipts. The suddenness of the candidacy gave little time to raise sufficient funds; at the outset some money was

[4] Aggregate spending for candidate and delegate candidates was officially reported at $97,863.

[5] See Oregon's official *Summary Report of Campaign Contributions and Expenditures: 1964 Primary Election* (Compiled and published by Howell Appling, Jr., Secretary of State of Oregon, July 15, 1964), p. 16. This shows only $447,884.85 contributed by National Committee, Rockefeller for President.

borrowed, and the Scranton family contributed some funds. After the convention there was a deficit of $150,000, all of which was paid by early 1965.

The Scranton expenditures, totaling $827,000, were: TV-radio—$245,000; candidate travel—$110,000; convention —$200,000; printing—$58,000; polls—$12,000; fundraising—$10,500; hotels—$27,000; miscellaneous—$164,525.

The campaign on behalf of Henry Cabot Lodge cost over $100,000, raised primarily from Boston and New York supporters; an early effort was started in December 1963 in Washington, D. C., and ultimately raised some $10,000. Some funds were raised in New Hampshire, and $4,000 locally in Oregon; the Lodge family apparently contributed some money. A deficit of $17,000 existed after the New Hampshire primary; it was $9,600 after the Oregon primary, and by the end of 1964 was reduced to about $4,000, which was subsequently paid up. In addition, campaigners received no salaries and paid their own expenses. Actual expenditures for the New Hampshire primary were $32,000; for Oregon $54,300; for other primaries, relatively small amounts.

For the unannounced candidacy of former Vice President Richard M. Nixon there is little information. Most money was raised for the Oregon primary, with at least $10,000 coming from a California group; there were repeated reports of difficulties in raising funds. Known expenditures came to $71,800: $15,285 for the New Hampshire primary; $49,000 for Oregon; and about $7,500 for a write-in campaign in Nebraska.

Almost half the funds spent by Harold Stassen in his quest for the nomination were his own contributions. Expenditures came to over $70,000, including $44,833 for

New Hampshire, $10,000 for Indiana, and $15,000 for California.

Senator Margaret Chase Smith received numerous contributions, all of which were returned to the donors. Of her own funds, she spent $250 in the New Hampshire primary and $85 for air travel to Illinois. In Oregon $1,171 was spent on her behalf by others; elsewhere, small amounts also were spent in her support.

Throughout the Republican campaigns in 1964 there were frequent charges of excessive spending. Some of the allegations concerning primary costs were extravagant, with Governor Rockefeller bearing the brunt of charges about high levels of spending. One in Oregon went: "Don't let your vote be bought by Eastern money" (which applied to Lodge as well as Rockefeller). Rockefeller responded that "he cared enough" to spend enough to win.

Except in California, Goldwater supporters won by seizing state delegations, not by winning primaries. The organizational route these supporters followed has been thought to be cheaper than the primary or media route, but the Goldwater prenomination costs were so high that we must conclude that in modern-day campaigning even the organizational route is expensive.

The Goldwater movement appears to have attracted many more contributors than did Dwight D. Eisenhower in 1952. This impressive financial support, though widespread in terms of historical financial support for candidates of either party, may nevertheless have been limited to a relatively small portion of the population. The moderates may have given Rockefeller and Scranton and Lodge less active financial support in part because they *are* moderate and perhaps less passionately concerned about the consequences of Democratic rule. Foreseeing an inevitable Johnson victory in November, some Republicans saw little reason to contribute.

The Democrats

Governor George Wallace of Alabama entered presidential primaries in Wisconsin, Indiana, and Maryland. He was not directly opposed by President Johnson in any of them, but by various state officials acting as stand-ins.

Governor Wallace reported receiving $321,344 in contributions toward his primary campaign expenses,[6] and on behalf of the unpledged electoral vote campaign in Alabama. According to the Governor, all funds were furnished by voluntary contributions from individuals; there were isolated reports of funds raised in certain cities on his behalf and sent to his headquarters. Officials in the Wallace campaign frequently denied using any state funds; and just as frequently they claimed that he received many small contributions for his campaign, with many coming from non-southern states. The sparse official reports that are available, however, indicate that only small sums of local money were raised for the Wallace campaigns in Wisconsin, Indiana, and Maryland. Instead, large amounts were reported to have been sent from national Wallace headquarters in Alabama: $19,989 of $20,000 reported in Indiana; $88,575 of $90,000 reported in Maryland. Observers estimated that the Wallace media campaign in Wisconsin cost between $25,000 and $30,000, and that most of the funds came from outside the state, with perhaps $5,000 raised locally.

President Johnson's stand-in for Wisconsin was John Reynolds, the Governor. His campaign received no monetary (but some working) help from the national and state Democratic parties. The campaign cost $16,000, derived wholly from a Citizens for Johnson Committee fundraising dinner.

After Governor Wallace made his remarkable showing in the Wisconsin primary, greater effort and larger funds were

[6] *Evening Star* (Washington), Aug. 5, 1964.

expended on the Indiana and Maryland primaries by both sides. Governor Matthew Walsh of Indiana campaigned against Wallace largely on funds supplied by the Democratic State Committee of Indiana, amounting to $100,000. The campaign on behalf of Senator Daniel B. Brewster of Maryland cost about $70,000. His campaign committee reported receipts and expenditures of $42,186, and the Senator personally borrowed $25,000, which was repaid after a major fundraising dinner in early 1965.

It seems obvious that funds were also spent in promoting the Democratic vice-presidential possibilities, although few figures are available. Projecting images of the various hopefuls was done quietly, even furtively, yet scores of thousands of dollars were spent on public opinion polls, staff, telephone calls for support, and on adequate communications facilities and hotel space at Atlantic City. President Johnson's elimination of Robert F. Kennedy from consideration for the vice-presidential nomination may have forestalled costly organizational efforts on his behalf. But one comprehensive and reliable report indicates that the President through aides told Senator Hubert Humphrey well before the convention to start gaining "exposure" and to drum up public support.[7] Friends of Humphrey were active on his behalf, including volunteered public relations help. Among the exposure gained were several speaking engagements for Senator Humphrey before groups of businessmen and bankers in Chicago, New York, and Washington.

Financing the Conventions

The Republican National Convention of 1964 cost $664,750, slightly more than the $642,800 cost in 1960. Of the total, $650,000 was guaranteed and paid by the host

[7] *New York Times*, Aug. 27, 1964.

city, San Francisco, which provided the money as follows: $400,000 from local city hotel tax funds, and $250,000 from Republican Convention Program proceeds and other means. The Convention costs above the guarantee were also paid by San Francisco from proceeds of ticket sales to special affairs and other donations, and adequate money remained to pay for the printing and distribution of the Convention Proceedings later.

Spokesmen for the Democrats assert their National Convention of 1964 cost about $2 million, 267 percent more than the Democratic Convention of 1960. Accounting for the high costs, the Democrats pointed out that the 1964 Convention was larger than ever before in numbers of delegates, alternates, and spectators; that it was better staffed; that it included expensive films, construction, and special programs; and that it required costly protection and security for President Johnson when he attended because Atlantic City had only a small police force. Atlantic City and New Jersey groups pledged and paid $625,000 in cash, plus fringe benefits such as air-conditioning the Convention Hall, to secure the convention.

If Democratic Convention costs were high, so were income and expenditures of the Program Book Committee, which published the volume as a memorial edition dedicated to the memory of President John F. Kennedy. The Program was published by a special committee rather than by the host city as in the case of the Republican convention, and Program revenues were not credited to the funds pledged by the host city.

Corporate advertising in the Program was $15,000 per page, three times higher than was charged in 1960, and on a circulation basis higher than comparable advertising costs in national magazines. There were ninety-six pages of advertising, including front and back covers, and at least $1,500,000 must have been received from this source. About 300,000 copies were published, and while some were distributed free to delegates and others, some were sold at a retail price of ten dollars. Total receipts, publication costs, and net profits are not known. Democrats state that profits went to pay for Convention costs above the $625,000 guaranteed by Atlantic City, and they confirm that $50,000 of the profits were contributed to the Public Affairs Institute and transferred by it to the National Council for Civic Responsibility to help counter so-called right-wing propaganda. Rumors have circulated that some profits were channeled into Negro registration drives.

The General Election Campaign

Both the Democratic and Republican campaigns were highly centralized, with auxiliary committees well integrated with party committees, and with the direction of campaign activity and financial operations centered in party headquarters. One exception was the National Television for Goldwater Committee, located in Los Angeles, which operated with some independence from other party and Washington-based allied committees.

Receipts and expenditures of various national-level committees affiliated with the major parties are summarized in Tables 5.2 and 5.3. Several of the committees approached the legal limit of $3 million. At no point before or during the campaign did the Democrats seem to be hurting for funds, but there were reports of dwindling treasuries and of scurrying for money to meet broadcast commitments, which were higher than anticipated.[8] At the Inauguration National

[8] Drew Pearson, *Washington Post*, Nov. 2, 1964.

Table 5.2. Receipts and Expenditures, Democratic National Campaign Committees, January 1-December 31, 1964

(In thousands of dollars)

Committee	Gross Reported Receipts	Adjusted Receipts[a]	Gross Reported Disbursements	Total Transfers Out	Direct Expenditures[b]
National..............	$ 2,989	$2,961	$ 2,992	$ 424	$2,568
National congressional	67	3	93	—	93
Congressional campaign..............	310	45	306	306	—
Senatorial campaign...	463	51	484	329	155
Democrats for sound government........	39	5	38	38	—
Subtotal.........	$ 3,868	$3,065	$ 3,913	$1,097	$2,816
President's club for Johnson...........	$ 2,733	$2,613	$ 2,730	$1,304	$1,426
Johnson-Humphrey...	1,623	1,508	1,623	312	1,311
Johnson for president..	710	691	702	—	702
Humphrey for vice-president..........	723	696	678	189	489
Subtotal.........	$ 5,789	$5,508	$ 5,733	$1,805	$3,928
23 Miscellaneous[c].....	$ 1,523	$1,245	$ 1,327	$ 314	$1,016
Total[d]..........	$11,180	$9,818	$10,973	$3,216	$7,760

[a] Adjusted for lateral transfers from national-level Democratic, labor, and miscellaneous committee groupings included in the tables.

[b] Direct expenditures were determined by subtracting all transfers of funds from gross disbursements.

[c] Artists & Entertainers for Johnson-Humphrey; All Americans Council; Americans Abroad for Johnson; Builders for Johnson-Humphrey; Business & Professional Men's Division of Citizens for Johnson-Humphrey; Citizens for Johnson-Humphrey; Committee for Responsible Leadership; District Attorneys for Johnson-Humphrey; Educators for Johnson-Humphrey; Friends of LBJ; Independent Citizens for Johnson-Humphrey; Industrial Relations Committee for Johnson-Humphrey; Lawyers for Johnson-Humphrey National Committee; National Committee of Small Businessmen for Johnson-Humphrey; National Independent Committee for Johnson-Humphrey; National Committee of Republicans & Independents for Johnson-Humphrey; Pharmacists for Johnson-Humphrey; Rural Americans for Johnson; Republicans for Johnson; Scientists & Engineers for Johnson-Humphrey National Committee; Senior Citizens for Johnson-Humphrey; Veterans for Johnson-Humphrey; Women for Johnson-Humphrey.

[d] Minor discrepancies between items and totals are due to rounding.

Table 5.3. Receipts and Expenditures, Republican National Campaign Committees, January 1-December 31, 1964

(In thousands of dollars)

Committee	Gross Reported Receipts	Adjusted Receipts[a]	Gross Reported Disbursements	Total Transfers Out	Direct Expenditures[b]
National.............	$ 2,949	$ 2,949	$ 2,640	$ —	$ 2,640
National finance operations.........	1,947	1,947	1,928	113	1,814
National congressional	1,686	1,269	1,633	544	1,089
Congressional boosters	190	190	141	141	—
Senatorial campaign...	465	430	480	258	223
Subtotal.........	$ 7,237	$ 6,785	$ 6,822	$1,056	$ 5,766
Citizens for Goldwater-Miller.......	$ 2,957	$ 2,957	$ 2,648	$ 20	$ 2,627
Republican campaign.	2,057	2,052	2,048	6	2,042
Republican television.	2,790	2,690	2,697	8	2,690
National TV.........	2,516	2,516	2,009	5	2,004
5 Miscellaneous campaign[c].............	784	761	759	24	737
Subtotal.........	$11,104	$10,976	$10,161	$ 63	$10,100
4 Miscellaneous non-party[d].............	$ 171	$ 171	$ 204	$ 44	$ 160
Total[e]..........	$18,512	$17,932	$17,187	$1,163	$16,026

[a] Adjusted for lateral transfers from national-level Republican, labor, and miscellaneous committee groupings included in the tables.

[b] Direct expenditures were determined by subtracting all transfers of funds from gross disbursements.

[c] Brothers for Goldwater; Citizens' Campaign Committee for Goldwater-Miller; National Federation of Republican Women; Solid South Speaks for Goldwater Committee; Women Voters for Goldwater-Miller.

[d] Committee for the Election of Republican Candidates; Committee to Support Moderate Republicans; Committee for Forward-Looking Republicans; Republican Citizens Committee of the United States.

[e] Minor discrepancies between items and totals are due to rounding.

Chairman John Bailey complained of ". . . a sort of a little financial deficit."[9] The Republican National Committee entered 1964 with a deficit of $400,000, yet ended the general election campaign with a surplus. This resulted from large sums received too late to be spent advantageously: a Republican survey indicates that $2.8 million was received in the last six days before the election. Some of the expenditures are discussed in the following sections.

Campaign Publicity

The Republican committees for 1964 spent over $7.3 million on items identifiable as publicity. These included the following: TV and radio time and production, $5.6 million; printing and reproduction, $555,000; printed advertising, $530,000; promotion and campaign supplies, $380,000; motion pictures, $125,000; and outdoor productions, $100,000.

No comparable data for the Democrats are available. The Democrats utilized a firm called Campaign Aids in the production and distribution of campaign materials, including those exhibited at the national convention. During the campaign, materials distribution—totaling several million bumper strips, 7 million brochures, and 4 million posters—was based on census data featuring location and population concentration. One high Democratic official stated that $2 million was spent on Johnson-Humphrey literature; the National Committee share cost about $750,000, while spending by other national, state, and local committees for this purpose comprised the remainder.

[9] *New York Times*, Jan. 20, 1965. The Democrats announced on April 14, 1965, payment of bills totaling $149,000 for use by the President of Air Force aircraft in connection with the 1964 campaign. DNC Press Release, April 14, 1965.

Political Broadcasts

Much less free broadcasting time was provided in 1964 to the presidential and vice-presidential candidates than in 1960, because the Senate killed the bill providing suspension of the equal-time requirement of the Federal Communications Act.[10] Accordingly, most radio and television time had to be bought, at much higher rates than four years before.[11]

A Federal Communications Commission study reported that total network and station charges for political broadcasting at all levels in the 1964 general election were $24.6 million—an increase of 73 percent from the $14.2 million spent in 1960, and 150 percent from the $9.8 million spent in 1956.[12] Figures for broadcasting costs in primary election campaigns are not available for 1956 or 1960; for 1964 they were $10 million, making a total of $34.6 million for candidates and committees at all levels.

Network and station costs attributable to presidential and vice-presidential campaigns totaled $12.8 million, or about 37 percent of all broadcast costs. Total TV and radio network charges in the general election campaign, for broadcasts devoted exclusively to the presidential, vice-presidential, and national party tickets, were $3,926,000, of which the Republican portion was $2,000,000 and the Democratic $1,926,000.

The networks were able to some extent to bypass the equal-time requirement by stressing interview and docu-

---

[10] See above, pp. 127-32.

[11] From 1959 to 1964, basic rates increased 31 percent in network television, 41 percent in spot television, 9 percent in network radio, and 21 percent in spot radio. "The Decade of Incentive: Marketing Review and Forecast, '64-'65," based on studies prepared by Marplan, a market research component of the Interpublic Group of Companies, Inc. (January 1965), p. 31.

[12] Federal Communications Commission, *Survey of Political Broadcasting: Primary and General Election Campaigns of 1964* (July 1965, mimeo.), Table 3.

mentary programs, which are exempt from Section 315 of the Communications Act; thus they could deny time to minority party candidates. The amount of sustaining time reported by the networks for the general election period was substantially less than in 1960: 4 hours 28 minutes by the TV networks, compared with 39:22 in 1960; 21:14 by the radio networks, compared with 43:14 in 1960.

Both the Federal Communications Commission and the federal courts ruled against pleas by Republican managers for broadcast time equal to that provided free by the networks to President Johnson for a report on Khrushchev's ouster and the nuclear explosion set off by the Red Chinese.[13] Following his defeat, Senator Goldwater several times alleged that failure to receive "equal time" put the Republicans at a severe disadvantage. The Republicans, however, capitalized on the denial of free time by making paid television appeals for funds to permit buying of more time to "answer" the President's report.

The increasing controversy about so-called right-wing broadcasts, estimated to total more than 6,000 radio and television broadcasts weekly and carried by more than 1,300 stations, brought about the formation of a National Council for Civil Responsibility, consisting of more than 100 civic, educational, religious, and business leaders, to present opposing views. Efforts to raise funds in order to present "dignified, factual, documentary broadcasts to expose the daily distortions of the radical reactionary groups" [14] were abandoned after five months for lack of financial support. Spokesmen for the Democratic National Committee admit contributing $50,000 of Convention Program proceeds to the project.[15]

[13] See above, p. 153.
[14] *New York Times*, Oct. 18, 1964.
[15] Drew Pearson claims an additional $10,000 in cash was contributed. *Washington Post*, March 3, 1965.

The Right Wing

Democrats and others were not reluctant to link right-wing support to the Goldwater candidacy.[16] Even before his nomination, Senator Goldwater was moved to declare it a myth that the right wing's "big money" was coming his way.[17] Clearly, some well-known financial supporters of organizations usually classified as right-wing were active supporters of Senator Goldwater both before and after his nomination. Some believe the great outpouring of contributions to the Goldwater campaigns, while impressive in the context of two-party support in the past, emanated in large part from a relatively small base of ultraconservative enthusiasts. Obviously, some elements of the far right worked for the candidate of the Republican party rather than for a third-party effort, as in some recent years, and their output had an important bearing on the costs of the major party campaigns.

Political pamphleteering reached new heights with the sales of large numbers of "hate books," so called because of their tendency toward a one-sided and unbalanced presentation. Various claims about the size of orders and sales were made for four books in particular,[18] and a careful survey indicates a minimum of 17 million copies ordered and distributed.[19] While prices ranged as high as $1, some were sold for 35 cents, and many were given away. These mass-produced books were published at about 20 cents each

[16] See Special Report #17 of Group Research, Inc., "Barry Goldwater and the Organized Right Wing," dated Oct. 12, 1964.

[17] Joseph A. Loftus, *New York Times*, Oct. 28, 1963.

[18] J. Evetts Haley, *A Texan Looks at Lyndon* (Palo Duro Press, 1964); Phyllis Schlafly and Chester Ward, *The Gravediggers* (Pere Marquette Press, 1964); Phyllis Schlafly, *A Choice Not an Echo* (Pere Marquette Press, 1964); John A. Stormer, *None Dare Call It Treason* (Liberty Bell Press, 1964).

[19] "Fair Comment," Fair Campaign Practices Committee, Inc. (February 1965), p. 2.

by companies established especially for the purpose, with printing and binding contracted to trade publishers. Thus a minimum of $3.4 million was spent on these items alone, while some political committees raised campaign funds by selling the books at higher prices.

In any case, the Goldwater campaign did not seem to draw off money from right-wing organizations, though some of them experienced periodic reductions in finances in 1963-64. Careful studies indicate at least $14 million [20] is spent annually on right-wing activities, and estimates range to as much as $30 million a year. Since much of this income is from membership dues, costs of literature, and corporate support, the basic income of such organizations tends to be stable and appeared not to be greatly affected by the Goldwater candidacy. The experience in 1964 has led to the starting of new ultraconservative bids for recruits and money, partly within the two-party framework and focused upon selected campaigns for Congress in 1966.[21]

Private Public Opinion Polls

Political polling costs at all levels in 1964 are reliably estimated at $5 million,[22] an increase from 1960. The Republican nomination scramble among Goldwater, Rockefeller, Scranton, and others raised polling costs above those made by the Democratic contenders in 1960. In the general election, the Republican National Committee spent $165,400 for surveys and polls. Some polling was done on President Johnson's behalf, and the White House examined polls for other candidates containing questions on the presidential race. In addition, polls were made on behalf of Democratic vice-presidential hopefuls.

[20] Arnold Forster and Benjamin R. Epstein, *Danger on the Right* (Random House, 1964), pp. 272-80.

[21] Donald Janson, *New York Times*, Nov. 23, 1964.

[22] Earl Mazo, in a forthcoming book, *Polling for Political Power*, to be published by Doubleday and Co.

Labor and Miscellaneous Committees

In 1964, national-level labor committees made gross disbursements of $3.7 million (Table 5.1), compared with $2.3 million disbursed by 21 committees in 1960. Transfers, consisting mostly of allocations to other committees and candidates, were $2.9 million, or more than twice as much as in 1960; allocations to candidates for Congress were about twice their 1960 level. In both 1964 and 1960 numerous labor committees spent more than they raised, indicating accruals from collections in nonelection years.

Twenty-six miscellaneous committees reported disbursements totaling $1,963,000 in 1964 (Table 5.1), compared with $850,000 from 19 committees in 1960. There were three significant new committees: the American Medical Political Action Committee reported receipts of $301,000 and disbursements of $402,000; the Business-Industry Political Action Committee received $144,000 and spent $203,000; and the Council for a Livable World received $119,000 and spent $137,000. The National Committee for an Effective Congress significantly increased its 1964 receipts and expenditures over 1960, when its totals were combined with two special allied funds. In 1964, it reported receipts of $344,779 and expenditures of $311,346 (including its special 1964 Campaign Fund Account); it was allied with two other funds not required to report in Washington, whose combined receipts were about $69,000.

Sources of Funds

Both parties in 1964 raised money by the successful use of techniques previously tried but not uniformly productive, in addition to the time-honored expedients of fund-raising dinners and other events, large contributions, sustaining funds, and state payments by quotas or some other arrangement. The Republicans made effective use of direct mail drives and TV appeals. The most significant Democratic development was the President's Club.

According to the Michigan Survey Research Center, 10 percent of a national cross section of adult Americans said they had contributed to some party or candidate in 1964; an additional 1 percent knew of another member of their household who had contributed, making a combined percentage of about 11. A Gallup Poll indicated 12 percent who had contributed, or a member of whose family did. For 1964, these percentages would translate into about 12 million contributors at all levels.

Republican experience in 1964 was marked by the breakdown of the unified fund-raising structure developed by the party in recent decades. There was little change from 1960 in the number of large contributors (sums of $500 or more), but the proportion of their contributions to the dollar value of total individual contributions decreased substantially. In geographic terms there were scattered indications in 1964 of increased financial support in the South and Southwest, and decreases in the North and East. However, an unparalleled number of small contributors responded to the massive mail drives and TV appeals. The response was due partly to the special appeal of Senator Goldwater to enthusiasts, but also to the large investment of time, energy, and money which the Republicans since 1962 have consciously devoted to building a national sustaining fund. Its development beyond 1964 will surely test Republican ingenuity and signal its financial health.

The financial base of Democratic support was comprised mostly of a wide geographic and occupational diversity of large contributors. Their contributions proportionate to the dollar value of total individual contributions rose in 1964 by a significant amount. Most striking is the long-term growth in Democratic financial support from low points in the presidential elections in 1948 and 1956. From 1960 to 1964 the dollar value of contributions received in sums of $500 increased more than two and one-half times, while total receipts from all sources more than doubled from 1956 to 1964. The changing bases of Democratic financial support are significant, accentuated in 1964 by the easy willingness of certain businessmen and nominal Republicans to join the President's Club or otherwise contribute to Democratic committees. Of equal importance is the decrease in emphasis on small contributors, on the Democratic National Committee sustaining fund, and on the Dollars for Democrats program.

Direct Mail and TV Appeals

Of the Republican total 1964 income of $18.5 million, an unprecedented 32.4 percent came from the direct mail drives and 13.7 percent from TV requests made mainly by Ronald Reagan, Raymond Massey, and Dean Burch. In sums under $100, the number of direct mail contributions was 380,000 (an additional 30,000 requests were returned without a contribution); the Reagan and Massey appeals brought another 134,000; Burch appeals collected about 100,000; while a separate Citizens for Goldwater accounting shows 37,000 more contributions—a total of about 651,000 contributions in small sums. In addition, from all these programs there were 10,000 individual contributions between $100 and $999, and 1,500 for $1,000 and over. Over 15 million pieces of fund-raising literature were mailed for party and citizens' programs during the year, bringing in more than $5.8 million.

It was remarkable indeed that so much was raised from so many in view of the widespread belief that Senator Goldwater would not win the election—a condition that usually hinders fund-raising appeals. To some extent, the large number of contributors to national-level Republican committees in 1964 must have reflected the political polarization within the Republican party. Goldwater supporters tended to give directly to Washington to avoid normal Republican state finance channels whereby funds would be shared with moderate candidates for other offices. Moderate Republicans were not anxious to have their funds shared with the national campaign, so many of them gave to individual moderate candidates and not to state finance committees.

The President's Club

President Johnson developed a Kennedy fund-raising innovation called the President's Club into a personal financial-political organization dedicated to his own election. The Club consists of about 4,000 contributors of $1,000 or more, and has become in effect a finance arm of the Democratic party and an operating committee for the President. Often, the President has combined an appearance at a $100-a-plate dinner with a President's Club function, such as a pre-dinner reception. President's Club dinners and receptions alone, as estimated on the basis of attendance, accounted for receipts of almost $2.3 million. When the Club was small, efforts were made to invite members to White House affairs. Special briefings or seminars led by federal government officials were arranged in some cities. During 1964 the Club grew so large its membership was no longer exclusive. Arrangements were made for members to attend the National Convention, and special events were held for them each day.

In several states, the regular party organization grumbled because the Club attracted a number of large contributors away and focused their attention on Washington. Some Club leaders have risen to prominence and in some instances may have supplanted state leaders with respect to patronage and other matters; some state and county committees have had to contribute in order to ensure that their leaders could attend Club events.

In December 1964, the Democrats announced that their 1965 Inaugural Gala would be sponsored by the Democratic National Committee and that campaign workers and members of the President's Club would be invited free, an indication of confidence that 1965 would bring new funds. Letters soliciting Club renewals were mailed within a month, but the response was not as good as expected.

Fund-Raising Dinners and Events

The appeal of the President's Club points up the utilization of a "star" system of attraction in political fundraising, illustrated in both parties by their dinners and similar events.

A wide but by no means complete collection of newspaper clippings indicates that a minimum of $26.6 million can be accounted for as receipts at political fund-raising events in 1964 for candidates and committees at all levels in all states. Remarkably, totals indicate Democratic and Republican receipts of $13.3 million each, though raised in different combinations at events ranging in price from $5,000 for cocktail parties to $1 tickets to galas, rallies, and clambakes.[23] The President, of course, was the star attraction, appearing at events where almost $7.9 million was collected.[24] After his nomination, Senator Humphrey attended events at which at least $455,450 was raised.[25]

By comparison, Barry Goldwater attended events in 1964 at which at least $1.6 million was raised before his nomina-

---

[23] In newspaper accounts, some figures are gross and some are net; some events could not be included when only amount per ticket but not number attending were stated, and vice versa.

[24] This amount includes the $2.3 million reported on p. 180. Proceeds were usually divided in varying proportions between national, state, and perhaps local committees.

[25] For a whole year, Humphrey attended events totaling $855,540.

tion, and $2.6 million afterwards.[26] Other Republican leaders whose personal appearances benefited the GOP were: former President Eisenhower, $1.1 million; Richard M. Nixon, $1.6 million; and vice-presidential candidate William Miller, at least $237,000. Republicans used closed-circuit TV for holding dinners simultaneously in different cities on one night each in January and November, but the circuits were considerably smaller than in 1960 when Eisenhower was still President. For the combined national party campaign committees in 1964, Republicans attributed 13.8 percent of their income to net national proceeds from dinners.

Large Contributions

The combination of the President's Club and fund-raising dinners provided the Democrats with much of their money for the national-level campaign. Despite their large numbers of contributors in smaller sums, the Republicans also received substantial funds from their Associates Program, consisting of contributors of $1,000 or more, which provided 12 percent of their total national income.

The data collected permit the following comparisons: more than 6,700 individual contributions of $500 and over were counted for the 107 committees filing with the Clerk of the House of Representatives. Of these, more than 3,400 were Democratic contributions totaling $5.2 million, while more than 3,000 were Republican contributions totaling $3.7 million. The Democrats received approximately 69 percent of the dollar value of their total individual contributions (aggregating $7.5 million) in amounts of $500 and over. The Republicans, by contrast, received only 28 percent of the dollar value of their total individual contributions

[26] One estimate puts Goldwater's fund-raising totals at Republican functions from 1960 to 1963 at $6.3 million, mostly for party coffers in local areas. David Kraslow, *Chicago Sun-Times*, July 12, 1964.

(aggregating $13.2 million) in these large sums. The dollar value of total Republican individual contributions received in sums of $500 and over was at the same level as in 1960, whereas total Democratic contributions in these sums increased from $2 million in 1960 to $5.2 million in 1964. In 1960 the proportions of the total Republican and Democratic individual contributions that stemmed from gifts of $500 or more were 58 percent and 59 percent respectively.[27] It is clear that in 1964 the Democrats relied on large contributions to a much greater extent than the Republicans. To the extent that such contributions come from special interests, they create an unhealthy state of affairs for a party so solidly in power.

Sustaining Funds

The Republican financial achievements of 1964 resulted in part from Goldwater's attraction, but also from a serious effort to build a national sustaining fund of $10-a-year memberships. Introduced in March 1962, the sustaining fund attracted 70,000 contributors in that year. In 1963, gross receipts were $1.1 million from over 100,000 contributors. In the first six months of 1964, prior to the Republican convention, another $1 million had been raised through this means. During some months, sustaining fund income provided the bulk of money available to keep the national party operating. Following the Goldwater nomination, another $1.3 million was raised through sustaining fund mailings. For the year, $2,369,000 was raised through the Republican National Committee sustaining fund, approximating the $2.5 million goal projected for 1964 regardless of the presidential nominee.

[27] In 1956, while Republicans were in power, of total amounts contributed by individuals to national-level committees, 74 percent was contributed in sums of $500 and over. In 1948, while Democrats were in power, their proportion was 69 percent.

In contrast to the Republicans, the Democrats, who had originated their sustaining membership program in 1957, permitted it to languish in 1964. Mailings totaling only one million were reported by officials, bringing perhaps 50,000 members at $10 each per year, compared with 65,000 members in 1960.

State Quotas and Contributions

The Republican national leadership solicited the states in 1964 more energetically and deeply through mail drives, phone blitzes, and other means than in recent campaign years. State committee quota payments or contributions to support the national party amounted to about 15 percent of total income, which can be estimated at about $2.7 million. There was increased financial support in the West and South, and a drop in contributions from the East. Illustrations of some national quota performance records for 1964, compared with 1960, are as follows:

Eight southern states increased; Florida, North Carolina, and Tennessee decreased.

California increased from 78 percent in 1960 to 118 percent in 1964; New York decreased from 132 percent to 62 percent.

Illinois, Ohio, Pennsylvania, Michigan, and Minnesota decreased; Indiana, Oklahoma, and Wisconsin increased.

Seven northeastern states decreased; Maine, Vermont, and New Jersey showed small increases.

All eleven western states increased, Arizona, Idaho, Montana, and New Mexico by sizable amounts; Nevada increased from 42 percent in 1960 to 262 percent in 1964.

The Democrats no longer have a quota system but negotiate with each state for national party support. In 1964, approximately $2.3 million was received in transfers from the states; from some nothing was demanded, since their needs were greater than those of the national committees.

Labor and Business in Politics

The concern of organized labor and corporate business with registration, get-out-the-vote, and contributions drives continued in 1964. In direct relationships or in parallel activities, labor gave more powerful support to the Democrats than ever before; the Goldwater candidacy drove some normally Republican unions to endorse President Johnson. At the same time, significant elements of the business and financial communities supported the President with votes and money.[28]

Labor

Financial and other relationships of labor with the Democratic national campaign were intimate. Coordination was effected in registration drives and also in financial and other matters, including the allocation of funds to candidates for Congress. Many labor leaders joined the large contributors in the President's Club as readily as did many business and financial leaders.

Registration. Greater emphasis was placed on voter registration by Democratic, labor, and Negro groups than had been done previously.[29] In national-level disbursements, the AFL-CIO Committee on Political Education (COPE) spent over $1 million on registration alone (compared with

[28] Herbert E. Alexander and Harold B. Meyers, "The Switch in Campaign Giving," *Fortune*, Vol. 72 (November 1965), p. 170; and David T. Bazelon, "Big Business and the Democrats," *Commentary*, Vol. 39 (May 1965), pp. 39-46.

[29] The RNC planned a special registration effort in ten major cities before Goldwater's nomination, but it floundered.

$535,000 spent in 1960), concentrating on marginal congressional districts. Efforts to match national money were made by locals and through state and local labor councils, but no estimate of total costs is possible. Other unions, such as the Teamsters, carried on their own activities.

The Democratic national command states it spent approximately $500,000 in registration activities in 1964,[30] compared with $200,000 reported in 1960. Furthermore, President's Clubs in Minnesota and California and other Democratic groups not reporting in Washington spent significant sums on registration.

In addition, large sums, not reported in sources noted above, are known to have been channeled into Negro registration drives, particularly in the South.[31] One such sum appears to have come from proceeds of the Democratic Convention Program. Negro organizations also received substantial amounts from quasi-political groups, including *both* labor and corporate sources.

Labor Spending. COPE spent almost another $1 million in funds voluntarily contributed by members, and claimed that 264 candidates for Congress—68 percent of those supported by COPE—were elected.[32] The Teamsters reported spending $270,000 nationally, and some locals are known to have spent substantial sums. The Teamsters opposed Senator Goldwater without specifically endorsing President Johnson.

[30] One report stated $250,000 of national party money for registration efforts in twelve key states was matched by $500,000 in local funds. *Newsweek*, Oct. 12, 1964, p. 44. Filed reports show national Democrats sent a minimum of $271,222 to eleven state groups for registration purposes.

[31] According to one report, the Negro campaign in the South cost $500,000 and produced 265,000 registrants, mostly in the cities. Charles Bartlett, *Evening Star* (Washington), March 25, 1965.

[32] It was reported that 65 million copies of campaign leaflets were distributed by the AFL-CIO, including 10 million copies of voting records of members of Congress. Other labor groups at all levels distributed literature, contributed funds, and volunteered personnel on behalf of candidates.

Considerable money was spent in various states for and against right-to-work laws. The Right-to-Work Committee declared a budget of $450,000 for 1964, while its opposite, the labor-supported Council for Industrial Peace, budgeted $150,000 to fight such legislation. To these amounts must also be added substantial funds raised and spent by proponents and opponents in various states, and among businessmen and labor unions. Following the Johnson victory, one of the first goals labor spokesmen pressed for as a reward for having supported the Democratic ticket was a revision of federal law to prohibit right-to-work laws in the states.

Business

Polls showed strong business and professional support for the Democratic ticket, and influential members of the Business Council, comprising some of the nation's top executives, endorsed President Johnson. Business supporters of the President included former Eisenhower cabinet members and other former Republican subcabinet officials and White House assistants. Demonstrated business support for Johnson was so marked that the National Independent Committee for Johnson and Humphrey, consisting of numerous big businessmen (many of them members of the President's Club), considered making a massive mailing soliciting funds from businessmen, on the theory that many Republican-oriented businessmen had never been asked by Democrats to contribute. The size and cost of a mailing and the late stage of the campaign caused the plan to be rejected, despite strong advocacy among certain top Democratic campaigners.

BIPAC. For the first time, a political fund called Business-Industry Political Action Committee was organized to support, financially and otherwise, congressional candidates of its choice and to encourage citizens to be more active and effective in politics. It contributed $203,000 to Republican and Democratic candidates in 86 House contests and 12 Senate races, including some primary contests. Supported candidates won in 40 percent of the House contests and in only one Senate contest.

Corporate Bipartisan Efforts. Once again, numerous corporations undertook bipartisan campaigns urging their employees to register, to vote, and to contribute. Some of these campaigns were directed toward the general public as well.

One impressive effort to attract new sources of small contributions, although with generally unfavorable results, was undertaken on the basis of an idea proposed by the R. L. Polk Company of Detroit, Michigan. Former President Dwight D. Eisenhower and his two-time opponent, Adlai E. Stevenson, jointly signed a letter soliciting contributions for the national parties. An experiment was made through a 300,000 mailing to a scientifically selected geographic sample of automobile owners and telephone subscribers. Special efforts were made in several cities in a media support test, time trend tests were made from July to October, and selected special lists were tried. A business campaign to distribute in-plant solicitation material to employees was also conducted. The latter two efforts were the most successful, though getting a late start. Both major parties agreed to the experiments, and special funds were raised for each to assume part of the costs. The parties received all contributed funds, amounting to about $30,000.

The Aerojet-General program continued to be the most far-reaching and successful bipartisan corporate in-plant solicitation. Since 1958, when $24,000 was raised for parties and candidates, the effort has produced $60,000 in 1960, $97,000 in 1962, and over $136,000 in 1964. In 1964, approximately $66,100 was contributed to Democratic party candidates, while about $63,800 went to the Republican party and candidates. The average contribution was $6.85 (much higher than the $4 average of 1962), while 20,000 employees, or 72.5 percent of the firm's personnel, contributed.

Hughes Aircraft Company inaugurated an Active Citizenship Campaign in 1964, and its employees probably established a national record for a first-year contribution program, raising a total of $86,053. The average contribution was $13.76, from 6,256 employees or 26 percent of total personnel. Contributions were designated for three political parties and ninety-nine individual candidates in twenty states, and could be arranged through payroll deductions. All contribution cards were immediately coded to prevent identification of contributors, recorded by data processing, and then placed in locked storage pending a final audit, which was made of every facet of the program. Returns from a questionnaire, which received a more than 50 percent response, indicated that an additional 18 percent of employees contributed *outside* the Hughes ACC program; 19 percent contributed through the ACC program *and* outside it; and 64 percent of the total number who contributed in 1964 did so for the *first time*. Thus 44 percent of Hughes employees contributed in 1964. If these figures accurately reflect the potential in other corporations and industries, the possible significance of in-plant bipartisan solicitation for the political parties and for campaign financing is obvious.[33]

---

[33] Some company programs, like those of Aerojet and Hughes, are designed to reach all employees. Other programs penetrate down only to middle-level clerical employees. Without reference to kind of program or degree of penetration, the following companies are known to have undertaken some fund solicitation in 1964: American Cyanamid, Bell Telephone Laboratories, Champion Paper, Ford, General Electric, Kimberly-Clark, Koppers, Monsanto Chemical, Pacific Gas & Electric, Pittsburgh Plate Glass, Thiokol Chemical, Thompson Ramo Wooldridge, Travelers Insurance Company, TWA, Western Electric, Westinghouse, and Whirlpool.

The Financial Future

With the Democrats in power everywhere, their ability to obtain funds would seem to be greatly enhanced. Yet despite significant financial support from certain Republicans in 1964, and national money withheld in the states, they still raised and spent less than the Republicans at the national level. The growth of the President's Club came at a time when the Republicans nominated a candidate with limited appeal for certain regular Republican contributors. This confrontation between a consensus and a nonconsensus candidate may not be repeated often; yet in recent years the Democrats have shown little initiative in developing a wider financial constituency to match their widening voter constituency.[34]

Assuming the continued success of the President's Club, Democratic galas, and other fund-raising events, attention will focus on the 1966 congressional elections and on the states. The Democratic interest in retaining the many marginal congressional seats won in the Johnson landslide suggests that large sums will be spent for their retention in 1966. The stakes in control of the party are now so high in some areas of the country that factional fights for command can be expected and will be costly. In key states, the weight of the party financiers may be crucial. The nationalizing tendencies inherent in the President's Club operations in the states will be worth watching, while the inevitable pull and tug between Club managers and state-oriented finance managers could turn into major battles in the larger states.

Under President Kennedy, separate congressional dinners were eliminated and national fundraising was centralized,

[34] Belatedly in mid-1965 the DNC announced a contest with prizes for members of the Sustaining Fund, in an effort to enlarge its membership; the effort was not successful.

with the DNC responsible for supplying funds to the Capitol Hill committees. Under President Johnson these committees once again held dinners. But the National Committee continued to supply other funds and in imaginative ways provided important services for incumbent congressmen. DNC funds retained in certain states, raised through presidential appearances at fund-raising dinners and President's Club functions, were released late in the 1964 campaign at the direction of the National Committee to help congressional candidates when it appeared the money would not be needed for the presidential campaign in those states. Under the central direction of the DNC, the President's Club for Johnson Committee disbursed $52,000 to various congressional candidates in the final five days of the campaign.[35] The Humphrey for Vice-President Committee also disbursed $100,000 to the Democratic Senatorial Campaign Committee and $53,000 to Minnesota congressional candidates, after receiving part of its funds from the Minnesota President's Club.[36] Earlier, the DNC helped pay travel expenses for incumbent congressmen who returned weekends to their constituencies while Congress was still in session.

In February 1965 the DNC announced that a staff of writers and publicists had been retained to help congressmen prepare constituent newsletters, press releases, speeches and scripts, to coach congressmen on media and public relations techniques, and to help disseminate materials to constituents by mail, teletype, and voice recordings.[37] Some of these programs had been available for incumbents in 1964. A weekly radio program was offered to stations willing to carry the show.[38] Although these programs were undertaken

[35] Eileen Shanahan, *New York Times*, Jan. 15, 1965.
[36] *Pioneer Press* (St. Paul), Oct. 27, 1964.
[37] *New York Herald Tribune*, Feb. 25, 1965.
[38] *Broadcasting Magazine*, March 22, 1965, p. 88.

with the cooperation of the Senatorial and Congressional Campaign Committees, these committees continue to subsist in part on grants from the DNC, and the interests of the White House in the congressional arena would seem to be well-protected. In addition, the Democrats have an asset money cannot buy—the ability to attract public attention via the mass media through the forums of public office in Washington and the state houses which they now control so overwhelmingly.

Campaigning is especially expensive for the challenger, and fundraising is normally difficult for a party out of power. Yet despite heavy electoral losses, in some ways the Republicans were in better financial shape in 1965 than in 1961. Their ability to raise funds was demonstrated, and they were not saddled with a deficit. The large number of contributors in 1964 gave the party a greater potential financial constituency than ever before. The Republican National Committee had built a solid list of sustaining members before the Goldwater candidacy, and undoubtedly will be able to attract some of his contributors. Mail solicitations to 1964 contributors brought satisfactory results throughout 1965.

The Republicans will need large sums to compete with the Democrats and to reshape their image. The RNC agreed to finance a Republican Coordinating Committee, a new policy arm with a membership composed of the National Chairman, congressional leaders, governors, and former presidential candidates, allotting it a minimum of $25,000 per year, and more was made available when the effort was well received. Efforts to match Democratic assistance to incumbent members of Congress were undertaken.[39]

In 1965 money was provided for revitalizing the Republican party. A bare-bones budget of $2.7 million was adopted,

---

[39] The Republican Congressional Boosters Club, a separate effort patterned on the President's Club, sought 2,000 contributors of $1,000 each, and earmarked its funds for Republican candidates for Congress in 1966.

but a larger victory budget of $4.7 million was projected if funds were available.[40] Upon retiring, Chairman Burch called for several items: a $250,000 increase in the research budget; additional amounts beyond those adopted to finance the Republican Coordinating Committee; an additional $100,000 to staff ten task forces; a $100,000 public opinion survey on national issues and a profile of the motivations of Republican workers; increases in spending for public relations;[41] and a field staff to assist local committees with registration, fundraising, and other activities. He also suggested that volunteer contributions be sought in a "buy a brick" campaign to construct a permanent headquarters building for the Republican party in Washington [42]—an endeavor which the Democrats might consider conducting simultaneously. The Burch proposals were ambitious and were partially adopted; they could contribute to the nationalizing and institutionalizing of party politics, now evident also in aspects of Democratic operations, and perhaps a portent of the future. The concept of continual campaigning, patterned on politics in other democracies, may now be coming into vogue in the United States.

Unified fundraising through the Republican National Finance Committee broke down in 1964. Multiple solicitation took place because the polarization of conservative Republicans (behind certain state and local candidates)

[40] The Republican Sustaining Fund for 1965 was projected at $1.2 million and brought in $1.7 million.

[41] In March, the RNC launched a five-minute weekly radio show, featuring the voices of Republican leaders, tapes of which are sent to about 160 broadcasters who provide free time.

[42] Burch also proposed for 1968 that the two major parties share equally the anticipated $6 million cost for joint one-hour programs on three networks, in half-hour segments for each party, in each of the eight weeks before election. Debates could take place within this framework, and presumably there would be no other paid broadcasts by the presidential candidates or national parties. Dean Burch, "Speaking Out," *Saturday Evening Post*, Vol. 238 (March 27, 1965), p. 14.

magnified the importance of the soliciting agency, and funds were not as effectively raised or shared as is normal through the traditional united finance committees. This diversity carried into 1965, when many Republican agencies competed for funds. The Republican Associates (a RNC program) and the Congressional Boosters Club both sought larger contributions; the Congressional and Senatorial Campaign Committees each planned to sponsor separate spring fund-raising events, until the Congressional group agreed to cancel theirs.[43] The RNC Sustaining Fund sought small sums apart from the Congressional Newsletter. In the aftermath of the election, the Republicans went for months without a national finance chairman.

Clearly, some Republicans will prefer to give their financial support to the moderate organizations grouped in the Council of Republican Organizations, each with its own membership and program, which are becoming more active. One, called Republicans for Progress, was organized during the election campaign as the Committee to Support Moderate Republicans, to generate creative and constructive ideas for party members in Congress. At least three such groups made postelection fund-raising mailings to similar lists of persons.

At the same time, right-wing groups sought to expand their fund-raising activities. The John Birch Society announced a goal of $12 million before the 1966 elections.[44] A new American Conservative Union sought $400,000.[45] Thus the spectrum was comprised of organizations of all shades and varieties, all seeking funds, some pointing their efforts toward independently influencing the nomination and

---

[43] Newspaper reports indicate the Senatorial Campaign Committee dinner, entitled "A Salute to Senator Everett M. Dirksen," grossed $400,000 and netted $350,000. *Washington Post*, April 29, 1965.

[44] John W. Fenton, *New York Times*, March 8, 1965.

[45] Sterling F. Green, *Evening Star* (Washington), March 19, 1965.

election processes, some seeking to promote conservatism in the Republican party. Most focused on the 1966 elections, while several of the Goldwater citizens committees announced that they were being reorganized into permanent bodies. By late May 1965, the Republican leadership complained that competing splinter groups were diluting the sources of party income.[46] Later, Barry Goldwater supported the establishment of a Free Society Association, purportedly organized for conservative educational purposes and not for political activities that would compete with the Republican party. Some conservative groups seem to have been formed to exploit the momentum and lists of contributors gathered in the Goldwater movement. Any effort of the national party to divorce itself from ultraconservative elements would probably encounter some financial difficulty because of the demonstrated fund-raising ability of Goldwater enthusiasts, who can withdraw support from the party at any time.

Clearly, the major problem for the Republicans will be to control the diffusion of energy and money within the mainstream of American thought and to channel diverse efforts into meaningful political action.

Issues of Public Policy

In 1961 President Kennedy established a nine-member bipartisan Commission on Campaign Costs, which reported to him in April 1962.[47] With some exceptions, the Commission advocated expanding the financial base of support for the parties, and also proposed a system of limited tax credits and deductions for political contributions, designed to give an

---

[46] John D. Morris, *New York Times*, May 28, 1965.

[47] President's Commission on Campaign Costs, *Financing Presidential Campaigns* (Government Printing Office, April 1962).

incentive to the potential donor.[48] A tax deduction bill in another form passed the Senate, but not the House. Some members of Congress have given support to the Commission suggestions, but the position of the Johnson administration is unknown. Some businessmen have favored the proposals; organized labor has opposed aspects of the plan.

The President's Commission furthermore recommended a limited subsidy to provide federal funds for the President-elect and Vice-President-elect to cover certain expenses from Election Day until Inauguration Day. This proposal limits financial pressures upon the parties at a time following a campaign when there may already be deficits to pay off, by permitting the federal government to assume limited costs for the new President in selecting and assembling his administration and in preparing to assume responsibility for government. Legislation to effect this change passed both houses of Congress and was signed into law by President Johnson. Funds were thus available for paying salaries of the Vice-President-elect's staff during the transition period, permitting Senator Humphrey to resign his Senate seat to allow the early appointment of his successor.

The Commission failed to endorse the concept popular in other democracies that registration and voting drives are proper or exclusive functions of government.[49] Yet if financial pressures on parties and candidates are to be relieved in America by other than tax incentives, the next

[48] As a result of a President's Commission recommendation, the Internal Revenue Service made a ruling authorizing federal tax deductions for expenses incurred by a corporation or business as part of an impartial effort to encourage employees or the public to register, vote, and work for and contribute to the party of their choice. Rev. Rul. 62-156, in *Internal Revenue Bulletin* (Government Printing Office, Sept. 24, 1962), pp. 7-10.

[49] Another group appointed by President Kennedy, the President's Commission on Registration and Voting Participation, went little further in the direction of state support. See *Report on Registration and Voting Participation* (Government Printing Office, November 1963).

step is likely to be in the direction of government assistance in bipartisan activities such as registration and voting drives.

The Democrats were parsimonious regarding financial information beyond that required by federal law. This attitude was linked to the problem of legal provision for more effective disclosure and publicity concerning political contributions and expenditures. Along with voluntarily divulging certain financial information, as practiced by the Republicans in 1964, goes the need for statutory requirements for mandatory reporting. The President's Commission recommended a comprehensive system of disclosure and publicity which President Kennedy proposed to the Congress. No hearings have ever been held on the measure in either House, and no action is in prospect.

President Kennedy had agreed to call a nonpartisan White House Conference on Campaign Finance to focus attention on the problems involved, and to signalize certain new approaches that would be made during 1964. Following Kennedy's assassination, higher governmental policies and priorities occupied President Johnson, valuable time was lost, and nothing was done.

During 1964, in lieu of debates between the presidential candidates, the Democrats appeared willing to pay for whatever broadcast time they desired, so long as this forced the Republicans to do likewise. Accordingly, Section 315 of the Federal Communications Act was not suspended for the presidential and vice-presidential campaigns; political broadcast costs for these offices were substantially higher than in 1960; and no steps were taken to alleviate the resulting financial pressures.

The allegations in the Bobby Baker case point up potential dangers in present fund-raising practices, as do a series of alleged violations of the Hatch Act in seeking contributions from government employees.[50] The present climate is not one to foster confidence. More democratic ways to finance American politics are one component still missing in the blueprint for the Great Society. The issue is one challenge which the administration may yet meet, or the Congress could take it up independently of the administration. But to do this, Congress must muster an initiative not now in sight.

[50] The Senate voted without dissent on May 26, 1964, to request the Attorney General to investigate reported solicitations. *Congressional Record*, daily ed., March 8, 1965, pp. 4222-23.

6

Nominations and Elections for the Senate

MILTON C. CUMMINGS, JR.

The 1964 presidential results gave President Lyndon Johnson a full four-year term in his own right. The 1964 elections for the House of Representatives and Senate gave him something he probably valued almost as highly: the opportunity to govern decisively for at least the first two years of that term with top-heavy majorities of his own party in both houses of Congress. Yet, though the basic consequences of the election were the same for both the House and Senate, they were achieved in different ways. The 1964 Democratic victories for the Senate were primarily defensive victories; they enabled the Democrats to retain an already heavy majority of the 100 Senate seats. The 1964 Democratic victories for the House included many offensive victories; for in 1964 the Democrats added substantially to their strength in the House. In this chapter attention will be focused on the primary and general election results for the United States Senate. The next chapter will be focused on the results for the House.

Patterns of Competition in Senate Primaries

The 1964 Senate primaries produced several contests that combined drama and suspense with results of exceptional closeness. Some of the results almost certainly had important consequences for the outcome of the general election; and on the Republican side there were several major battles which pitted the party's right wing against candidates from the moderate-to-liberal wing. Nevertheless, the bulk of the nominating contests conformed to a broad general pattern. In most cases where the incumbent senator stood for reelection, he was renominated with ease. In two of the three primaries where the incumbent did not stand for reelection, there was a spirited contest for the defending party's nomination. And primaries of the party that did not hold the Senate seat ranged from several close hard-fought contests to those in which one candidate received the nomination unopposed.

In the twenty-two primaries for Democratic-held seats where the incumbent stood for reelection, nineteen senators were renominated by margins of 2-1 or larger; eight of these were unopposed, and seven more won with better than 80 percent of the vote (Table 6.1). The close contests were in Texas, Nevada, and Oklahoma. Texas once again was the scene of a sensational and bitter primary campaign, with Senator Ralph Yarborough's main opponent, Gordon McLendon, charging that Yarborough had received $50,000 in cash from Billie Sol Estes. The day before the primary, Yarborough, who had immediately labeled the charge an "infamous lie," released news of a report from the Federal Bureau of Investigation that one of McLendon's witnesses had admitted lying. In the end Yarborough defeated McLendon with about 57 percent of the vote.[1] In Nevada,

---

[1] *New York Times*, April 26 and May 2, 1964. Many observers believed that Yarborough might have had a tougher primary opponent than McLendon, if President Johnson had not personally intervened to discourage a challenge to Yarborough by a major conservative Texas political figure. Such a challenge would have exacerbated the divisions between liberal and conservative Democrats within Texas, and would have dismayed liberal Democrats outside the state whose allegiance Johnson now sought to hold.

Senator Howard W. Cannon also ran into considerable opposition (he received only 59.3 percent of the total primary vote), but he had the advantage of having the opposition vote split between two major opponents.[2]

Oklahoma was the only state where a senator seeking the nomination was defeated in 1964. But the senator in question, J. Howard Edmondson, had had a tenuous hold on his Senate seat from the start. Edmondson was Governor when Senator Robert Kerr, long a dominant figure in Oklahoma politics, died. Edmondson resigned the governorship to enable his Lieutenant Governor to succeed him and to appoint him to Kerr's Senate seat. He then promptly ran into the same problem encountered in recent years by most politicians who have tried this route to the Senate.[3] After leading in the first primary, where three candidates polled heavy votes, Edmondson lost to Fred R. Harris in the runoff. Yarborough, Cannon, and Harris all had hard fights in the general election.

The Democratic primaries for the two Senate seats that were already controlled by the Democratic party were also hotly contested. In California Pierre Salinger bested Alan Cranston in a contest that had strong overtones of a power struggle between California Assembly Speaker Jesse Unruh on the one hand and Governor Pat Brown and the Cali-

[2] Senator Cannon's candidacy was apparently weakened by charges that he had been closely associated with Senate Majority Secretary Bobby Baker and by internal feuding within the state Democratic party. See "Poor Tactics Hurt Senator Cannon," *Carson City Appeal*, Nov. 16, 1964.

[3] From 1933 to 1964 only one of the six governors who resigned so that they could be appointed to the Senate was able to retain his Senate seat at the next election. The one exception was A. B. (Happy) Chandler, who resigned as Governor of Kentucky in 1939 to take a Senate appointment and was then elected to the Senate in 1940. In 1964, both Edmondson and former Governor Edwin L. Mechem of New Mexico, a Republican who had also been appointed to the Senate in this manner, were defeated. *Washington Post*, April 22, 1965.

Table 6.1. Percentage of Total 1964 Primary Vote Polled by Winning Candidates for Nominations for Senate Seats Held by Democrats Before the Election [a]

Winner's Percentage of Total Vote[b]	Democratic Primaries		Republican Primaries (No Incumbent Could Stand for Reelection)
	Incumbent Stood for Reelection	No Incumbent Stood for Reelection	
35–39	—	—	1[c]
40–44	—	—	—
45–49	—	1[d]	—
50–54	—	1[e]	3[f]
55–59	2[g]	—	—
60–64	1[h]	—	1
65–69	1	—	1
70–74	2	—	—
75–79	1	—	3
80–89	4	—	3
90–99	3	—	—
Unopposed	8	—	11
Total	22	2	23[i]

Source: *Congressional Quarterly Weekly Reports,* March–October, 1964.

[a] Two states with Democratic Senators up for reelection in 1964 (Connecticut and Indiana) where candidates were nominated by conventions rather than in primaries are excluded. Nominations for two-year Senate terms are included.

[b] In primary contests where a runoff election was required, the winner's percentage at the runoff election is used.

[c] Elly M. Peterson, Michigan.

[d] Pierre Salinger, California, not incumbent at the time of the primary.

[e] Ross Bass, Tennessee.

[f] George Murphy, California; Ernest Wilkinson, Utah; and John S. Wold, Wyoming.

[g] Howard W. Cannon, Nevada; and Ralph Yarborough, Texas.

[h] The winner in this cell, Fred R. Harris of Oklahoma, was not an incumbent. He defeated the incumbent, J. Howard Edmondson, in a runoff.

[i] The Republicans did not nominate a candidate for the Democratic Senate seat in Mississippi.

fornia Democratic Council on the other.[4] In Tennessee, Representative Ross Bass, who had voted for the 1964 Civil Rights Act, surprised many observers by winning 51 percent of the vote in the first primary and thus avoiding a runoff.[5]

The amount of competition that developed in Republican primaries among contenders who hoped to capture Democratic-held Senate seats varied widely from state to state, ranging from two very close contests won by less than 2,000 votes (in Utah and Wyoming) to eleven where Republicans were nominated unopposed. Not all Republicans who won uncontested nominations entered the campaign without real hope of winning in November. But in some states one can well understand why the competition for the Republican nomination was less than spirited. To most members of the GOP, the Republican nomination to oppose a Ted Kennedy in Massachusetts, a John Pastore in Rhode Island, or a

[4] Salinger won the nomination on June 2 (the incumbent Clair Engle having withdrawn in April) and was appointed on August 4 to succeed Engle, who died on July 30. Salinger was therefore the incumbent at the time of the November election but not at the time of the primary.

Many observers also thought they saw in Salinger's California candidacy an attempt by Robert F. Kennedy to establish a potential base of support on the West Coast. Salinger declared that he had discussed his decision to run with Mrs. John F. Kennedy and with the Attorney General; and six days before the primary President Kennedy's widow granted an interview in which she said that Salinger had been "very close" to President Kennedy. It was also reported that she had consulted Robert Kennedy before making her statement; *San Francisco Examiner*, May 25 and 28, 1964. Although Mrs. Kennedy did not formally endorse Salinger, Mrs. Clair Engle, the wife of the seriously ill Democratic incumbent, did endorse him, in a statement made the day after the Jacqueline Kennedy interview; *San Francisco Examiner*, May 29, 1964. Unruh's first public endorsement of Salinger came just three days before the primary. Said Unruh: "Since Mrs. John F. Kennedy and Mrs. Clair Engle have made known their choices, I cannot help but humbly add my own name below those of two great ladies who have suffered so deeply and so inspired our state and the nation"; *San Francisco Examiner*, May 31, 1964.

[5] Bass's main opponent, Governor Frank G. Clement, apparently suffered from a fairly common liability hindering governors who are bent on continuing their political career—Clement had put through a sales tax.

Harry Byrd in Virginia must have appeared to be a prize of dubious value. As it turned out, no nonincumbent Republican who was nominated for the Senate without opposition was elected.

In primary contests for the handful of Republican-held seats in the Senate class of 1964, much the same general pattern can be detected (Table 6.2). Only one incumbent, J. Glenn Beall of Maryland, encountered serious opposition, and he defeated his closest opponent by nearly 2-1. The one Republican primary for a Republican-held seat not involving an incumbent was in Arizona. There, when Senator Goldwater stepped out to run for higher office, the state's Republican Governor, Paul Fannin, stepped in, and there was no contest.

In several of these states where Republican senators were up for reelection, Democratic prospects looked reasonably bright in 1964, and a number of hard-fought contests among Democrats developed. Both Joseph Tydings in Maryland and Genevieve Blatt in Pennsylvania took on candidates backed by the established Democratic organizations in their states and won the nomination. Tydings also went on to win in November; but the Blatt-Musmanno fight, where, due to the closeness of the vote, Miss Blatt's victory was not assured until midsummer, may well have left scars that played a major role in her narrow defeat by Senator Hugh Scott in the general election.

The Democrats had few serious primary clashes that pitted candidates of markedly different ideology against each other, although the Yarborough-McLendon race in Texas did amount to a clear-cut liberal-conservative confrontation. On the Republican side, however, there were a number of primary battles that echoed San Francisco, between right-wing and more liberal elements in the party.

The results of these skirmishes were mixed. In Texas, George Bush, a moderate Republican and the son of a

*Table 6.2.   Percentage of Total 1964 Primary Vote Polled
by Winning Candidates for Nominations for Senate Seats
Held by Republicans Before the Election* [a]

Winner's Percentage of Total Vote	Republican Primaries		Democratic Primaries
	Incumbent Stood for Reelection	No Incumbent Stood for Reelection	(No Incumbent Could Stand for Reelection)
35–39	—	—	—
40–44	—	—	1[b]
45–49	—	—	1[c]
50–54	—	—	—
55–59	1[d]	—	1[e]
60–64	—	—	1[f]
65–69	—	—	—
70–74	—	—	1[g]
75–79	—	—	—
80–89	1	—	—
90–99	1	—	—
Unopposed	3	1	2
Total	6	1	7

Source: *Congressional Quarterly Weekly Reports,* March-October, 1964.

[a] Two states with Republican Senators up for reelection in 1964 (Delaware and New York) where candidates were nominated by conventions rather than in primaries are excluded.
[b] Roy L. Elson, Arizona.
[c] Genevieve Blatt, Pennsylvania.
[d] J. Glenn Beall, Maryland.
[e] Joseph D. Tydings, Maryland.
[f] Thomas P. Gill, Hawaii.
[g] Frederick J. Fayette, Vermont.

former Republican senator from Connecticut, defeated Jack Cox, a staunch conservative, in a victory that was all the more noteworthy because of the pronounced conservatism of most Republicans who have been nominated for high office in Texas in recent years. In Ohio, Representative Robert A. Taft, Jr., who has sought to move the Taft image in American politics closer to the middle of the road, swamped his right-wing opponent, Ohio Secretary of State

Ted Brown. On the other hand, right-wing Republicans won victories in several states, including Utah, where Ernest Wilkinson defeated Representative Sherman L. Lloyd, a more moderate candidate, in a race decided by fewer than 2,000 votes.[6] In past years some Republican Senate classes have been notable for their conservatism. Others have been considerably more liberal. If a national tide to the Republican senatorial ticket had developed in November, the Republican Senate class of 1964 would have been a mixed breed.

General Election Results:
The Republicans' Lost Opportunity

In November, however, there was no electoral tide to the Republican party's senatorial nominees. In fact, perhaps the most noteworthy feature of the Senate general election results was not what did happen, but what did not happen. The net change in the number of Senate seats was small. In partisan terms, only four seats changed hands. In California, where Pierre Salinger had the job of defending the Democratic seat vacated by the death of Clair Engle, George Murphy captured the seat for the Republican party. Democrats took seats from the Republicans in Maryland, in New Mexico, and in New York, where Senator Kenneth Keating was defeated by Robert F. Kennedy in a race that attracted

[6] There is some evidence that, despite his primary victory, Wilkinson was not a strong candidate in Utah in the November general election. The incumbent Democratic Senator, Frank Moss, ran 2.6 percentage points ahead of President Johnson's Utah showing against Barry Goldwater, and defeated Wilkinson handily. In 1958 Moss had required the intervention of a major independent Senate candidate, who split the Republican vote, to win his Senate seat with 38.7 percent of the total vote.

national attention.[7] Yet, although the net change was small, the results added up to a major defeat for the Republican party and a broad electoral verdict destined to have a significant effect on the character of the Senate for the next six years. The group of Senators up for election in 1964 was heavily Democratic with many of the Democratic incumbents holding marginal seats potentially vulnerable to capture by Republicans. The elections thus gave the Republican party its best chance since 1958 to make important gains in the Senate; but in 1964 it was an opportunity they were unable to seize.

A look at the special features of the seats that were to be filled makes clear how much was at stake in the Senate contests of 1964. Since the Great Depression, the election results for the group of seats up for election in 1964 have been the most volatile of the three classes of Senate seats

[7] Robert Kennedy's success in being elected Senator from New York less than three months after establishing a residence in the state raised an interesting question about the current importance of the residence rule in American national politics. Was the Kennedy victory just a freak, an event made possible by the special magic of the Kennedy name in the aftermath of President Kennedy's brutal assassination, or does it portend a greater nationalization of American politics? Other candidates have also bucked the residence rule in recent years. Both the Kennedy experience and that of Kenneth Hechler, a Democrat who moved to West Virginia after the 1956 election and was elected to Congress from that state in 1958, suggest that for men who are able to mix the requisite daring with the right electoral circumstances, the barrier of the customary residence rule need not always be insurmountable. Yet, as Robert Kennedy himself pointed out, New York has had something of a tradition of elevating migrants into the state to high public office. Thomas E. Dewey, for example, spent his boyhood in Michigan rather than New York State; and Adlai Stevenson was seriously considered for the Democratic senatorial nomination in 1964. And what was possible—even for a Kennedy in 1964—in New York State might not have been possible in Wisconsin, or Indiana, or even in Pennsylvania. Moreover, even in New York State Kennedy clearly was on the defensive on the carpetbagger issue. The length of time required to become a New Yorker or a Californian for political purposes is undoubtedly shorter than that required to become a Virginian; but until there is further evidence to the contrary, one must still conclude that the customary adherence to the residence rule remains a highly potent force in American politics.

that are filled for staggered terms. And during this period it has been the wide shifts in party strength from one election to the next in this group of seats that have done the most to alter the balance between liberal and conservative forces within the Senate.

Data underpinning the first of these propositions appear in Table 6.3, where the numbers of senators elected by each party in each election year since 1920 are set forth for the three Senate classes up for election in 1960, 1962, and 1964. As the data indicate, all three groups of seats were swept by successive Democratic landslides during the peak years of the Depression (1932-1936). But then, although Democratic strength in the groups last filled in 1960 and 1962 has varied considerably, these seats have been substan-

Table 6.3. Senate Election Results, 1920-1964, in the Three Classes of Senate Seats Filled in 1960, 1962, and 1964 [a]

Class of 1960				Class of 1962				Class of 1964			
Election Year	Demo-cratic	Repub-lican[b]	Percent Demo-cratic	Election Year	Demo-cratic	Repub-lican	Percent Demo-cratic	Election Year	Demo-cratic	Repub-lican[b]	Percent Demo-cratic
1960	20	13	60.6	1962	24	10	70.6	1964	26	7	78.8
1954	21	10(1)	65.6	1956	17	15	53.1	1958	24	8	75.0
1948	23	9	71.9	1950	15	17	46.9	1952	12	20	37.5
1942	15	17	46.9	1944	21	11	65.6	1946	11	21	34.4
1936	23	6(3)	71.9	1938	22	10	68.8	1940	21	10(1)	65.6
1930	20	12	62.5	1932	27	5	84.4	1934	24	7(1)	75.0
1924	13	19	40.6	1926	14	18	43.8	1928	14	17(1)	43.8
				1920	7	25	21.9	1922	21	10(1)	65.6

Sources: "Complete Returns of the 1964 Elections by Congressional District," *Congressional Quarterly Special Report*, March 26, 1965; biennial reports of the Clerk of the House of Representatives containing statistics of the congressional and presidential elections, for 1936-1962; *Congressional Directory* (Government Printing Office), 1920-1934.

[a] Tabulation includes elections for full six-year terms only. The size of the Senate classes expanded after 1958 when Alaska and Hawaii were admitted to the Union.

[b] Figures in parentheses following the number of Republicans elected denote victories by independent or minor-party Senate nominees.

tially less volatile than the Senate class of 1964. In the post-Depression years, Democratic strength in the seats up for election in 1964 has varied from one-third Democratic in 1946 to nearly four-fifths Democratic in 1964.

In 1940, the year Franklin Roosevelt won a third term as President, the Democrats also scored an important defensive victory in contests for these Senate seats. By winning a number of highly marginal races and holding most of the seats they had won six years earlier in the Depression year of 1934, the Democrats were able to retain a top-heavy majority in the Senate, with 66 of the 96 seats in the body. Six years later, however, Franklin Roosevelt was dead and the political climate had changed considerably. In a major Senate landslide, the famous Republican class of 1946 was sent to Washington. Among the Republicans elected in 1946 were an unusual number of pronounced conservatism, including William F. Knowland, John W. Bricker, William E. Jenner, George W. Malone, and Joseph R. McCarthy.

When this Republican class of 1946 came up for reelection in 1952, Eisenhower headed their ticket and most of these Senators were reelected.[8] The 1952 results thus insured that the Republicans elected in the extraordinary Republican sweep of 1946 would continue to have a significant effect on the character of the Senate for another six years. In 1958, however, Eisenhower was off the ticket, and this time the balance swung sharply to the Democratic party. Democrats won 24 seats in this group; Republicans won 8. And

[8] There were signs even in 1952, however, that the electorate was exercising some selectivity between the Republican presidential ticket and the more conservative members of the Republican Senate class of 1946. Republican Senators Harry P. Cain of Washington, James P. Kem of Missouri, and Zales N. Ecton of Montana were sent to involuntary retirement by the voters, despite Eisenhower victories in their states. In addition, one liberal Republican, Henry Cabot Lodge, was beaten by John F. Kennedy. Nevertheless, Republican gains in other states, including the victory of Barry Goldwater in Arizona, kept the group almost as heavily Republican as in 1946.

just as the 1946 Republican landslide kept the Senate close to half Republican from 1946 to 1958, the 1958 Democratic sweep, reinforced and extended in 1964, has kept the Senate close to two-thirds Democratic ever since.

Of the 33 contests for full six-year terms in 1964, Democrats won 26, Republicans 7. Democrats also won two hard-fought contests for two-year Senate terms (Ross Bass in Tennessee and Fred Harris in Oklahoma), to bring their overall 1964 Senate score to 28-7. Of the 28 Democratic victories, 10 were won with less than 55 percent of the vote. The Senate seats that are to be filled in 1966 and 1968 contain fewer Democratic seats potentially vulnerable to capture by the Republicans than did the Senate class of 1964. Thus by their 10 close victories in 1964, the Democrats were virtually assured of continuous control of the Senate until 1971.

The Impact of the Johnson Landslide

In the days before the election the expectation of a heavy vote for President Johnson led to much discussion about how much help he would provide for the Democratic senatorial ticket. Aggregate election statistics do not indicate how many votes polled by Democratic Senate candidates can be attributed to Johnson's strength in their state, but Table 6.4 suggests something of the advantage the President may have given Democrats defending Senate seats in marginal constituencies. Johnson carried every state where Democrats were defending Senate seats but Mississippi, and there the conservative southern Democrat, John Stennis, had no Republican opponent. In all but six of the Senate contests where the Democrats were the defending party, Johnson carried the state with more than 55 per cent of the vote.

Table 6.4.   Senatorial Election Results in Relation to Popular Presidential Vote, 1964 [a]

State Democratic Presidential Percentage	Democratic Seats		Republican Seats		All Seats	
	Number	Number Held	Number	Number Lost	Number	Number Democratic
0–39	1	1[b]	—	—	1	1
40–44	—	—	—	—	—	—
45–49	—	—	1	—	1	—
50–54	3	3	1[c]	—	4	3
55–59	9	8[d]	1	1[e]	10	9
60–64	6	6	1[f]	—	7	6
65–69	5	5	4	2[g]	9	7
70–74	—	—	—	—	—	—
75–100	2	2	1[h]	—	3	2

Source: "Complete Returns of the 1964 Elections by Congressional District."
[a] Tabulation includes two elections for two-year Senate terms.
[b] John Stennis, Mississippi, who had no Republican opponent.
[c] Roman Hruska, Nebraska.
[d] The Democrat who lost was Pierre Salinger, California.
[e] Edwin Mechem, New Mexico.
[f] John Williams, Delaware.
[g] The Republican losers were Kenneth Keating, New York, and J. Glenn Beall, Maryland. The two Republican winners were Hugh Scott, Pennsylvania, and Winston Prouty, Vermont.
[h] Hiram Fong, Hawaii.

It would be absurd to attribute all of the close Democratic Senate victories to Johnson's strong presidential race. The number of incumbent Democratic senators defending these seats was undoubtedly a potent factor in the results.[9] (The only Senate seat the Democrats lost in 1964 was in California, where Clair Engle, the popular Democrat elected in 1958, died before the election.) And even in 1964, some Democratic senatorial candidates demonstrated that they had

[9] V. O. Key found that in 1960 most incumbent senators were reelected regardless of which party won the presidential vote in their state. V. O. Key, Jr., "Interpreting the Election Results," in Paul T. David (ed.), *The Presidential Election and Transition 1960-1961* (Brookings Institution, 1961), p. 171.

independent sources of electoral strength that were clearly not attributable to the vote for Johnson. Thus, in eight states, despite the Johnson national landslide, there were Democratic Senators who ran ahead of Johnson—Spessard Holland in Florida, John Stennis in Mississippi, Harry F. Byrd in Virginia, Stuart Symington in Missouri, Mike Mansfield in Montana, John D. Pastore in Rhode Island, Frank Moss in Utah, and Henry Jackson in Washington.

In eighteen contests where the Democrats were the defending party, however, the President led the Democratic Senate nominee. One can never be sure from the aggregate figures that Johnson saved the seat for the Democrats, but in some states the Democratic senatorial candidate was so much weaker than Johnson that it seems unlikely that he could have won without a strong surge to Johnson in the presidential balloting. In Ohio, Senator Stephen M. Young withstood a strong challenge from an opponent with a name long magical in Ohio politics, Robert A. Taft, Jr., to win by 16,827 votes while Johnson was sweeping the state by 1,027,466 votes (62.9 percent).[10] In Nevada, Senator Howard W. Cannon survived by the slimmest Senate margin of 1964, 48 votes, while Johnson was carrying his state by 23,245 (58.6 percent). And in Oklahoma, Fred Harris edged to victory over the Republicans' Bud Wilkinson by 21,390 votes while Johnson was winning the state by

---

[10] Without detracting from his tenacity in the face of heavy odds or from his achievements, one must nevertheless be struck by the exceptional good luck of Senator Young. In 1958, when he challenged Ohio's redoubtable Republican Senator, John W. Bricker, he won a victory few observers expected, in the wake of a statewide Democratic landslide triggered in part by organized labor's furious opposition to a referendum on the "right to work" issue. In the spring of 1964, Young appeared headed for a serious primary challenge from an authentic American hero, John Glenn. After announcing his candidacy, however, Glenn injured himself in a fall in his bathroom and was forced to withdraw from the race. Then, in the November general election, Young was aided by the heaviest vote ever cast for a Democratic presidential candidate in Ohio.

107,169 (55.7 percent).[11] The GOP would have done substantially better in Senate contests in 1964, if only Goldwater had not done so badly.[12]

So high was the Johnson tide that all but one of the nine Republicans defending Senate seats also had to stand in states carried by the President. Of these eight Republicans who ran in Johnson territory, five survived—including Hugh Scott who won by 70,635 votes in Pennsylvania where Johnson won by 1,457,297 (65.2 percent), and Hawaii's Senator Hiram Fong, who won by 13,958 votes while Johnson got an astounding 78.8 percent of the Hawaii presidential vote. (In percentage terms, Hawaii may well have produced the greatest amount of split-ticket voting for President and Senator of any state.) The Republican casualties in 1964 were New Mexico's Senator Edwin Mechem, defeated by Joseph Montoya; Maryland's J. Glenn Beall, defeated by Joseph D. Tydings; and New York's Kenneth Keating, who lost to Robert F. Kennedy. Kennedy's margin over Keating was 719,693; Johnson carried New York by 2,669,597.

[11] Focusing attention on Democratic Senate candidates who were markedly weaker than Johnson but still survived probably gives only a minimal estimate of the number of Democratic Senate seats that were saved by the Johnson landslide in 1964. As Warren E. Miller has noted, races where candidates below the top of the ticket poll votes that closely parallel the presidential vote may indicate that the presidential nominee has been of greater help to his running mates than races where candidates for lower offices trail far behind. And survey data, not aggregate electoral statistics, would be necessary to explore the precise effects the presidential contest had on the Senate contests, and vice versa. See Warren E. Miller, "Presidential Coattails: A Study in Political Myth and Methodology," *Public Opinion Quarterly*, Vol. 19 (1955-1956), pp. 353-68. Nevertheless, without a Johnson landslide in 1964, it still seems unlikely that Democratic senatorial candidates such as Young, Cannon, and Harris would have won.

[12] One irony of the 1964 election was that in the five Deep South states where Goldwater did best and where he might have helped a GOP senatorial nominee, four had no Senate contest, and in the fifth, Mississippi, the Democratic incumbent had no Republican opponent.

Safe Seats and Marginal Seats

As we have seen, the group of Senate seats up for election in 1964 has fluctuated widely between the two parties since the Depression. The 1964 results left them still potentially highly competitive. In terms of the voting results, about 46 percent of the seats filled in 1964 were in the marginal category—won by less than 55 percent of the vote (Table 6.5). About a third of the Democratic victories were in this technically marginal category, but several other seats where the Democratic vote exceeded 55 percent in 1964 could well be hotly contested in another election year or with a different

Table 6.5.   Sure and Close Senate Races, 1964: Distribution According to Democratic Percentage of Two-Party Vote

Democratic Percentage of Vote	Number of Elections[a]	Percent of Elections	Distribution by Winning Party	
			Percent of Republicans	Percent of Democrats
0–34	—	—	—	—
35–39	1	2.9	14.3	—
40–44	—	—	—	—
45–49	6	17.1	85.7	—
50–54	10	28.6	—	35.7
55–59	3	8.6	—	10.7
60–64	8	22.9	—	28.6
65–69	3	8.6	—	10.7
70–74	2	5.7	—	7.1
75–79	—	—	—	—
80–84	1	2.9	—	3.6
85–100	1	2.9	—	3.6
Total	35	100.0	100.0	100.0

Note: Details may not add to totals because of rounding.
Source: "Complete Returns of the 1964 Elections by Congressional District."
[a] Tabulation includes two elections for two-year Senate terms.

Democratic Senate candidate. It is hard, for example, to regard the Senate seats of Edmund Muskie of Maine (66.6 percent Democratic in 1964) or Harrison Williams of New Jersey (62.4 percent Democratic in 1964) as irrevocably "Safely Democratic." And Senators Frank Moss of Utah, Ralph Yarborough of Texas, or Quentin Burdick of North Dakota, all of whom polled between 56 and 58 percent of the vote, might well expect a closer contest in any other election year. The Republicans' position in the Senate class of 1964, however, was even more precarious. Five percent more Democratic votes in the 1964 Senate contests, evenly distributed, would have enabled the Democrats to win every seat up for election but one.

It is clear that the Senate as an institution is now potentially very responsive to shifts in the relative balance of party strength in the country. The election of 1964 left the chamber as a whole with a very sizable number of marginal seats. The distribution of the Democratic vote in contests which involved the three groups of incumbent Senators (those elected to full six-year terms in 1960, 1962, and 1964) is indicated in Table 6.6. As the data make plain, 41 percent of all these contests were won by less than 55 percent of the vote; and the percentage of the major-party vote ranged between 40 and 60 percent in nearly six of every ten Senate contests during these years.[13]

Again one must note that the Democrats have more safe seats (in terms of the percentage of the vote polled) than the Republicans. Half of the Republican seats during this period were won with less than 55 percent of the vote, compared with just over a third of the Democratic seats. But the figures also reflect the Republicans' growing strength in

[13] H. Douglas Price stresses that a large number of Senate seats have been competitive in recent years and that the proportion of such seats in the Senate is markedly higher than in the House. See H. Douglas Price, "The Electoral Arena," in David B. Truman (ed.), *The Congress and America's Future* (Prentice-Hall, 1965), pp. 32-51.

Table 6.6. *Sure and Close Senate Races, 1960-1964: Distribution According to Democratic Percentage of Two-Party Vote* [a]

Democratic Percentage of Vote	Number of elections				Distribution of Total by Winning Party	
	1960	1962	1964	Total	Percent of Republicans	Percent of Democrats
0–34	—	1	—	1	3.2	—
35–39	2	2	1	5	16.1	—
40–44	6	3	—	9	29.0	—
45–49	5	5	6	16	51.7	—
50–54	5	12	8	25	—	36.3
55–59	3	2	3	8	—	11.6
60–64	3	3	8	14	—	20.3
65–69	1	3	3	7	—	10.1
70–74	2	1	2	5	—	7.2
75–79	1	1	—	2	—	2.9
80–84	1	—	1	2	—	2.9
85–100	4	1	1	6	—	8.7
Total	33	34	33	100	100.0	100.0

Sources: Richard M. Scammon (ed.), *America Votes*, Vols. 4 and 5 (University of Pittsburgh Press, 1962 and 1964); and "Complete Returns of the 1964 Elections by Congressional District."
[a] Tabulation includes elections for full six-year terms only.

certain southern senatorial contests, a trend which, if continued, could have a profound effect on the Senate.

Even now, there are signs that the Democratic hold on the Senate seats of the South is less overwhelmingly one-sided than at any time since Reconstruction. Thus, from 1920 to 1958, over a quarter (27.1 percent) of all Senate seats won by Democrats—mostly southerners—were carried by 80 percent or more of the vote (Table 6.7). In the 1960-64 period about a tenth (11.6 percent) of the Democratic seats were won by similar margins. Texas, South Carolina, Tennessee, and Alabama are all southern states where in recent

Table 6.7. *Sure and Close Senate Races, 1920-1958: Distribution According to Democratic Percentage of Two-Party Vote* [a]

Democratic Percentage of Vote	Number of Elections	Percent of Elections	Distribution by Winning Party	
			Percent of Republicans	Percent of Democrats
0–9	5	0.8	1.9	—
10–19	6	1.0	2.2	—
20–29	28	4.4	10.4	—
30–39	50	7.9	18.6	—
40–44	72	11.4	26.8	—
45–49	108	17.2	40.1	—
50–54	91	14.4	—	25.1
55–59	81	12.8	—	22.4
60–69	62	9.8	—	17.1
70–79	30	4.8	—	8.3
80–89	26	4.1	—	7.2
90–100	72	11.4	—	19.9
Total	631	100.0	100.0	100.0

Source: Adapted from V. O. Key, Jr., *Politics, Parties, and Pressure Groups* (Thomas Y. Crowell, 1964), p. 548.
[a] Tabulation includes elections for full six-year terms only; it excludes eight elections in which independent or third-party candidates won.

years the Democratic senatorial nominee has known he was in a serious fight at the general election. And in 1964 the largest Democratic percentage of the vote in a contested Senate race was not in Virginia, Texas, or Florida, but in Rhode Island.

The 1964 Election and the Liberal-Conservative Balance in the Senate

Yet perhaps the most striking feature of the 1964 Senate results lay in their implications for the amount of legislative support President Johnson could expect for the more liberal measures in his domestic program. For the group of Senators up for election and for the most part reelected in 1964 was, in marked degree, the most liberal of the three senatorial classes. In Table 6.8, data are presented on the number of times the classes elected in 1960, 1962, and 1964 cast votes which Americans for Democratic Action, a liberal organization, considered "correct" on a series of roll-call votes which it selected. Such roll-call vote indexes have distinct limitations as indicators of the full range of behavior by legislators. But they do give a rough indication of broad differences in outlook among legislators, including those nominally from the same party. Thus, in 1964, the ratings given by the ADA to Senators Philip Hart, Eugene McCarthy, and Mike Mansfield were 96, 90, and 80, respectively, while Virginia's Senator Harry Byrd was rated 4 and Senators Barry Goldwater and Edwin Mechem were rated 0. Table 6.8 indicates that the group of senators up for

Table 6.8. *ADA Ratings on Selected Roll-Call Votes for Three Groups of Senators Up for Election in 1960, 1962, and 1964* [a]

Election Year[b]	Number of Senators	ADA Roll-call Vote Ratings of Senators (in Percentages)		
		0–29	30–69	70 and Over
1960	33	48.5	21.2	30.3
1962	34	44.1	17.6	38.2
1964	33	21.2	27.3	51.5

Source: *Congressional Quarterly Weekly Report*, Oct. 23, 1964, p. 2548.
[a] Roll-call vote ratings based on the percentage of the time each Senator voted in accordance with the position of Americans for Democratic Action, a "liberal" organization, on selected issues during the term each Senator was serving in 1964—covering six, four, or two years.
[b] Senators were assigned to the class of 1960, 1962, or 1964 according to when their seat was last filled for a full six-year term.

election in 1964 was heavily weighted in the liberal direction (over half had ADA ratings of 70 or higher), and that this class was notably more liberal than either of the other two classes. Only 21 percent of the senators who were up in 1964 had ADA scores under 30, compared with nearly half of the group last elected in 1960, and 44 percent of the group elected in 1962.[14]

This liberalism was so pronounced because both the Democrats and the Republicans who came up for election in 1964 were decidedly more liberal than the groups within their own parties who were elected in 1960 and 1962. Among Democrats, the distribution of the ADA ratings given to senators who were elected in 1960, 1962, and 1964 was as follows:[15]

Election Year	0-29	30-69	70 or over
1960	7 (36.8%)	3 (15.8%)	9 (47.4%)
1962	7 (30.4%)	5 (21.7%)	11 (47.8%)
1964	3 (12.5%)	4 (16.7%)	17 (70.8%)

The comparable ratings given the Republican classes were:

Election Year	0-29	30-69	70 or over
1960	9 (64.3%)	4 (28.6%)	1 (7.1%)
1962	8 (72.7%)	1 (9.1%)	2 (18.2%)
1964	4 (44.4%)	5 (55.6%)	—

The Democratic class of 1964 was unusually liberal because it included only three conservative southerners—Byrd,

[14] Analysis based on use of a roll-call vote rating given senators by Americans for Constitutional Action, a strongly conservative organization, reveals much the same general pattern as the ratings made by ADA.

[15] The ADA roll-call vote ratings used in the two analyses that follow are identical to those used in Table 6.8.

Holland, and Stennis. In the Republican group of Senators up for reelection in 1964, Beall, Fong, Keating, Prouty, and Scott all tended to be aligned with the moderate-to-liberal wing of their party.

Overall, the balance between liberal and conservative forces in the Senate was not greatly changed by the 1964 elections, although, if anything, it was the liberals who gained.[16] The replacement of Clair Engle of California by George Murphy was a clear gain for the conservatives, but this was almost counterbalanced by the defeat of New Mexico's Republican Senator Edwin Mechem by Representative Thomas Montoya. (Montoya's 1964 ADA rating in the House was 72.) Senators Keating and Beall, the other GOP losses, were in the moderate-to-liberal wing of their party, thus lessening the impact on the ideological balance in the Senate caused by their replacement by Demo-

---

[16] Analyses of Senate roll calls that rest on the assumption that all Senators' votes would have remained unchanged in different circumstances have their dangers. If the balance in the Senate between Democrats and Republicans had been closer in 1965, it is possible, for example, that some Democrats who did not back the President because their vote was not absolutely necessary might have been induced to come to his support. Nevertheless, the vote on one of the proposed amendments to the Medicare bill affords a rough indication of the importance the 1964 Senate election results had for passage of some of the more controversial items in the President's program. On July 8, 1965, Senator Carl Curtis of Nebraska, a Republican, offered an amendment that struck at the administration's determination to avoid any semblance of a means test in the administration of Medicare benefits. The Curtis amendment would have provided that a hospital patient under the basic health insurance plan pay a deduction of either $40 or the amount of his previous year's income tax liability, whichever was greater, and that a patient under the supplementary health care plan pay an annual deduction of $50 or his previous year's income tax liability, whichever was greater. The amendment was defeated by the fairly close vote of 41-51, with only four Republican Senators voting against it. Among Senators elected in 1964, the vote was: for the amendment, 10; against the amendment, 21. Among Democratic Senators elected in 1964, the margin against the amendment was 21 to 4. *Congressional Quarterly Weekly Report,* July 9, 1964, p. 1347.

crats.[17] Yet in both cases, their successors, extremely ener-
getic men, were likely to have even higher support scores for
ADA-approved legislation.

This overall pattern of little change, however, conceals
some shifts within each party's 1964 Senate delegation. The
addition of Montoya, Tydings, and Kennedy, with only the
loss of Engle, gave an even stronger liberal cast to the 1964
vintage Democrats. But on the Republican side, Murphy
replaced Mechem, leaving Keating and Beall as clear losses
for the moderate-liberal wing. Goldwater made a poor showing for conservatism in presidential politics, but an additional result of the 1964 elections was probably to weaken
the more liberal wing of the Republican party in the Senate.

[17] Keating's 1964 ADA rating was 67, Beall's was 36.

7

Nominations and Elections for the House of Representatives

MILTON C. CUMMINGS, JR.

Of the three organs of government for which national elections were held in 1964, the House of Representatives was probably changed most by the results of the voting. The presidential results confirmed and strengthened Johnson's already firm grip on the power of the American Presidency. The nominations and elections for the Senate retained a liberal majority in that body. But the net effect of the hundreds of House primaries and elections spread over the better part of a year was to bring about a pronounced change in the balance between liberal and conservative elements in the House. That this would be the outcome of the House elections, however, was by no means readily apparent at the beginning of the campaign year.

Patterns of Competition in the Primaries

In the primary elections for the House of Representatives most of the results conformed to the same broad pattern as the Senate primaries. Where a party did not control the House seat—and hence no incumbent could be involved

—the primary campaigns varied widely: from hard-fought contests decided by narrow margins to primaries in which the candidate was unopposed. Primaries for seats a party controlled but for which the incumbent failed to run again also produced varying amounts of competition. On the other hand, wherever an incumbent stood for reelection, the odds were strong that he would be renominated with ease.

Of the 384 incumbents who stood for reelection in 1964, only 30 polled less than 65 percent of the total primary vote, and 8 of these were defeated in the primary (Table 7.1). In Michigan, where there was a major redistricting shortly before the election, four incumbent Democrats were thrown into two newly created districts, and two, John L. Lesinski and Harold M. Ryan, were perforce defeated. The contest between Representatives Lesinski and John D. Dingell attracted considerable national attention. Lesinski was one of only two Democratic congressmen from districts outside the South and Border States to vote against the Civil Rights Act of 1964, and his position angered Negro and

Table 7.1. 1964 Primary Races in Which Incumbent Democratic Representatives Were Defeated

District	Incumbent	Percent of Vote	Chief Opponent	Percent of Vote
Tennessee 9	Clifford Davis	40.7	George W. Grider	49.7
Michigan 16	John L. Lesinski	45.4	John D. Dingell	54.6
New York 23	Charles A. Buckley	45.9	Jonathan B. Bingham	54.1
Louisiana 8	Gillis W. Long	46.0	Speedy O. Long	54.0
New York 21	James C. Healey	47.0	James H. Scheuer	53.0
Michigan 14	Harold M. Ryan	47.2	Lucien N. Nedzi	52.8
Oklahoma 6	Victor Wickersham	49.3	Jed Johnson, Jr.	50.7
Alabama AL	Carl Elliott[a]	—	—	—

Source: *Congressional Quarterly Almanac, 88th Congress, 2nd Session—1964* (Congressional Quarterly Service, 1965), p. 1068.

[a] Elliott finished last in a statewide race among nine contestants for eight House nominations on the Democratic ticket.

labor groups as well as leaders of the Michigan Democratic organization. Dingell, a supporter of the act, defeated Lesinksi by about 5,000 votes, despite the fact that a majority of the voters in the new district had been in Lesinski's district before 1964.[1] In the 6th district of Oklahoma, another Democratic Representative, Victor Wickersham, also lost the primary. His opponent attacked him for absenteeism and for involvement in real estate transactions in the Washington area, and during the campaign he urged Wickersham to make a public statement of his investments.[2]

Special factors loomed particularly large in both the Michigan and the Oklahoma primary overturns. Most of the other primaries where an incumbent was defeated, however, were of two types: fights between "reform Democrats" and the established local Democratic organization in New York City; and contests where moderate-to-liberal Democrats were pitted against more conservative candidates in House districts in the South.

Warfare Among New York City Democrats

Representative Charles A. Buckley, the leader of the Bronx Democratic organization, was defeated by reform Democrat Jonathan Bingham. Buckley had been a member of Congress for thirty years and had become chairman of the House Public Works Committee. During the campaign he was the recipient of cordial public statements on his behalf from both President Lyndon Johnson and Robert F. Kennedy. Bingham had the active backing of Mayor Robert F. Wagner.

[1] *Congressional Quarterly Weekly Report,* Sept. 4, 1964, p. 2055.

[2] In recent years the Oklahoma 6th has had the most consistently precarious House seat at primary election time in the country. Wickersham, who first entered the House in 1941, also lost the primary in 1946 and 1956. Both times he won his seat back the following election year; and he held it in two hotly contested primary battles in 1960 and 1962. *Congressional Quarterly Weekly Report,* May 29, 1964, pp. 1066-67.

In another Bronx constituency, Representative James C. Healey, a Buckley ally, also was defeated by a reform Democrat; and in New York's 19th district (Manhattan) Representative Leonard Farbstein was hard pressed by William Haddad, another candidate with reform group backing,[3] who polled 45.7 percent of the vote.

These internecine wars within the New York Democratic party have been reflected at the congressional level for several years. The reform Democrats also defeated a House candidate backed by the regular organization in 1960 and again in 1962. Over time they may be slowly transforming the character of the New York City delegation in the House.[4]

Liberals v. Conservatives in the South

Both reform and organization Democrats from New York City tend to support President Johnson's legislative program. But in the South there were several 1964 primary contests that had important implications for the balance between liberals and conservatives within the Democratic membership in the House. In the Tennessee 9th (Memphis) George W. Grider, a liberal, defeated Clifford Davis, a nine-term Democratic Representative who had often been allied with the conservative southerners in his party. In Louisiana's 8th district, however, the liberals suffered a loss in a statewide contest involving two branches of the Long family. There

[3] Unlike Healey's and Buckley's opponents, however, Haddad did not have the public support of the Mayor.

[4] In 1964 one of the newer breed of New York Democrats in the House, Benjamin Rosenthal, astounded observers of the City's delegation by announcing that he planned to buy a house and live in Washington so that he could devote more time to his legislative duties. Reporters could not recall another instance when a New York City Democrat had moved to Washington. Representative John Lindsay, a Republican, had moved to Washington two years before. *New York Times,* March 16, 1964.

Representative Gillis W. Long (with a 1964 ADA roll-call vote rating of 60) was defeated by a distant cousin, Speedy O. Long. But the southern liberals suffered their most costly defeat in Alabama, when Carl Elliott, an eight-term member and generally an administration supporter on the House Committee on Rules, ran last in a statewide race among nine contestants for eight House nominations on the Democratic ticket.[5]

Not all close Democratic primary contests involving a liberal-conservative choice resulted in defeat for the incumbent (Table 7.2). Representative Phil Landrum in Georgia and T. Ashton Thompson in Louisiana were both challenged by more conservative opponents and won, as did Louisiana's liberal Congressman James Morrison, who also benefited from having the opposition vote split several ways. Representatives Walter Baring (D-Nev.) and Joe Pool (D-Tex.), both conservatives, also survived substantial opposition in their primaries. Baring, who has the most conservative voting record of any Democrat outside the South, was renominated by only 1,600 votes.[6]

Yet when all the 1964 primaries were over, perhaps the most notable feature of the results was how little net change in the ideological complexion of the Democratic House ticket had occurred. Before the primaries there were news-

[5] In the statewide Alabama primary campaign, a conservative segregationist group called "Constitutional Coalition of Alabama" distributed sample ballots listing eight names while omitting Elliott's. The ballot contained a slogan often used by Governor George Wallace, "Stand Up for Alabama," although Wallace publicly repudiated the group and asserted that he was neutral. In the primary Elliott's nearest opponent (a nonincumbent) received 194,987 votes. Elliott received 191,964. *Congressional Quarterly Weekly Report,* June 2, 1964, p. 1089.

[6] See "Nevada Primary Results," *Congressional Quarterly Weekly Report,* Sept. 4, 1964, p. 2035.

Table 7.2. Close 1964 Primary Races Where the Incumbent Was Renominated by Less than 65 Percent of the Vote

District	Incumbent	Percent of Vote	Chief Opponent	Percent of Vote
Democratic Primaries				
Hawaii AL	Spark M. Matsunaga	38.3	Patsy T. Mink	22.0 [a]
			Walter M. Heen	19.8
Nevada AL	Walter S. Baring	50.6	Ralph L. Denton	47.8
Ohio 20	Michael A. Feighan	50.6	Ronald M. Mottl	39.9
Georgia 9	Phil M. Landrum	52.2	Zell Miller	42.0
Michigan 14	Lucien N. Nedzi	52.8	Harold M. Ryan	47.2
Louisiana 6	James H. Morrison	52.9	John E. Jumonville	20.7
New York 19	Leonard Farbstein	54.3	William F. Haddad	45.5
Texas 7	John Dowdy	54.5	Benton Musslewhite	45.5
Michigan 16	John D. Dingell	54.6	John Lesinski	45.4
Louisiana 7	T. Ashton Thompson	56.4	Gary Tyler	43.6
Texas AL	Joe Pool	57.2	Robert W. Baker	42.7
Maryland 3	Edward A. Garmatz	58.3	John A. Pica	41.6
North Carolina 4	Harold D. Cooley	59.0	R. Mayne Albright	41.0
Maryland 2	Clarence E. Long	59.1	Joshua F. Cockey	17.8
Arkansas 4	Oren Harris	59.3	Dean E. Murphy	40.6
Texas 3	Lindley Beckworth	60.4	L. E. Page	29.5
Georgia 5	Charles L. Weltner	61.0	Wyman C. Lowe	39.0
Mississippi 5	William M. Colmer	61.2	Edward A. Khayat	31.9
Mississippi 4	Arthur Winstead	61.8	Tom Dunn	19.1
Oregon 4	Robert B. Duncan	62.8	Charles O. Porter	37.1
Republican Primaries				
Wisconsin 6	William Van Pelt	54.1	Jack Steinhilber	45.8
Michigan 2	George Meader	55.2	Stanley G. Thayer	41.5

Source: *Congressional Quarterly Almanac, 1964,* pp. 1068-69.
[a] From a four candidate field, the two leading contenders were nominated for Hawaii's two at-large seats. Matsunaga was renominated, and State Senator Mink was nominated to run for the other at-large seat.

paper reports of plans by nationally oriented Democratic groups to try to "purge" some of the more conservative southern Democrats in the House.[7] As it turned out, only one of the conservative southerners who was reported to be

[7] *New York Times,* April 11, 1963. Thirteen Democrats were reported to be on the "purge" list.

on the "purge" list was defeated in a primary.[8] Whatever change there was to be in the balance between liberals and conservatives would have to come about in the general elections, not through the primary process.

General Election Results

During the course of the fall general election campaign, predictions of the probable outcome of the House contests became increasingly encouraging for supporters of the Democratic party.[9] Yet in the end the scope of the Democratic victory equalled or exceeded their most optimistic advance assessments of the possible gains for the House. Democrats, who entered the election with a nominal majority of 79, captured 48 seats from Republicans while losing 10.[10] This net gain of 38 seats gave the Democratic party a 295-140

---

[8] This was Clifford Davis of Tennessee. Another Democrat on the list, Representative Arthur Winstead of Mississippi, was defeated by a Republican in November. By allowing news of their plans to assist liberal challengers to conservative House Democrats to leak to the press, proponents of the plan probably did the one thing most likely to undermine whatever chances they had had of success. Representatives who reportedly were on the "purge" list were quick to emphasize it and to denounce it in statements aimed at their constituents. Said Representative W. J. Bryan Dorn of South Carolina shortly after news of the plan appeared in the paper: "It is utterly incredible that some little Caesars in Washington would openly and boldly threaten money, manpower and influence to oppose me in a South Carolina Democratic primary in John C. Calhoun's old Congressional district. It will be a pleasure to run for re-election against any candidate they might select." *New York Times,* April 12, 1963.

[9] *New York Times,* Oct. 30, 1964.

[10] Of the 48 seats gained by Democrats, 47 were in districts previously controlled by the Republicans and 1 was a seat previously accounted for by a Republican in Michigan but not identifiable because of redistricting. Of the 10 seats gained by Republicans, 9 were from districts previously controlled by Democrats and one was a Wisconsin seat previously accounted for by a Democrat but not identifiable because of redistricting. "Complete Returns of the 1964 Elections by Congressional District," *Congressional Quarterly Special Report,* March 26, 1965, p. 522.

margin over the Republicans—the most heavily Democratic House since Franklin Roosevelt's landslide reelection in 1936.[11]

There was an extraordinary amount of ticket-splitting between the presidential and House races in 1964. If the outcome of the House contests had paralleled the presidential results in every district, the Democratic margin would have been 375-60, not 295-140, and the Republican party would have been all but wiped out in the House. In about one district in every four, the voters elected a Republican candidate while returning a Democratic majority in the presidential race. In all, 113 of the 140 Republicans elected to the House won despite a Johnson victory in their district. And these Republican defensive victories were of crucial importance in enabling the GOP to retain at least some base of support in the House from which to try to launch a counterattack against the Democrats in 1966.[12] In another 33 districts—all but one of them in the South—Democratic House candidates won despite Goldwater margins in their constituencies. The number of districts with split election results—146—was almost certainly the largest in any election year in the last half century.

The results also reversed the relationship between the relative strength of the congressional and presidential wings of the Democratic party that had prevailed since World War II. Johnson ran ahead of his party's House nominee

---

[11] The Democratic margin in the House became 294-141 in June 1965, when former Democratic Representative Albert W. Watson of South Carolina, who resigned from the House after the Democratic caucus stripped him of his seniority, was reelected as a Republican.

[12] Despite their heavy losses, the Republicans clearly did better in House contests in 1964 than in 1936, the only other year when there has been a Democratic presidential landslide of comparable magnitude. In 1936 the Democrats' edge over the GOP in the House was 333-89. The much greater amount of ticket-splitting in 1964, which on balance worked to the advantage of the defeated party, was one of the major differences between the electoral verdicts of 1964 and 1936.

in 274 of the 435 House districts. He thus became the first Democratic presidential candidate to lead a substantial majority of his party's House ticket since Franklin Roosevelt.

House Results and the Johnson Landslide

Yet important and extensive as this ticket-splitting was in 1964, there was nevertheless a broad general relationship between the Johnson presidential tide and the showing made by the Democratic House ticket. Six days before the opening of the Republican National Convention, the names of 62 Republican House members appeared in a full-page advertisement in the *New York Times* endorsing Barry Goldwater for the Republican nomination for President. After listing some of the personal qualities which they felt qualified Senator Goldwater for leadership of the Free World, they also turned to more practical matters: "As Members of Congress, we are vitally interested in the success of our Party, at all levels of Government, at the polls in November . . . We are convinced that the nomination of Senator Barry Goldwater by the Republican Party will result in substantial increases in Republican membership in both Houses of Congress."[13] As it turned out, the nomination of Barry Goldwater had disastrous consequences for the Republican congressional ticket in every major region except the South.[14]

In November the Johnson tide was so strong that outside the South there were only 16 House districts which Gold-

[13] *New York Times,* July 7, 1964.

[14] The signers of the Goldwater endorsement in the *New York Times* were particularly hard hit by the Democratic landslide in November. Of the 62 Representatives who made the endorsement, 57 ran for reelection, and 20 were defeated. Of the 5 who retired, 3 saw their House seats captured by Democrats. Many of the defeated incumbents had been elected by comfortable margins in 1962: 9 had polled between 55 and 59.9 percent of the vote, 3 had received between 60 and 65 percent, and 1 had been elected by over 70 percent.

water carried—6 in southern California, 5 in Chicago suburban areas, and 1 each in Arizona, Idaho, Nebraska, Oklahoma, and Kentucky. In district after district which the Republican presidential ticket has usually carried, from upstate New York and upstate Michigan to downstate Illinois, Johnson's strength in effect gave Democratic House candidates a broad umbrella under which to run their own campaigns. And many Democratic nominees, particularly those seeking to oust an incumbent Republican, seemed to alternate between trying to link themselves closely with the President and attempting to tie a close association with Senator Goldwater tightly around their opponent's neck.[15]

In most presidential election years there is a fairly regular relationship between the vote for President and the results of House elections: the larger the winning presidential candidate's margin in a given district, the greater are the chances that a House nominee of his party will also win in the district.[16] As the data in Table 7.3 indicate, in 1964 there were some exceptions to this relationship in the country as a whole. In most districts where the Johnson tide was strong (over 60 percent) Democratic nominees were elected. But there were also a number of Democratic House victories in districts where Johnson was weak; and in some of the groups of districts that Johnson carried, the relationship between Democratic presidential strength and Democratic House victories was irregular.

---

[15] In Louisville, Kentucky, the Democratic House nominee, former Mayor Charles P. Farnsley, was quoted as saying that if elected he planned to support President Johnson "morning, noon, and night." In New York's 25th district (Westchester County), where Democrat Richard L. Ottinger opposed the incumbent Republican, Representative Robert R. Barry, Ottinger made references during the campaign to the opposition's "Barry-Barry ticket."

[16] For a demonstration of this relationship between the presidential vote and House results in 1952 and 1956, see V. O. Key, Jr., *Politics, Parties, and Pressure Groups,* 5th ed. (Thomas Y. Crowell, 1964), p. 560.

Table 7.3. Distribution of 1964 House Election Results in Relation to the Two-Party Presidential Vote

District Democratic Presidential Percentage	Number of Districts[a]	Number Electing Democrats	Percent Democratic
0.0–4.9	—	—	—
5.0–29.9	8	7	87.5
30.0–34.9	2	2	100.0
35.0–39.9	3	1	33.3
40.0–44.9	13	10	76.9
45.0–47.4	9	3	33.3
47.5–49.9	17	7	41.2
50.0–52.4	19	8	42.1
52.5–54.9	26	15	56.0
55.0–59.9	89	45	50.6
60.0–64.9	89	65	73.3
65.0–69.9	72	55	76.4
70.0–74.9	39	33	84.2
75.0–94.9	40	40	100.0
95.0–100.0	1	1	100.0
Total	427	292	

Source: "Complete Returns of the 1964 Elections by Congressional District," *Congressional Quarterly Special Report*, March 26, 1965.
[a] The eight districts in Alabama, where there was no slate of presidential electors pledged to Johnson on the ballot, are excluded from this tabulation.

The Democratic House victories in areas where Johnson was weak, however, occurred almost exclusively in the South. Many southern Democratic congressmen won regardless of the size of the vote for Goldwater in their district. And as the figures in Table 7.4 make clear, outside the South the Democrats' prospects of victory in the local House contest went up with each increase in the size of Johnson's vote in their district.

The strong Democratic congressional tide brought about a marked shift in the relative strength of the Democratic and

Table 7.4. Distribution of 1964 House Election Results in Relation to the Two-Party Presidential Vote, in the South and Outside the South

District Democratic Presidential Percentage	South			Outside the South		
	Number of Districts[a]	Won by Demo-crats	Percent Demo-cratic	Number of Districts	Won by Demo-crats	Percent Demo-cratic
0.0–4.9	—	—	—	—	—	—
5.0–29.9	8	7	87.5	—	—	—
30.0–34.9	2	2	100.0	—	—	—
35.0–39.9	2	1	50.0	1	—	—
40.0–44.9	11	10	90.9	2	—	—
45.0–47.4	4	3	75.0	5	—	—
47.5–49.9	9	6	66.7	8	1	12.5
50.0–52.4	7	6	85.7	12	2	16.7
52.5–54.9	10	10	100.0	16	5	31.3
55.0–59.9	16	14	87.5	73	31	42.5
60.0–64.9	14	13	92.9	75	52	69.3
65.0–69.9	6	6	100.0	66	49	74.2
70.0–74.9	8	8	100.0	31	25	80.6
75.0–94.9	1	1	100.0	39	39	100.0
95.0–100.0	—	—	—	1	1	100.0
Total	98	87		329	205	

Source: "Complete Returns of the 1964 Election by Congressional District."
[a] The eight districts in Alabama, where there was no slate of presidential electors pledged to Johnson on the ballot, are excluded from this tabulation.

Republican congressional parties in the country, leaving the Democratic party with a stronger hold on an absolute majority of 218 seats in the 435-member House than at any other time since 1936. The 1964 results moved many Democratic House seats that had been closely contested in 1962 out of the statistically marginal category. They also cut sharply into the number of safe Republican seats. In 1962 the GOP won 85 House seats with more than 60 percent of the vote. After the 1964 balloting there were only 37 seats on which the Republican party had a similar hold. The number of Democratic House seats won by 60 percent or more of the vote in 1964 was 210—just 8 seats short of a majority of the House (Table 7.5).[17]

The Democrats' chances of retaining a House majority in the near future thus looked exceedingly bright following the 1964 elections. But their chances of retaining the kind of decisive margin that gave the liberal wing of the Democratic party effective control of the House in the 1965 session were much less certain. In 1964 Democrats were elected from a number of normally Republican districts where the new Democratic congressman must feel anything but comfortable as he contemplates the 1966 midterm election, with no Lyndon Johnson on the Democratic ticket or Barry Goldwater on the Republican ticket. In all, the Democrats won 61 House seats in 1964 with less than 55 percent of the vote. Included among these were 37 districts where the Democrat was elected by an extremely narrow margin—under 52.5 percent. If a midterm trend to the Republican House ticket develops in 1966, an unusually large number of Democratic seats will be highly vulnerable.

Major Trends in the 1964 House Elections

Although the Democratic congressional tide enabled the party to pick up House seats in almost every region, the

[17] Charles O. Jones has emphasized this erosion of the number of safe Republican seats and the increased number of safe Democratic seats in 1964. See his "The 1964 Presidential Election—Further Adventures in Wonderland," in Donald G. Herzberg (ed.), *American Government Annual, 1965-1966* (Holt, Rinehart and Winston, 1965), pp. 26-27. The "safe seat" categories used in the text above, it should be added, are statistical categories only. The unusual character of the 1964 Democratic congressional sweep made it clear that many of the individual House results deviated markedly from more normal levels of party strength. Moreover, some of the seats where the Democratic vote exceeded 60 percent in 1964 could potentially be vulnerable to capture by the Republicans in a more normal congressional election year.

Table 7.5. Democratic House Strength by Districts, 1962 and 1964

Democratic Percentage of Two-Party House Vote	1962		1964	
	Number of Districts[a]	Percent of Districts	Number of Districts	Percent of Districts
0.0–4.9	1	0.2	1	0.2
5.0–29.9	11	2.6	2	0.5
30.0–34.9	25	5.9	7	1.6
35.0–39.9	48	11.2	27	6.2
40.0–44.9	57	13.3	56	12.9
45.0–47.4	20	4.7	26	6.0
47.5–49.9	14	3.3	21	4.8
50.0–52.4	21	4.9	37	8.5
52.5–54.9	19	4.4	24	5.5
55.0–59.9	46	10.8	26	5.6
60.0–64.9	33[b]	7.7	39	9.0
65.0–69.9	28	6.6	46	10.6
70.0–94.9	53	12.4	81	18.6
95.0–100.0	51	11.9	44	10.1
Total	427		435	

Source: "Complete Returns of the 1964 Elections by Congressional District."

[a] Data for the eight Congressmen from Alabama, who were all elected at large in 1962, are excluded from this tabulation. All eight Alabama seats were filled by Democrats in 1962: the lowest statewide vote for a Democratic House nominee was 257,299; the highest statewide vote for a Republican House nominee was 141,202.

[b] Included in this cell is the Tennessee 5th district where all House candidates ran as independents in 1962 and where the winner, Richard Fulton, polled 60.3 per cent of the vote. Fulton took his seat in the House as a Democrat.

strength of this movement across the country was far from uniform; and in the Deep South there was a strong counter-trend to the Republican party. The states where the biggest Democratic gains of House seats were registered were New York (+7), Iowa (+5), Washington (+4), Ohio (+4), Michigan (+4), and New Jersey (+4). In fourteen other states the Democrats made net gains of one or two seats. At the other extreme was Alabama, where the Republicans cap-

tured five seats from the Democratic party. The details of
the Democratic House gains and losses, by states, appear in
Table 7.6. Hidden in these state-by-state figures were several
more general electoral trends that affected whole regions or
groups of broadly similar House districts. The following
were some of the more salient patterns in the returns for
the House.

Formerly Republican Eastern Suburban Districts

Net Democratic gain, 6 seats. In districts in suburban
areas of the Northeast that had long been predominantly
Republican, an important trend to the Democratic party
developed in 1964.[18] Most of these districts were in the areas
around New York City and Philadelphia; others were close
to Buffalo, Pittsburgh, and Boston. Of 19 northeastern suburban districts which had Republican representatives going
into the election, 6 elected Democrats in 1964, and in another 3 the Democratic House candidate came within two
percentage points of winning (Table 7.7).

Although these districts had been considered Republican
territory ever since the New Deal, in some of them Democratic strength has been growing in recent years. The Democrats' gains in the suburbs may have reflected in part this
long-term trend to the Democratic party, as well as the
peculiarities of the 1964 political situation; and the outcome
of the House contests in these districts in 1966 will thus
be of particular interest.

---

[18] For purposes of this discussion, the Northeast is comprised of the
six New England states, plus the mid-Atlantic states of New York, New
Jersey, Pennsylvania, and Delaware. In addition to the 19 normally
Republican suburban districts in the Northeast, there were seven other
northeastern districts classified as suburban by the *Congressional Quarterly*
which had elected Democratic Representatives before 1964. Most of these
predominantly suburban districts already controlled by the Democrats,
however, had a sizable group of voters from normally Democratic cities
such as Newark or Jersey City within the district. See *Congressional
Quarterly Weekly Report,* Sept. 20, 1963, pp. 1642-57.

Table 7.6. Democratic Gains and Losses of House Seats in 1964, by States

State	Seats Shifting Party Control[a]		Net Democratic Gain or Loss
	Democratic Gain	Republican Gain	
New York	7	—	+7
Iowa	5	—	+5
Michigan	4	—	+4
New Jersey	4	—	+4
Ohio	4	—	+4
Washington	4	—	+4
Colorado	2	—	+2
Indiana	2	—	+2
Pennsylvania	2	—	+2
Texas	2	—	+2
Connecticut	1	—	+1
Illinois	1	—	+1
Kentucky	1	—	+1
Maine	1	—	+1
Nebraska	1	—	+1
New Hampshire	1	—	+1
North Dakota	1	—	+1
Utah	1	—	+1
Wyoming	1	—	+1
Wisconsin	2	1	+1
California	1	1	—
Georgia	—	1	−1
Idaho	—	1	−1
Mississippi	—	1	−1
Alabama	—	5	−5
Total	48	10	+38

Source: "Complete Returns of the 1964 Elections by Congressional District."

[a] Seats listed as having shifted party control include one seat formerly accounted for by a Democrat in Wisconsin and one seat formerly accounted for by a Republican in Michigan which are not identifiable by specific district numbers because of redistricting.

Table 7.7. Democratic Percentage of Two-Party House Vote in Traditionally Republican Eastern Suburban Districts, 1962 and 1964 [a]

Democratic Percentage of Two-Party House Vote	Number of Districts, 1962	Districts Shifting Democratic in 1964	Number of Districts, 1964
30.0–34.9	3	—	—
35.0–39.9	6	2 [b]	4
40.0–44.9	8	3 [e]	6
45.0–47.4	2	1 [d]	—
47.5–49.9	—	—	3
50.0–52.4	—	—	2
52.5–54.9	—	—	2
55.0–59.9	—	—	2
Total	19	6	19

Source: "Complete Returns of the 1964 Elections by Congressional District."

[a] Districts included in this tabulation are: Mass. 6; N. J. 1, 5, 6, 7, 9, 12; N. Y. 2, 3, 4, 5, 25, 26, 39; Penna. 7, 8, 13, 18, 27. All but two of these districts were classified as suburban in an analysis by the *Congressional Quarterly*, with at least 50 percent of their population being suburban as defined by *CQ*. In the remaining two districts the 1960 suburban population percentages were 46.9 (N. Y. 25) and 49.0 (Penna. 8). *Congressional Quarterly Weekly Report*, Sept. 20, 1963, pt. 2, pp. 1642-57.

[b] N. Y. 25 and 39—Robert Barry and John R. Pillion defeated.

[e] N. Y. 3 and 5—Steven Derounian defeated and Frank Becker retired; N. J. 9—Frank Osmers defeated.

[d] N. J. 12—George Wallhauser retired.

Plains States Districts

Net Democratic gain, 7 seats. Since 1954 the results of House elections in the states of Iowa, North Dakota, South Dakota, Nebraska, and Kansas have been highly volatile, as the number of seats won by each party in the area attest:

Year	Democratic	Republican	Year	Democratic	Republican
1954	—	22	1960	3	19
1956	3	19	1962	1	18
1958	11	11	1964	8	11

As these figures indicate, as late as 1954 the Republican party controlled every House seat in the area. From 1956 to 1958, when there was considerable evidence that some of the area's voters had their doubts about Republican farm policy and Secretary of Agriculture Ezra Taft Benson, there was a marked improvement in the Democratic position. Most of these Democratic gains were wiped out in 1960, however, when John F. Kennedy made a poor showing for the Democratic presidential ticket in these states. (In several districts, the incumbent Democratic House candidate ran as much as 10 percentage points ahead of Kennedy, yet still lost.) The strong Democratic tide that developed in 1964 brought the area's Democratic House strength almost, but not quite, back to the level the party had reached in 1958.[19] It also left the plains states with an unusually large number of marginal House seats, and the prospect of further shifts in party control in future elections (Table 7.8).

Western Districts

Net Democratic gain, 7 seats. In 1964, the western states, like the plains states, showed a definite trend to the Democratic congressional ticket.[20] But whereas the plains states have been highly volatile in congressional voting in recent years, the western states have undergone a pronounced and

[19] The Democrats did almost as well in the plains states in 1964 as they had done in 1958 largely because of their strong showing in Iowa, where they won 6 of the 7 House seats; they fared better in Iowa in 1964 than in 1958. In South Dakota, Nebraska, and Kansas, they did not do as well in 1964.

[20] In the subsequent discussion, states described as western include the Rocky Mountain states of Idaho, Montana, Wyoming, Colorado, Utah, Nevada, New Mexico, and Arizona, and the Pacific Coast states of Alaska, Washington, Oregon, and California, plus Hawaii.

Table 7.8. Democratic Percentage of Two-Party House Vote in Plains States Districts, 1962 and 1964 [a]

Democratic Percentage of Two-Party House Vote	1962		1964	
	Number of Districts	Percent of Districts	Number of Districts	Percent of Districts
30.0–34.9	4	21.1	—	—
35.0–39.9	2	10.5	1	5.3
40.0–44.9	7	36.8	4	21.1
45.0–47.4	5	26.3	2	10.5
47.5–49.9	—	—	4	21.1
50.0–52.4	—	—	3	15.8
52.5–54.9	—	—	4	21.1
55.0–59.9	—	—	—	—
60.0–64.9	1[b]	5.3	—	—
65.0–69.9	—	—	1[b]	5.3
70.0–100.0	—	—	—	—
Total	19		19	

Source: "Complete Returns of the 1964 Elections by Congressional District."

[a] Tabulation includes all House districts in Iowa, North Dakota, South Dakota, Nebraska, and Kansas.

[b] Neal Smith, Democratic incumbent in Iowa 5.

fairly steady shift to the Democratic party since 1952.[21] Democratic House candidates did unusually well in the West in 1964, and their party will probably be on the defensive in the region in 1966. Nevertheless, the marked change in the relative strengths of the two parties in the

[21] Part, but not all, of the improved Democratic position in western House contests stemmed from the Democrats' success in winning control of the California state government in 1958. They were able to control the state's redistricting process following the 1960 Census, which gave California 8 more House seats; and they made full use of their opportunity. The House results in California in 1952, following a redistricting which the Republicans controlled, were: Democrats, 11; Republicans, 19. The results in 1962 were: Democrats, 25; Republicans, 13.

West is reflected in the number of House seats won by each party in western districts from 1952 to 1964:[22]

Year	Democratic	Republican	Year	Democratic	Republican
1952	19	38	1960	33	26
1954	20	37	1962	42	27
1956	28	29	1964	47	22
1958	32	26			

Southern Districts

Net Republican gain, 5 seats. The South was the one major region in the country in 1964 where the Republican party increased its House strength over 1962. And no other region better illustrates the effect of the Goldwater-Johnson presidential contest on the fortunes of the two parties' congressional tickets. In the six states that rim the Deep South (Virginia, North Carolina, Florida, Tennessee, Arkansas, and Texas), the predominant swing of the presidential tide compared with 1960 was to the Democratic party: there were 57 House districts in these states where the Democratic presidential percentage increased between 1960 and 1964, and 12 districts where it decreased.

In the five Deep South states of South Carolina, Georgia, Alabama, Mississippi, and Louisiana, on the other hand, there was a swing to the Republican presidential ticket in every district except the two in the Atlanta, Georgia, area: [23]

[22] After 1962, Democrats lost two California House seats; their margin in the West fell from 42-27 to 40-29 going into the 1964 election.

[23] Georgia was redistricted shortly before the 1964 election, and Atlanta was the only area of the South where there was some doubt concerning the net movement of the presidential vote between 1960 and 1964 where it was not feasible to obtain the 1960 presidential vote within the new 1964 district boundary lines. If the two Atlanta area districts are lumped together, the 1960 Democratic presidential vote in them was 51.0 percent. In 1964 it was 51.8 percent. Data sources for the presidential vote in southern House districts in 1960 and 1964 were: U. S. Bureau of the Census, *Congressional District Data Book (Districts of the 88th Congress)* (Government Printing Office, 1963) and special supplements to it for states redistricted in 1963-64; and "Complete Returns of the 1964 Elections by Congressional District."

in those 2 districts the Democratic presidential percentage increased, but in 35 other districts the percentage decreased.

The shifts in the 1964 House election results tended to parallel this trend in the presidential voting. In the rim of the South, Republicans actually lost 2 of the 11 southern House seats they had won in 1962; and in another Republican district in the area, the Virginia 10th, the Republican candidate came closer to losing his seat than at any time since his first election in 1952. On the other hand, in the Deep South, where the Republicans held no House seats before 1964, the party elected 7 congressmen—five in Alabama, and one each in Georgia and Mississippi; and the odds are they missed an opportunity to win even more. In 1964, the Republicans failed to contest four House seats in each of four Deep South states—Louisiana, Mississippi, South Carolina, and Georgia. They also left 2 seats uncontested in Alabama. Had the Republicans run more House candidates in the Deep South in 1964, their gains in the area might well have been larger.

The 1964 elections changed the basic pattern of the Republican party's strength in southern House contests—a pattern that had prevailed since World War II. The main source of southern Republican House strength before 1964 is illustrated by Table 7.9, which lists the Negro percentage of the population and other characteristics of the southern districts where Republican House nominees did best in 1962. The great majority of these districts where the 1962 southern Republican House vote was highest were districts where the Negro population was relatively low, many in the Appalachian plateau, or else they were districts in the growing urban areas of the South. By contrast, in the most strongly rural and small-town districts of the black belt, where the densest Negro populations in the South are found, there were no Republican House candidates or Republican House strength in 1962 (Table 7.10). This pattern of Republican

Table 7.9. Southern House Districts in Which Republican Candidates Polled 40 Percent or More of Two-Party Vote in 1962

District	Republican Percentage of Two-Party House Vote	Percent of Population Urban	Percent of Population Negro	Location of District in State
Tennessee 2	70.6	51.5	6.0	E. Central (Knoxville)
Virginia 6	65.4	60.1	13.5	W. Central (Roanoke)
Florida 12	64.5	91.1	8.8	W. Central (St. Petersburg)
Texas 5	56.3	97.5	14.5	Dallas
North Carolina 8	56.0	53.5	25.2	S. Central (Charlotte)
Virginia 10	55.4	88.8	6.1	Washington D.C. suburbs
Tennessee 1	55.1	32.1	2.6	Northeast
Texas 16	53.8	84.9	3.9	West (El Paso)
Florida 11	51.9	68.9	15.8	E. Central (Orlando)
Tennessee 3	51.1	56.1	13.2	Southeast (Chattanooga)
North Carolina 9	50.5	34.9	12.1	N. W. Central
Virginia 3	49.7	82.8	25.7	Richmond and environs
Tennessee 9	49.4	87.8	36.3	Memphis
Virginia 7	49.4	29.4	8.1	N. Central (Winchester)
Texas 3	48.0	48.0	24.7	East (Tyler)
South Carolina 2	47.2	47.7	37.2	Central (Columbia)
Texas 22	46.5	98.1	14.7	Houston—South and suburbs
North Carolina 10	44.9	42.3	12.2	W. Central (Gastonia)
North Carolina 11	44.8	26.0	6.0	West (Asheville)
Georgia 5	44.4	90.0	26.5	Atlanta
Texas AL	43.9	75.0	12.4	Texas
Florida 3	42.4	98.8	17.8	N. Dade Co. (Miami)
North Carolina 4	41.9	40.8	22.6	Central (Raleigh)
Texas 18	41.2	69.2	3.9	N. Panhandle (Amarillo)
North Carolina 5	40.8	40.9	22.4	N. Central (Winston-Salem)
North Carolina 6	40.1	67.5	23.0	N. Central (Durham)

Sources: *Congressional District Data Book (88th Congress);* and Richard M. Scammon (ed.), *America Votes*, Vol. 5 (University of Pittsburgh Press, 1964).

weakness in the black belt and growing Republican strength in urban centers and the Appalachian plateau was the basic pattern that had prevailed in southern House contests since 1945.[24]

[24] One exception to this general pattern occurred in 1962. In the South Carolina 2nd district, an area with a 1960 Negro population of 37.2 percent and a number of small-town counties of the black belt, a Republican polled 47.2 percent of the House vote against the then Democratic candidate, Albert W. Watson. *Congressional District Data Book (88th Congress),* p. 454. For an analysis of congressional elections in the South, see Gerald Pomper, "Future Southern Congressional Politics," *Southwestern Social Science Quarterly,* Vol. 44 (June 1963), pp. 14-24.

Table 7.10. 1962 Republican House Vote in Southern Districts Where Negro Percentage of Population Exceeded 40 Percent in 1960

District	Percent of Population Negro	Republican Percentage of Two-Party House Vote	Percent of Population Urban	Location of District in State
Mississippi 2	59.1	—	28.0	Northwest
North Carolina 2	48.4	—	31.9	Northeast
Virginia 4	47.9	—	27.4	Southeast
South Carolina 6	46.5	—	27.8	East
Mississippi 3	46.4	—	53.8	Southwest
South Carolina 1	43.8	—	44.5	South (Charleston)
Georgia 6	41.3	—	53.8	Central (Macon)
Louisiana 5	40.4	—	44.8	Northeast
Mississippi 4	40.3	—	25.8	Central

Sources: *Congressional District Data Book (88th Congress)*; and Scammon (ed.), *America Votes*, Vol. 5.

In 1964 the Republicans lost ground in southern House districts outside the black belt. But for the first time since Reconstruction the GOP made a major breakthrough at the congressional level in black-belt House districts, districts which heretofore had tended to send conservative Democrats to Washington. Table 7.11 provides a listing of some salient characteristics of the southern House districts where the Republican party did best in 1964. The Republican strength in certain urban areas and the Appalachian upland remains; but to it has been added Republican strength in the black belt. The victory as a Republican of South Carolina's former Democratic representative, Albert W. Watson, in a special election in June 1965 added one more district with a heavy element of black-belt counties to the Republican total.

This establishment of a congressional beachhead in the black-belt districts of the South may be one of the most

Table 7.11. Southern House Districts in Which Republican Candidates Polled 40 Percent or More of Two-Party Vote in 1964

District	Republican Percentage of Two-Party House Vote	Percent of Population Urban	Percent of Population Negro	Location of District in State
Tennessee 1	71.7	32.1	2.6	Northeast
Alabama 2	62.8	55.7	35.8	S. Central (Montgomery)
Florida 12	60.6	91.1	8.8	W. Central (St. Petersburg)
Florida 11	60.6	68.9	15.8	E. Central (Orlando)
Alabama 6	60.6	86.5	31.7	N. Jefferson Co. (Birmingham)
Alabama 1	59.9	68.2	37.0	Southwest (Mobile)
Alabama 7	59.6	34.8	7.7	N. Central (Gadsden)
Alabama 4	59.1	40.5	30.5	E. Central (Selma)
Georgia 3	57.4	51.9	36.9	S. W. Central (Columbus)
Virginia 6	56.2	60.1	13.5	W. Central (Roanoke)
Mississippi 4	55.7	25.8	40.3	Central
North Carolina 9	55.2	34.9	12.1	Northwest
Tennessee 2	54.8	51.5	6.0	East (Knoxville)
Tennessee 3	54.6	56.1	13.2	Southeast (Chattanooga)
North Carolina 8	54.3	53.5	25.2	S. Central (Charlotte)
Virginia 10	50.7	88.8	6.1	Washington D.C. suburbs
Virginia 3	49.6[a]	82.8	25.7	Richmond and environs
North Carolina 5	48.4	40.9	22.4	N. Central (Winston-Salem)
North Carolina 4	48.2	40.8	22.6	Central (Raleigh)
Tennessee 9	47.4	87.8	36.3	West (Memphis)
Alabama 5	47.0	49.3	42.5	W. Central (Bessemer)
Georgia 5	46.0	91.4	33.4	Atlanta
Louisiana 8	45.5	36.7	28.9	Central (Alexandria)
Georgia 7	45.3	39.4	8.8	Northwest
Arkansas 3	45.3	38.6	2.2	Northwest
Texas 18	45.0	69.2	3.9	N. Panhandle (Amarillo)
Louisiana 2	45.0	79.3	30.8	W. New Orleans and suburbs
Texas 16	44.3	84.9	3.9	West (El Paso)
Georgia 4	43.1	88.7	19.8	Atlanta suburbs
Texas 5	42.5	97.5	14.5	Dallas
Texas 22	41.9	98.1	14.7	Southern Houston
Virginia 9	41.8	19.3	2.7	Southwest
North Carolina 10	41.4	42.3	12.2	West Central
Texas 3	40.7	48.0	24.7	East (Tyler)
Tennessee 5	40.2	87.7	19.1	Nashville

Sources: *Congressional District Data Book (88th Congress)* and special supplements to it for states redistricted in 1963-64.

[a] The Republican House nominee polled 49.6 percent of the major-party vote in Virginia's 3rd district, but there was also a large vote (31.5 percent of the total) cast for independent nominees. The Republican's share of the total House vote was 34.0 percent.

important legacies of the 1964 election to the Republican party, although members of that party will differ on whether its effects on the GOP in other areas of the country are an advantage or a liability. The base of support for the Republican congressional ticket in some of the urban districts and the Appalachian plateau region of the South seems sufficiently well established that it is likely to endure and in all probability will grow. The prospects for the Republicans in the black belt, however, are less certain, and, in short run at least, turn on the question whether, once Goldwater is off the Republican ticket, these districts will support conservative Democratic or conservative Republican candidates for representative.

The stakes involved are high. For if there is enduring Republican House strength in these districts, the areas in the South that will be opened up to an effective Republican challenge to traditional Democratic control will be substantially increased.[25] Over time, too, such a trend could sharply reduce the size of the dissident conservative wing of the Democratic congressional party, while increasing the number of conservatives in the congressional ranks of the GOP. Yet even these speculations, it should be added, may apply only to a relatively short "short run." They are essentially an extrapolation of black-belt trends during a period when many Negroes in these areas were deprived of the vote. If Negroes vote in large numbers in these districts, some of the districts might actually switch from sending opponents of federal welfare and civil rights legislation to sending supporters of such measures to Washington. The emergence of large numbers

---

[25] The number of southern congressional districts where the Republican House candidate polled 35 percent or more of the vote may give a rough indication of the districts in the South where the Republicans must be taken seriously in a congressional race. There were 9 districts of this type in 1944. In 1954 there were 17. In 1964, after the Republican breakthrough in the black belt, there were 44.

of Negro voters in the black belt could also constitute a powerful additional force laying a basis for two-party competition in black-belt House districts.

Victory for the Liberal Democrats

The 1964 results also had important effects on the balance between the liberal and conservative wings of the two congressional parties. On the Democratic side the effects of the election were clear-cut. All but 2 of the 48 new Democrats elected in districts captured from the Republicans came from outside the South, thus adding a sizable new block of Democratic legislators likely to support most of the more liberal measures in the President's legislative program. Moreover, from the liberals' standpoint, some of the Democratic congressmen who lost would hardly be missed. This was not true of the three northern Democrats who were replaced by Republicans, and Rains and Elliott of Alabama (also replaced by Republicans), all of whom tended to vote with the northern liberal Democratic congressmen on most roll-call votes. Representative Kenneth A. Roberts, who also lost in Alabama, had given less support to liberal measures in 1963-64 than had Rains or Elliott, but he also had been one of the more liberal of the Alabama congressmen.[26] The four other Democrats who were replaced by Republicans, however, were conservatives.[27] The net effect of the election was

[26] The three northern Democrats who were replaced by Republicans had 1963-64 ADA roll-call vote ratings of 88. Rains and Elliott had ratings of 60 and 64, while that of Roberts was 40. Roberts' ADA scores in earlier Congresses had been higher; he may have modified his voting record somewhat in 1963-64 out of fear of the current political climate in Alabama. *Congressional Quarterly Weekly Report,* Oct. 23, 1964, pt. 2, pp. 2546-47.

[27] The four conservative southern Democrats who were succeeded by Republicans had 1963-64 ADA roll-call vote ratings of 24, 20, 8, and 0. *Ibid.*

to strengthen markedly the liberal wing of the Democratic congressional party, and to reduce the ranks of the conservative southern Democrats in the House.[28]

Barry Goldwater and the Fate of Liberal and Conservative Republicans

The effects on the liberal-conservative balance within the Republican party in the House are more difficult to trace. In some respects the 1964 elections were for Republicans like a great downpour in which both liberals and conservatives alike were drowned. In Connecticut, where Representative Abner Sibal lost, and in New Jersey, where three Republicans with moderate-to-liberal voting records were replaced by Democrats, the small band of House Republican liberals sustained some losses. At the same time the net gain of five Republican House seats in the South added five more staunch conservatives to the Republican membership. But while Republican liberals sustained some losses and conservatives scored some victories, the great majority of the defeated Republican congressmen were conservatives. In all, 40 Republican representatives with ADA ratings of under 20 were replaced.[29]

---

[28] There is undoubtedly an interesting story to be told concerning the efforts made by liberal Democrats already in the House to help bring about their 1964 gains. In November 1963, House Democratic liberals set up a fifteen-member committee headed by Representative Richard Bolling to help elect new liberal Democratic congressmen and to protect vulnerable seats already held by liberal Democrats. *New York Times,* Nov. 26 and Dec. 12, 1963.

[29] As Robert L. Peabody has noted, the election dragged to defeat an unusual number of conservative senior Republicans, including the first- and second-ranking Republicans on the House Appropriations Committee, the second-ranking member of the Committee on Rules, and the fourth-ranking member of the Ways and Means Committee. "The Ford-Halleck Minority Leadership Contest, 1965," Eagleton Institute Cases in Practical Politics, No. 40 (McGraw-Hill, 1966).

There is also some evidence that liberal Republican House members were more successful than conservatives in withstanding a heavy Johnson presidential tide in their district. In 1964, 137 incumbent Republican congressmen outside the South had to stand for reelection in districts that went Democratic in the presidential race. In Table 7.12, these Republican incumbents are grouped according to the magnitude of the vote for Johnson in their district. The data also indicate the number of these Republicans seeking reelection who won or lost, and the average ADA roll-call vote rating of the winners and losers in each group. There was some

Table 7.12. ADA Ratings of Republican Representatives Outside the South Who Won and Lost in 1964, in Relation to Presidential Vote in Their District

Democratic Percentage of Two-Party Presidential Vote	Republican Representatives Seeking Reelection		Mean ADA Roll-Call Vote Rating of Republican Representatives[a]	
	Winners	Losers	Winners	Losers
0.0–39.9	1	—	—	—
40.0–44.9	2	—	4	—
45.0–47.4	3	—	3	—
47.5–49.9	6	—	7	—
50.0–52.4	8	—	6	—
52.5–54.9	10	1	9	—
55.0–59.9	40	12	16	4
60.0–64.9	22	17	18	14
65.0–69.9	14	7	39	15
70.0–74.9	6	—	51	—
75.0–100.0	—	—	—	—
Total	112	37		

Sources: *Congressional Quarterly Weekly Report*, Oct. 23, 1964, pt. 2, pp. 2546-47; and "Complete Returns of the 1964 Elections by Congressional District."

[a] Based on roll-call vote ratings for 1963-64 compiled by Americans for Democratic Action. Data are based on the ratings given all incumbent Republican House members who stood for reelection in 1964.

tendency for the survivors to have slightly more liberal voting records than the losers in each of the groups of districts that Johnson carried. But it was among the Republican congressmen who had to run for reelection where there was a Democratic presidential landslide that a clear tendency for the Republican winners to be more liberal than the losers developed. In districts where the Johnson vote ranged between 65 and 70 percent, the ADA average of the winners was 39, that of the losers was 15. The six Republicans who were reelected in districts where Johnson received over 70 percent of the vote had an average ADA score of 51. Among the winners in districts the President carried by two to one or more were Stanley Tupper of Maine, William Mailliard of California, William Bates of Massachusetts, and Frank Horton and John Lindsay of New York. Among the losers in such districts were Victor Knox of Michigan, Jack Westland of Washington, and R. Walter Riehlman and John Pillion of New York.

The extent of the Republican liberals' achievement is underscored if one considers the magnitude of the threat to the liberal GOP wing in the House that the Goldwater candidacy posed. Most of these liberals represented districts where Goldwater was extremely weak. Yet in November most of them survived. To do so, some of them induced the electorate in their districts to indulge in an extraordinary amount of ticket-splitting. In New York's 17th district John V. Lindsay polled 71.5 percent of the House vote, while Johnson's share of the presidential vote in the district was 71.8 percent. In the Massachusetts 5th, Representative Bradford Morse polled 65 percent of the vote, while Johnson got 74.2 percent. And in the 22nd district of Pennsylvania, the vote totals were Representative John P. Saylor 57 percent, and President Johnson 65.9 percent.

The 1964 Elections and the Changed
Balance of Power in the House

Yet in retrospect 1964 may be best remembered as one of those relatively few congressional elections that resulted in a major shift in the balance of power within the House of Representatives. For the 1964 elections transformed the House from a body closely divided on the more controversial and liberal measures in the Johnson administration's legislative program to one in which there was a clear majority for the bulk of the President's program. In 1964, measures like the Urban Mass Transportation Act, the anti-poverty program, and a number of other important bills sponsored by the administration passed the House by narrow margins.[30] The administration's Medicare program never reached the floor of the House. The election results virtually assured the passage of measures such as these by the new Congress. They also shifted the terrain of meaningful congressional battle to legislative proposals such as rent subsidies, amendment of the Taft-Hartley Act to prohibit state right-to-work laws, and modification of the immigration laws—measures that would have had little chance of passage by the Congress before 1964.[31]

[30] Some of the close House votes on measures backed by the administration in 1964 were: the wheat-cotton bill (Agricultural Act of 1964), passed April 8 by 211-203; the food stamp bill, passed April 8 by 229-189; the Urban Mass Transportation Act, passed June 25 by 212-189; the motion to recommit the Foreign Aid Appropriations Bill with instructions to cut the funds for economic aid, defeated (as desired by the administration) on July 1 by 208-198; and the anti-poverty bill (Economic Opportunity Act of 1964), passed Aug. 8 by 226-185. *Congressional Quarterly Weekly Reports,* April 10-Aug. 14, 1964.

[31] One main result of the 1964 congressional elections may have been to bring about a closer balance between the amount of liberal strength in the House and in the Senate. A major result of the Senate elections was to retain firm majorities for liberal legislative measures in the Senate. A major result of the House elections was to create them. For an analysis

Thus, on April 8, 1965, in a key vote affecting Medicare, the House rejected by a vote of 191-236 the motion by Republican Representative John W. Byrnes of Wisconsin to recommit the bill to the House Ways and Means Committee, with instructions to report back a substitute bill providing for a voluntary health insurance program for the aged financed by general revenues and contributions from participants. A vote against the Byrnes motion was a vote supporting the Johnson administration's Medicare program tied to the Social Security system. Of the 48 new Democrats who replaced a Republican in 1964, 46 opposed the Byrnes motion and 2 supported it. On final passage of the Elementary and Secondary Education Act of 1965, passed 263-153 on March 26, 1965, all 48 of these new Democrats supported the act. On the bill to repeal Section 14(b) of the Taft-Hartley Act (which permitted state right-to-work laws prohibiting the union shop), which passed the House 221-203 on July 28, 1965, the vote among these 48 new Democrats was 44 in favor of the bill, and 3 opposed. And on the motion to delete the authorization of rent supplements for low-income families from the administration's housing bill—a move that was rejected by only a 202-208 margin on June 30, 1965—the 48 new Democratic representatives voted 39 for rejection and six in favor.

Nor were these the only votes on key items in the Johnson legislative program where the new Democrats appeared to make a decisive difference. A study by the *Congressional Quarterly* of all new Democratic House members in 1965 indicated that on the average they supported President Johnson 89 percent of the time on twelve selected Great Society

of liberal strength in the House and Senate before the 1964 elections, see Lewis A. Froman, Jr., *Congressmen and Their Constituencies* (Rand McNally, 1963), Chap. 6, "Why the Senate is More Liberal than the House."

roll calls. The average presidential support score among all new Democrats from the North alone was 95 percent.[32]

The tabulation below gives a rough indication of the distribution of strength in the House before and after the 1964 elections, not in terms of party membership, but in terms of the number of congressmen who were likely to vote for or against the President on the more controversial measures in his legislative program.

Tendency of Representatives	House Elected in	
	1962[33]	1964
Support Johnson	188	228
Support sometimes, oppose sometimes	63	61
Oppose Johnson	179	146

The data are broken down into three categories: congressmen tending to support the President on most measures; congressmen opposing him most of the time; and congressmen supporting him part of the time, while opposing him on a sizable number of measures.[34] The figures reflect the closely divided balance of power that prevailed in the House before the 1964 elections. Of the 435 congressmen elected in

[32] See "New House Democrats Give President Strong Support," *Congressional Quarterly Weekly Report,* Aug. 27, 1965, pp. 1746-47.

[33] The total number of representatives listed for the House elected in 1962 is 430; there were five vacancies entering the 1964 election.

[34] As close observers of the subtleties of congressional politics will be quick to note, any division of the House membership into three broad categories such as these is an extraordinarily crude measure of the distribution of power among various types of congressmen. Many analysts of the House, for example, would distinguish among two or more types of "liberals" among the Democrats. Thus Leo M. Snowiss has emphasized the distinction between "ideological, issue-oriented liberal Democrats, who founded the Democratic Study Group, and the non-ideological machine liberals, who took much less interest and provided almost no leadership for the DSG during its formative years." "The Cities and Congress" (Paper prepared for delivery at the 1965 Annual Meeting of The American Political Science Association, Sept. 8-11, 1965), p. 13.

1962,[35] only 188—well under a majority of the House—generally supported the President; and it was primarily from these representatives and from the "in-and-outers" that the House Democratic leadership and the President were able to fashion some remarkable legislative victories in the 1964 session of Congress. The 1964 elections, as the data indicate, moved the number of usual presidential supporters up to an absolute majority of the House,[36] making possible the

[35] For the House elected in 1962, members were allocated into the Johnson support, Johnson opponent, and the sometimes support-sometimes oppose categories according to the ratio between their 1964 presidential support score and their 1964 presidential opposition score on 52 Johnson-issue roll calls as computed by the *Congressional Quarterly.* This meant that a representative with a presidential support score of 60 and a presidential opposition score of 20 would be given a presidential support index of 75. The cutting points used for the categories were: Johnson supporter—presidential support index of 80 or over; sometimes support and sometimes oppose—presidential support index of 60-79; Johnson opponent—presidential support index below 60. These cutting points were set fairly high in order to discriminate among supporters and opponents of the President on the more controversial measures in his legislative program. To do this, high cutting points were required because the 52 Johnson-issue roll calls analyzed included a number of votes on issues where most members of both parties supported the President. Republican Representative Charles Halleck, the House Minority Leader in the 88th Congress, for example, had a 1964 presidential support index of 40.4. *Congressional Quarterly Weekly Report,* Oct. 30, 1964, pp. 2596-97; and "Complete Returns of the 1964 Elections by Congressional District."

[36] The membership of the new House elected in 1964 was allocated among the three presidential support categories as follows: Where there was no change in a district's representative, the allocation remained the same as before the 1964 election. Where there was a switch in party control, newly elected Democrats outside the South were allocated as presidential supporters, newly elected Democrats in the South (two, in Texas) were allocated to the sometimes support and sometimes oppose category, and newly elected Republicans were allocated to the presidential opponents' category. Where a nonincumbent of the same party succeeded an incumbent representative, the new member was allocated to the same category as his predecessor, with two exceptions: in the Louisiana 8th district, where Speedy O. Long (D) replaced Gillis W. Long (D), and in the Virginia 3rd district, where David E. Satterfield (D) replaced J. Vaughn Gary (D), the allocations were changed from Johnson supporters to Johnson opponents. Gary, who was approaching retirement, had a presidential support index of 81.9 in 1964, higher than that of any

passage of many measures that had been on the legislative agenda for years and shifting the terrain of real contest in the House several degrees to the left.[37]

The House elections of 1964 opened up the opportunity for enactment of the most sweeping Democratic legislative program since 1935, and by the autumn of 1965, most of the President's Great Society proposals—including federal aid for primary and secondary schools, medicare, creation of a Department of Housing and Urban Development, establishment of an Appalachian regional redevelopment authority, and numerous other measures that increased the expenditures of federal funds for domestic programs—were on the statute books. The victories for the President's program that followed the 1964 voting highlighted one of the chief paradoxes of the 1964 election year. The nomination of Barry Goldwater was unquestionably the most dramatic victory scored by the conservative wing of the Republican party in a generation. But it was accompanied by the election of one of the most liberal Congresses in American history.

---

other member of the Virginia delegation, including Pat Jennings. *Congressional Quarterly Weekly Report,* Oct. 30, 1964, pp. 2596-97; and "Complete Returns of the 1964 Elections by Congressional District."

[37] Not the least of the virtues for the Democrats of their heavy majority was that it gave them margins so large that individual Democratic congressmen could afford to vote against the President on a few votes. They could thus give a demonstration for their constituents of their "independence."

8

Interpreting the Presidential Victory

ANGUS CAMPBELL

The election of Lyndon B. Johnson in November 1964 was one of the most decisive electoral choices in the recent history of presidential elections but the intention of the electorate and the significance of their collective decision are by no means clear. The aggregative data from the states and precincts give the general outline of the flow of the vote in relation to previous elections but they leave wide latitude to those who seek to interpret the meaning of the vote. A more precise understanding of the mood of the voters will become available only when the national sample surveys carried out at the time of the election are fully analyzed.

This chapter presents an array of preliminary findings from a study conducted in October-November 1964 by the Survey Research Center of The University of Michigan. This survey, based on a probability sample of the adult population of forty-eight states (excluding Alaska and Hawaii), is the most recent in a series of election studies carried out by the Center since 1952. It followed the general design of the earlier studies, and a number of direct comparisons of data from the successive election years are possible. The value of this presentation is largely descriptive; more intensive analysis of the survey findings will appear in subsequent publications.

Our program of research on the national vote has led to a theory of partisan competition, the basic proposition of which is that "fluctuations in turnout and partisanship (in the vote) derive from a combination of short-term political forces, superimposed on the underlying level of political interest and on the long-standing psychological attachments of the electorate to the two parties."[1] The short-term forces are those political facts which have more or less importance for the electorate during a specific election situation, the appeal of the candidates, the policy issues, the image of the competing parties, and the immediate domestic and international circumstances. If the total impact of these forces stands at a balance, with no net advantage to either party, the vote will be determined by the "standing party commitments," by what Lord Bryce called the "normal party strength" of the two parties. If the short-term forces do favor one party over the other, the actual vote will swing away from the "normal vote" toward the advantaged party. The greater this net advantage, the greater will be the deflection from the normal vote. In most cases a swing in votes toward a party profiting from immediately favorable circumstances will be followed in subsequent elections by a return to a division approximating the normal vote. In some unusual cases the swing in the vote is associated with a realignment of the basic partisan orientations of some significant part of the electorate and the displacement of the normal vote to a new level.

The following description of the national vote in the 1964 election begins with a consideration of public reaction to the presidential candidates, to the two parties, and to certain

---

[1] Angus Campbell, "Surge and Decline: A Study of Electoral Change," *Public Opinion Quarterly*, Vol. 24 (Fall 1960), pp. 397-418.

major issues of the campaign. We then ask whether the events of 1964 produced any realignment in the party identifications of the electorate. Finally, we consider the implications of the 1964 election for the immediate future of American politics.

Public Image of the Candidates

It has been the Survey Research Center's procedure in its election surveys to open the preelection interview with a series of free-answer questions intended to elicit from the respondents a statement of their perception of the positive and negative features of the candidates and parties. The questions read as follows:

Is there anything in particular that you like about the Republican Party?

Is there anything in particular that you don't like about the Republican Party?

Is there anything in particular that you like about the Democratic Party?

Is there anything in particular that you don't like about the Democratic Party?

Now I'd like to ask you about the good and bad points of the two candidates for President. Is there anything in particular about Goldwater that might make you want to vote *for* him?

Is there anything in particular about Goldwater that might make you want to vote *against* him?

Is there anything in particular about Johnson that might make you want to vote *for* him?

Is there anything in particular about Johnson that might make you want to vote *against* him?

As one might expect, these questions produce a great variety of answers. A set of categories has been developed, however, into which each item of response can be coded, and by maintaining the same definitions from study to study it is possible to compare the total number of positive and negative references to the candidates and parties made in the succeeding elections and also the relative importance given to specific statements of approval or criticism. Considering first the total number of responses given to the candidate questions over the last four presidential elections, we see the extraordinary quality of the public image of the two candidates in the 1964 contest (Table 8.1).

In the earlier elections from which survey data are available the respondents have in every case been more favorable than unfavorable in their comments regarding the candidates. This was particularly true of Mr. Eisenhower. The public was not as responsive to Mr. Stevenson as it was to his opponent; his total image was generally favorable in 1952 but became much less so in 1956. In 1960 both candidates

Table 8.1. Total Number of References to Characteristics of Republican and Democratic Presidential Candidates, 1952-1964 [a]

References	1952		1956		1960		1964	
	Eisen-hower	Steven-son	Eisen-hower	Steven-son	Nixon	Ken-nedy	Gold-water	John-son
Positive	3153	2154	3485	1703	2790	2678	1505	3271
Negative	1415	1243	1378	1567	1214	1836	2815	1463
Number of cases	1798		1762		1807		1570	

[a] The data in this table and those following have been adjusted to remove the effect of differences in the number of respondents in the four surveys. The 1960 sample was taken as the base.

attracted strong favorable reactions, but Mr. Kennedy stimulated a large number of unfavorable references, many of them having to do with his religion. In contrast to the pattern of these years, the two candidates in 1964 stood at polar extremes. Mr. Johnson's ratio of favorable to unfavorable comments approached that of Mr. Eisenhower; Mr. Goldwater's balance was negative by almost a 2-1 ratio.

One comes to a clearer appreciation of the public's perception of Mr. Johnson and Mr. Goldwater when he compares the specific comments made in answer to the free-answer questions. We have included in Tables 8.2 and 8.3 comparable data from 1960 so that the similarities and contrasts between the two elections may be seen.[2]

We need only summarize the detailed data of these tables. It seems clear that while Mr. Johnson's personal attributes did not stir unusual favor among the electorate, he profited greatly from his long experience and record as a public official. He also drew favorable comment because of his association with the Democratic party and with the Kennedy administration. He was criticized as a "politician," "lacking in integrity," and associated with "immorality in government," these criticisms coming very heavily from Republican partisans. As we have seen in our earlier studies, when people are asked what they like and dislike about a candidate they do not typically refer to his positions on specific policy issues.[3] Mr. Johnson's stands on issues, however, were more frequently referred to than those of either candidate in 1960

---

[2] Nearly a hundred categories are needed to code the types of references made to the candidates. Only the more important categories are included in Tables 8.2 and 8.3. The same is true of Tables 8.6 and 8.7 which present the more important favorable and unfavorable references to the parties.

[3] Donald E. Stokes and Warren E. Miller, "Party Government and the Saliency of Congress," *Public Opinion Quarterly,* Vol. 26 (Winter 1962), pp. 531-46.

Table 8.2. Favorable References to Candidates

References	1960		1964	
	Nixon	Kennedy	Goldwater	Johnson
Generally good man, capable, qualified	501	276	77	363
Record and experience				
Record as a public servant	74	29	9	293
Political experience	186	56	33	132
Qualifications and abilities				
Good leader, knows how to handle people	24	25	8	21
Good administrator	1	7	12	75
Strong, decisive	61	126	61	55
Educated	90	241	22	33
Good speaker	16	72	17	36
Understands the problems	73	56	16	79
Knows how to handle world problems	277	21	9	24
Personal qualities				
Integrity	83	122	182	76
Sincerity	60	95	61	37
Pleasant personality	55	107	43	69
Policies				
Like his policies, unspecified	61	91	75	63
Like his policy favoring civil rights movement	5	7	3	101
Like his policy opposing civil rights movement	7	—	55	1
Like his policy on medical care	7	17	6	64
Like his policy on social security	—	16	13	46
Believe he will keep the peace	29	1	25	62
Believe he will stop Communism abroad	79	22	28	2
Like him because he is liberal	1	32	3	35
Like him because he is conservative	18	—	51	3
Group associations				
Good for the common people	41	77	8	118
Good for all people	12	23	12	69
Party association				
Like him because he's a Democrat	—	183	—	150
Like him because he's a Republican	80	—	61	—
"Will continue Kennedy's policies," "don't change horses . . ."	—	—	—	232
No specific content				
"I just like him"	65	65	39	127

Table 8.3. Unfavorable References to Candidates

References	1960		1964	
	Nixon	Kennedy	Goldwater	Johnson
Generally not a good man, not qualified	43	170	81	25
Record and experience				
Poor record in public life	19	14	23	16
Inexperienced	5	34	14	10
Qualifications and abilities				
Poor leader	11	—	3	2
Poor administrator	1	1	16	7
Weak, indecisive	48	20	29	20
Poor speaker	10	12	24	29
Too much a "politician"	4	—	12	105
Don't like his speeches, campaign tactics	57	101	237	55
Positions unclear, don't know where he stands	—	—	214	46
Don't like his religion	—	362	10	—
Too young	10	122	—	—
Connection with immorality in government	—	—	—	100
Personal qualities				
Impulsive, doesn't think before he talks	7	47	192	1
Lacks integrity	74	48	39	133
Fanatic, unstable	—	—	107	1
Insincere	13	5	22	37
Policies				
Don't agree with his policies, unspecified	26	20	90	16
Too much for civil rights	3	8	6	72
Too much against civil rights	4	4	81	18
Don't like his stand on medical care	4	14	48	14
Don't like his stand on social security	3	—	177	5
Too militaristic	4	8	213	2
Too liberal	2	27	2	8
Too conservative	8	1	121	1
Party association				
Don't like him because he's a Democrat	—	53	—	30
Don't like him because he's a Republican	157	—	51	—
No specific content				
"I just don't like him"	93	74	259	107

and they were more commonly seen favorably than unfavorably.

A comparison of the public image of Mr. Johnson in 1964 with that of Mr. Kennedy in 1960 reveals a significant contrast in the way the two men were seen. While Johnson's strength was in his experience and his public record, this was Kennedy's area of weakness. Less well-known than his opponent and youthful in appearance, Kennedy was frequently seen as lacking the qualifications for high office. His strength lay in his attractive personal qualities, attributes which were less commonly associated with Johnson.

It has been pointed out that Mr. Goldwater was much more commonly spoken of unfavorably than favorably. While he was more often referred to as a man of integrity than Mr. Johnson, and less commonly as a "politician," in most other respects he suffered from the comparison. He was especially weak in the public assessment of his past record and experience. His speeches drew much more criticism than Johnson's. His policy positions, as they were seen by the public, drew an exceptional number of comments, most of them unfavorable. While Mr. Goldwater obviously had many ardent admirers, the total public reaction to his personal qualities, his campaign appearances, and the policies with which he was identified was on balance clearly negative.

It might be expected that any Republican candidate will be subject to a good deal of derogatory comment from the electorate simply because Democrats are much more numerous than Republicans. It was true in 1964 that Democrats were considerably more likely than Republicans or Independents to criticize Mr. Goldwater but it must be remembered that in the three preceding presidential elections the balance of positive and negative comments given by our respondents was considerably more favorable to the Republican candidates than it was to the Democratic. There can be little doubt that in 1964 the impact of candidate appeal strongly favored the Democratic ticket.

We cannot assess precisely how much the factor of candidate appeal actually moved the vote. Our studies of the Eisenhower elections have shown that many voters faithfully stay with their party ticket even when they greatly prefer the opposing candidate. We can see the interaction between party loyalty and evaluations of the Republican candidate in 1964 by comparing the votes of those Democrats, Independents, and Republicans who described themselves as "particularly happy" or "particularly unhappy" at the nomination of Mr. Goldwater in answer to the following series of questions (Table 8.4):

Was there anyone in particular that you hoped the Republicans would nominate (at the San Francisco Convention)? (If Goldwater) Were you particularly happy that Goldwater got the nomination or would some other candidate have been just about as good? (If other) Were you particularly unhappy that Goldwater got the nomination or did you think he was nearly as good as your man?

As one would expect, the vote is most nearly unanimous among those groups whose reactions to party and candidate are compatible, Democratic identifiers who found Mr. Goldwater particularly unattractive and Republicans who were particularly happy with his nomination. Where conflict between these attitudes occurred, major defections from normal party support resulted. Since the number of voters who called themselves "unhappy" about Mr. Goldwater's nomination was considerably larger than those who described themselves as "happy," even among people normally Republican in partisanship, we conclude again that Mr. Goldwater's personal impact on the Republican voter was clearly negative.

Table 8.4. Relation of Preconvention Preference for Republican Presidential Nomination to the Vote

Vote	Preferred Goldwater, Happy[a]	Preferred Another, Goldwater About as Good	Preferred Another, Unhappy	No Pre-convention Preference
		Democrats		
Voted for Johnson	43%	84%	96%	91%
Voted for Goldwater	57	16	4	9
	100%	100%	100%	100%
Number of cases	23	64	176	307
		Independents		
Voted for Johnson	7%	50%	82%	79%
Voted for Goldwater	93	50	18	21
	100%	100%	100%	100%
Number of cases	30	28	84	76
		Republicans		
Voted for Johnson	4%	9%	49%	32%
Voted for Goldwater	96	91	51	68
	100%	100%	100%	100%
Number of cases	47	69	92	93

[a] One percent of this sample of voters said they had preferred Goldwater but felt another candidate would have been just about as good. They have been omitted from this table.

Public Image of the Parties

Although the public perception of the two parties would not be expected to vary as much from year to year as the perception of the different candidates, still it is apparent from Table 8.5 that sizable fluctuations do occur. There is no doubt that over the 1952-1964 period the electorate has had a more favorable impression of the Democratic party than of the Republican. This advantage was seriously com-

Table 8.5. Total Number of References to Characteristics of the Republican and Democratic Parties, 1952-1964

References	1952		1956		1960		1964	
	Rep.	Dem.	Rep.	Dem.	Rep.	Dem.	Rep.	Dem.
Positive	1976	2485	1712	2185	1621	2043	1124	2076
Negative	1752	2272	1587	1304	1486	1199	1464	1297
Number of cases	1798		1762		1807		1570	

promised in 1952 when the Truman administration came under repeated and widespread criticism for its presumed tolerance of unsavory and sometimes corrupt practices in Washington. This cloud appeared to pass quickly, however, and in the succeeding election years the Democratic party was much more often spoken of favorably than unfavorably.

The Republican party, on the contrary, has not had a strongly positive image at any time during this period. Even in 1956 when Mr. Eisenhower was carrying 57 percent of the popular vote, his party was much less favorably seen than the Democratic party. In 1964 the terms in which the Republican party was described by our respondents turned sharply negative and for the first time became more unfavorable than favorable.

This deterioration of the image of the Republican party in the eyes of the electorate between 1960 and 1964 expressed itself in a variety of ways. A close examination of Tables 8.6 and 8.7 will show that, although the patterns of comments made by our respondents in 1960 and 1964 are generally quite similar, the Republican position was consistently weaker in the latter year. Those attributes which favored one party in 1960 tend to be seen favorably again in 1964. The same criticisms of the respective parties are offered in both years. There were certain major changes, however. The positive influence of Mr. Eisenhower faded

Table 8.6. Favorable References to Parties

References	1960		1964	
	Rep.	Dem.	Rep.	Dem.
Like people associated with party				
Eisenhower	78	—	30	—
Kennedy	—	—	—	62
Policies				
Like their policies, unspecified	56	48	40	68
Like their welfare programs	15	69	8	100
Like their stand on medical care	10	34	8	56
Times are better under them	65	134	12	90
They spend less money	89	4	72	6
They are good for employment	29	102	2	66
They are more for civil rights	9	11	1	67
Like their conservative philosophy	104	6	132	5
Like their liberal philosophy	7	57	9	36
Better chance for peace with them	150	13	40	33
Group association				
Good for common people	16	405	12	369
Good for all people	17	53	24	100
Traditional association				
"I've always been a Republican (or Democrat)"	102	192	97	227
No specific content				
"I just like them"	74	90	40	110

from the Republican image over the four-year period and the Goldwater association was generally negative. The advantage which the Republican party had held on the war-and-peace issue in 1960 had disappeared in 1964. The fact that this decline in the favor with which the public saw the Republican party occurred at the same time as the much more dramatic shift in the way they evaluated its presidential candidate leads one to doubt that these changes were inde-

Table 8.7. Unfavorable References to Parties

References	1960 Rep.	1960 Dem.	1964 Rep.	1964 Dem.
Don't like people associated with party				
Eisenhower	32	—	—	—
Truman	—	23	—	—
Goldwater (as candidate)	—	—	136	—
Johnson (as candidate)	—	—	—	25
Policies				
Would give dishonest government	2	22	22	85
They spend too much	18	145	2	100
Believe in too much governmental activity	4	28	—	71
Don't like their socialistic philosophy	4	55	2	79
Don't like their conservative philosophy	44	10	52	25
Times are bad under them	47	6	52	—
Don't like their campaign and/or convention	10	42	97	51
Too much for civil rights	26	22	5	74
Don't do enough for civil rights	16	6	17	3
They are the war party	4	95	25	25
Group association				
For big business, rich people	272	7	184	10
Bad for common people	142	6	133	7
No specific content				
"I just don't like them"	52	44	77	33

pendent of each other, and the nature of the criticisms made of the party in 1964 specifies the manner in which it suffered from its association with Mr. Goldwater.

The Policy Issues

Our earlier studies have shown that specific policy issues have not played a major role in recent presidential elections and that the electorate is generally much less ideologically oriented than is commonly supposed.[4] The public may become aroused by current circumstances such as the Korean War in 1952 or by some attribute of the candidate such as Kennedy's religion in 1960, but it is typically poorly informed and unconcerned about the interparty debates over specific policy decisions which agitate the party leadership and command copious space in the newspapers.

The campaign of 1964 stood in some contrast to those immediately preceding it in the degree to which the two candidates appeared to differ in their positions on certain questions of national policy. In the phrase of the moment, the voters were for the first time in many years being presented "a choice, not an echo." While Mr. Johnson did not depart remarkably from the moderate "welfare liberalism" of his Democratic predecessors, Mr. Goldwater seemed clearly less near the political center than the typical Republican candidate. The fact that he was so perceived by a significant proportion of the electorate is demonstrated by the comparison of the public's images of Goldwater and Nixon (Tables 8.2 and 8.3), especially in their unfavorable references to the policies they identified with the two men.

We cannot examine in this article the full range of data on the electorate's policy positions which our 1964 study will ultimately make available. We will look at only two questions, dealing respectively with two major dimensions of the ideological differences between the two candidates. Mr. Goldwater's writings and statements prior to the election made it clear that he objected to the extent to which various agencies of the federal government intervened in the lives of the citizenry. In enunciating his philosophy as a self-styled "conservative" he called for a revival of individual responsibility, a reduction of federal "welfare" programs, and a

[4] Angus Campbell, Philip E. Converse, Warren E. Miller, and Donald E. Stokes, *The American Voter* (John Wiley & Sons, 1960), Chap. 10.

decentralization of governmental power. Mr. Johnson wrote few books and was perhaps less explicit in his political doctrines than his opponent, but his commitment to large-scale governmental programs in the name of "public welfare" was apparent.

We approached this area of policy difference by posing to our respondents the following rather extreme statement of the concept of governmental responsibility for individual welfare:

In general, some people feel that the government in Washington should see to it that every person has a job and a good standard of living. Others think the government should just let each person get ahead on his own. Have you been interested enough in this to favor one side over the other?

Their responses are presented in Table 8.8, in which we have first divided the sample of voters into those who identified themselves as "usually" Republican, Democrat, or Independent, and then compared the votes of those who gave contrasting answers to our question.[5]

It is apparent from Table 8.8 that party identification is a much more powerful predictor of the vote than the attitudes expressed to this question of governmental policy. A majority of Democrats and Republicans support their respective candidates whatever position they take on this question. It is also clear that Republicans are much more likely than Democrats to support the position of individual responsibility as posed in this question. However, there is no doubt that the attitudes which this question tapped exerted an inde-

---

[5] We establish the respondent's party identification by a standardized series of questions as follows: "Generally speaking, do you usually think of yourself as a Republican, a Democrat, an Independent, or what? (If Republican or Democrat) Would you call yourself a strong (R) (D) or a not very strong (R) (D)? (If Independent) Do you think of yourself as closer to the Republican or Democratic Party?"

Table 8.8. Relation of Attitude Toward Governmental Welfare Programs to the Vote

Vote	North[a]			South[a]		
	Gov't. Should Help	Depends, Don't Know, No Interest	Person Get Ahead on Own	Gov't. Should Help	Depends, Don't Know, No Interest	Person Get Ahead on Own
			Democrats			
Johnson	35	26	32	37	22	24
Goldwater	1	1	5	4	3	10
Number of cases		378 = 100%			204 = 100%	
			Independents			
Johnson	20	23	28	17	7	17
Goldwater	3	6	20	5	7	47
Number of cases		181 = 100%			41 = 100%	
			Republicans			
Johnson	7	8	15	8	0	6
Goldwater	8	14	48	13	15	58
Number of cases		253 = 100%			53 = 100%	

[a] The South includes the eleven Confederate states, Oklahoma, Kentucky, West Virginia, and Maryland. The North includes all the remaining states except Alaska and Hawaii.

pendent force on the vote. The picture is complicated by the fact that there were numerous defections from both parties for reasons other than attitudes on this issue, but there were additional losses suffered by both parties among those individuals whose attitudes conflicted with the positions their candidates had taken. The total impact of this issue on voters in the North, including the independent voters, appears to have favored Mr. Johnson but in the South it favored Mr. Goldwater.

We have seen in the foregoing tables that in 1960 the electorate did not associate either the candidates or the parties with contrasting positions on civil rights. In 1964, partly at least because of Mr. Goldwater's widely publicized negative vote on the Civil Rights Act, this issue had acquired a partisan flavor. In order to see to what extent the voters' attitudes on civil rights were reflected in the vote, the following question was asked:

Some say that the civil rights people have been trying to push too fast. Others feel they haven't pushed fast enough. How about you: do you think that civil rights leaders are trying to push too fast, are going too slowly, or are they moving at about the right speed?

Despite rampant speculation during the campaign as to the size of the white "backlash" which the dispute over civil rights would stimulate among northern Democrats, it is clear from Table 8.9 that no such movement developed. The loss of normally Democratic votes which was associated with the feeling that the civil rights movement was being pressed too fast was minimal. The civil rights issue appears to have had a stronger impact on voters whose normal partisanship was Republican than it did on Democrats. Considering the northern voters only, we would estimate a deficit to Mr. Goldwater resulting from the party positions on the civil rights issue.

Table 8.9. Relation of Attitude Toward Civil Rights to the Vote

Vote for President	Democrats			Independents			Republicans		
	Too slow	About right	Too fast	Too slow	About right	Too fast	Too slow	About right	Too fast
					North				
Johnson	12%	28%	54%	5%	25%	41%	3%	9%	18%
Goldwater	1	1	4	1	4	24	2	11	57
Number of cases	369 = 100%			164 = 100%			226 100=%		
					South				
Johnson	7%	25%	51%	3%	20%	20%	2%	4%	8%
Goldwater	0	a	17	0	2	55	0	11	75
Number of cases	197 = 100%			40 = 100%			52 = 100%		

a Less than one percent.

Not surprisingly, the civil rights issue had a much greater impact on the vote in the South than it had in the North and the effect was unfavorable to Mr. Johnson. Although those Democrats and Independents in the South who accepted the pace of the civil rights movement as not too rapid held very solidly to the Democratic ticket (many of them were Negroes), there were sizable defections among the very much larger segment of the Southern electorate who did not accept it. It is apparent that it was only the fact that the "normal" Democratic majority in the South is so large that prevented these defections from throwing a larger number of states into the Goldwater column.

These preliminary explorations of issue positions associated with the 1964 vote lead us to limited conclusions which subsequent analysis will extend and make more precise. The broad issue of governmental responsibility does not have the immediate impact on the electorate that the civil rights issue has, but it is an issue on which the followers of the two parties show important differences. Its impact in the 1964 election was visible but not a major contributor to movements of the vote from normal party positions. Civil rights, on the contrary, moved a substantial number of votes, especially in the southern states. The partisan impact of the civil rights issue was one of the most striking aspects of the 1964 election; its specific relevance to region and race cuts crosswise of the traditional pattern of party attachments, with consequences which remain to be seen in subsequent elections.[6]

Although Mr. Goldwater was far less attractive to the electorate than Mr. Eisenhower or Mr. Nixon had been in the preceding elections, over 27 million Americans voted for him on November 3. The extent to which this sizable

[6] Results very comparable to those reported here were obtained from a second question in our questionnaire which read: "What about you? Are you in favor of desegregation, strict segregation, or something in between?"

fraction of the electorate was supporting Mr. Goldwater because it shared his political philosophy has been the subject of diverse interpretations, the most extreme of which assumes that these voters make up the "conservative" wing of contemporary American politics. A second look at Table 8.4 shows how exaggerated this assumption must be. Of the total Goldwater vote:

27% were "particularly happy" that Goldwater was nominated,

24% preferred someone else but thought Goldwater was "nearly as good,"

30% had no one in particular they hoped would be nominated,

19% were "particularly unhappy" that Goldwater was nominated.

If we attempt to isolate within the Goldwater total those votes which could reasonably be identified as showing conservative support for a conservative candidate, we must surely subtract the 19 percent of his votes which come from people who had not wanted to see him nominated. It also seems most unlikely that the 30 percent who had no special interest in who was nominated contained many voters who felt themselves strongly identified with Mr. Goldwater's conservative views. Of the remaining half of the Goldwater total, 24 percent had originally preferred some other candidate for the Republican nomination but were willing to accept Mr. Goldwater as "nearly as good" as their first choice. Since Mr. Goldwater was clearly more conservative in his political professions than any of the other candidates considered at the Republican Convention it is reasonable to conclude that in the degree to which the choices of this 24 percent were influenced by ideological factors their position at the time of the convention was less conservative than that of Mr. Goldwater. It is undoubtedly within the 27 percent who preferred Mr. Goldwater from the start and were pleased with his nomination that the core of his ideological support lay. We cannot assume that all of these people were supporting Mr. Goldwater because they understood his policy positions and agreed with them; indeed, our experience with such inquiries would lead us to expect that a good many of them preferred him because he was "sincere" or was "a good man," with very little awareness of what his views on policy might be. But we are probably safe in concluding that this 27 percent of the Goldwater vote contained the bulk of the people who self-consciously shared his conservative philosophy, along with a certain number of people who were less sophisticated about issues but were not offended by what they knew of his position.

Later analysis of the 1964 survey will make it possible to describe in detail the characteristics of these various components of the Goldwater vote and to estimate with some precision the extent to which they shared Mr. Goldwater's views on welfare, racial, and international policies. From the preliminary data presented here it seems doubtful that the "conservative vote" in 1964 could have exceeded 25 percent of the Goldwater total. We have no doubt the "ultras," who contributed the most vocal segment of Mr. Goldwater's support, were very much less numerous than this.[7]

Party Identification

Although short-term political forces are capable of moving the vote quite dramatically from one election to the next,

[7] The hazards of estimating the numerical strength of a sector of the electorate standing at an extreme of the political dimension from the contents of the "letters to the editor" which are written to the nation's press is dramatically demonstrated by Philip E. Converse, Aage Clausen, and Warren E. Miller in "Electoral Myth and Reality: The 1964 Election," *American Political Science Review,* Vol. 59 (June 1965), pp. 321-36.

the stability of the American electoral system rests on the enduring strength of the attachment felt by most of the electorate to the party of their choice. Despite the strong emotions which were stirred by the candidates and the issues of the 1964 campaign, the majority of the voters remained faithful to their parties (Table 8.10).

We have seen in earlier elections that when the political wind is blowing strongly, the extent of the response among the electorate is closely associated with the strength of their party identification. The pattern seen in the North in 1964 is very similar to the pattern of the vote in 1956, although the direction of the defections is reversed. The strong adherents of the favored party voted almost unanimously for their candidate; their less-committed copartisans were less faithful but still gave their candidate stronger support than they would in a normal election. The independent voters swung toward the favored party. Defections were high among the weak identifiers of the disadvantaged party, much lower but higher than normal among its strong partisans. This appears to be the archetypical picture when events conspire to the advantage of one party over the other.

The pattern of movement in the 1964 vote differed in one respect from what we have seen in the earlier elections.

Table 8.10. Vote for President by Party Identification Groups, 1964

Group	North			South		
	Johnson	Goldwater	Total	Johnson	Goldwater	Total
Strong Democrats	99%	1%	100%	90%	10%	100%
Weak Democrats	86	14	100	72	28	100
Independents	70	30	100	41	59	100
Weak Republicans	47	53	100	22	78	100
Strong Republicans	11	89	100	7	93	100

Where the swing of the vote in 1952 and 1956, and less clearly in 1960, had been relatively homogeneous in all parts of the country, in 1964 there was a strong regional contrast. The same short-term forces which worked to the Democratic advantage in the North worked to its disadvantage in the South. As has been noted above, the civil rights issue, and less importantly the issue of governmental intervention, cost the Democratic party votes in the South which it would not normally expect to lose.[8]

We have argued in earlier publications that a strong swing in the vote of the kind recorded in 1964 may either express a temporary reaction to immediate circumstances with no clear ideological component, or it may be a response to "a great national issue and the association of the two major parties with relatively clear contrasting programs for its solution." [9] In the former case the flow of the vote tends to be homogeneous throughout the electorate, the underlying distribution of party identification does not change, and the vote returns to "normal" in subsequent elections. In the latter case, the overriding issue of the moment tends to divide the electorate along lines relevant to the issue, and there is a shift in party identifications leading to a realignment of party strength and a movement in the level of the normal vote. We have seen that the civil rights issue in 1964 fulfilled in some degree the description of a great national issue with contrasting associations with the two parties and that it moved segments of the electorate in opposite directions. We may now ask if this

[8] The southern data in Table 8.10 are flawed by a substantial over-report of turnout and Democratic votes in our survey interviews. Preliminary analysis suggests that this came mainly from Negro southerners who did not actually vote. The proportion of defections among strong and weak Democrats in the South was probably higher than indicated in Table 8.10. The Survey Research Center is currently carrying out a precinct check of the voting records of these respondents in order to remove errors in reported turnout.

[9] Angus Campbell, "Voters and Elections: Past and Present," *Journal of Politics*, Vol. 26 (November 1964), pp. 745-57.

movement of the vote was associated with a movement in the distribution of party identifications.

Our national surveys have been recording the electorate's attachments to the two parties since October 1952. As Table 8.11 makes clear, there was great stability in this distribution throughout the Eisenhower period and into the preconvention period of 1964. There was, however, a visible shift toward the Democratic party in the latter stages of the 1964 campaign. Some part of this movement we must attribute to the tendency of a few politically detached people to associate themselves with a party they see to be a winner.[10] A similar "bandwagon" effect of much smaller proportion seemed to occur in 1956. But there remains a Democratic gain of several

Table 8.11. Distribution of Party Identification in the United States, 1952-1964

Identification	Oct. 1952	Oct. 1956	Oct. 1960	May 1964	Oct. 1964
Strong Democrat	22%	21%	21%	24%	27%
Weak Democrat	25	23	25	22	24
Independent Democrat	10	7	8	7	9
Independent	5	9	8	10	8
Independent Republican	7	8	7	5	6
Weak Republican	14	14	13	17	13
Strong Republican	13	15	14	11	11
Apolitical, other	4	3	4	4	2
	100%	100%	100%	100%	100%

[10] There was a remarkable degree of agreement among the electorate in October 1964 that Mr. Johnson would be elected President. Over 80 percent of our respondents predicted his election in our preelection survey, 8 percent predicted a Goldwater victory, 11 percent were uncertain. This far exceeds any of the previous years of our surveys, including 1956 when the corresponding figures were 68 percent Eisenhower, 19 percent Stevenson, and 13 percent uncertain. The relation of the high degree of public certainty regarding the outcome of these two elections to the relatively low turnout in these two years can hardly be merely coincidental.

percentage points which goes beyond what might have been expected from such "false" reports or from errors associated with sampling.[11]

Implications of the 1964 Election

As we have seen in Table 8.11, our numerous readings of the distribution of partisan attachments over the years preceding the 1964 election have shown a remarkably constant ratio of approximately 60-40 in Democratic and Republican partisans. Because of the lower level of political interest shown by Democratic identifiers, their effective strength is not as high as their proportion in the population. We have estimated the "normal vote" during the period 1952 to 1960 to be about 54 percent Democratic; that is, if there were no short-term forces moving the vote away from the division which would be expected on the basis of underlying levels of interest and partisanship, we would predict the Democratic presidential candidate would carry approximately 54 percent of the national vote.[12]

In 1964 the Democratic vote swung far beyond this normal expectation. We have seen that the Democratic presidential candidate was far more favorably perceived by the electorate than his opponent, an advantage much greater than that held by either candidate in 1960. The images of the two parties also showed a clear Democratic preference, again a stronger differentiation than was present in 1960. The two major issues which were prominent in the campaign, civil rights and governmental welfare activities, aroused contrasting reactions in different sections of the electorate, favoring the

[11] Preliminary analysis indicates that a strong contribution to this Democratic gain came from southern Negroes who had previously had no positive association with either party.

[12] Angus Campbell, Philip E. Converse, Warren E. Miller, and Donald E. Stokes, *Elections and the Political Order* (John Wiley & Sons, 1966), Chap. 2.

Democratic candidate in the North and the Republican candidate in the South. These are the major short-term forces in any presidential contest, and the evidence from our survey makes it clear that on balance they strongly favored the Democratic alternative in the 1964 election.

We have seen the impact of short-term forces on the vote in all the earlier elections studied, although in the previous years they have always been favorable to the Republican candidate. What we have not seen in the earlier years is the swing in the distribution of party identification which we find in the 1964 data. If this shift turns out to be a temporary reaction to the circumstances of the moment, the future of party competition in this country will probably not differ greatly in the near future from what has been seen in the recent past. If it is the first sign of a true realignment of party attachments, the implications for the future may be far-reaching.[13]

We do not have information on the partisan attachments of the electorate prior to 1952, but we know that in the hundred years of two-party competition for the Presidency the margin of victory has varied through a very narrow band. Stokes and Iverson have pointed out that during this period neither party has succeeded in winning more than 15 percent beyond an equal share of the presidential vote, and the average difference in the party division of the vote from election to election has been less than 6 percent.[14] Insofar as we can judge the underlying party strength from the records of the vote, there appear to have been three phases of party balance during this era. After the southern states reentered the electorate in 1876 there ensued a period when the two

[13] A national sample interviewed by the Survey Research Center in February 1965 produced a distribution of party identification almost identical with that recorded in October 1964.

[14] Donald E. Stokes and Gudmund R. Iverson, "On the Existence of Forces Restoring Party Competition," *Public Opinion Quarterly*, Vol. 26 (Summer 1962), pp. 159-69.

parties appeared to command approximately equal strength. In the 1890's the balance swung to the Republican party and over the period 1896 to 1916 (omitting the aberration of 1912) its advantage averaged about 54 percent of the presidential vote. This period of Republican ascendancy was extended through the 1920's, with increased margins associated with the extension of women's suffrage and the effect of minor party votes. The phase of Democratic dominance, beginning in 1932 and still continuing, has recorded an average of 53 percent of the vote.

It appears that since 1896, when the post-Civil War stalemate was broken, the standing strength of the two parties has departed from an equal balance by approximately 3 to 5 percentage points. During the same period, neither party has held the Presidency for fewer than eight consecutive years or for more than twenty. The party balance, first favoring the Republicans and then the Democrats, has stood at a point sufficiently beyond an equal division to give the ascendant party an adequate buffer to withstand passing embarrassments, but not a large enough majority to permit it to override challenges based on widespread public dissatisfaction. The party balance has been such as to prevent rapid turnover in national politics but to permit realistic competition between the two parties.

The question which the 1964 vote raises is whether we are entering a period of party realignment which will increase the prevailing Democratic advantage in the party balance. There are indications in our survey data of a movement of this kind. It appears, however, from the experience of the 1890's and the 1930's that major realignments do not take place in a single election, that there are "realigning eras" rather than "realigning elections." If the events of the last four years have indeed set the stage for a movement toward a new level of party balance, we may see profound changes in the nature of party competition in American politics.

Index

Taft, Robert A., 46

Taft, Robert A., Jr., 13, 205, 212

Taft-Hartley Act, amendments to, 251, 252

Tax reduction bill, 60

Television: campaigning by, 10, 122-25; convention coverage by, 36-38, 118-22, 125; cost of, 172; damaging influence on Republican party, 120-21; effect on election turnout, 150-51; "equal-time" requirements for, 117, 153, 173, 174; fundraising by, 125, 178, 179-80; future role of, 155; Goldwater's use of, 19, 122, 123; overcoverage by, 118-19; preconvention uses of, 115; permanent installation in White House, 117; use of, during primaries, 109, 122-23

Television debates: attitude of press toward, 133; attitude of Republicans toward, 128; in campaign of 1960, 127; in campaign of 1964, 112; controversy over, 127-34; Goldwater's position, 131, 132-33; Johnson's position, 128, 133; plans for future use, 151-53; report of American Political Science Association panel, 129-31; proposal for use by Republican presidential aspirants, 129

Tennessee primary, 225

Tennessee Valley Authority, 61, 113, 115

Ter Horst, J. F., 95n

Test Ban Treaty, 61, 127

Thompson, T. Ashton, 226

Thomson, Charles A. H., 10, 111, 117n

Thurmond, J. Strom, 7, 68, 155

Tillett, Paul, 8, 15

Time, allocation among states by candidates, 50-53, 64-66, 72, 73, 75-76

Truman, David B., 215n

Truman, Harry S., 74, 102

Tupper, Stanley, 250

Turnout, election, 150-51

Two-party system, 10; effect of 1964 election on, 107-08

Tydings, Joseph, 204, 213, 221

United Nations, 69, 92n, 115

Unruh, Jesse, 201, 203n

Urban Mass Transportation Act, 251, 251n

Vietnam, as campaign issue, 54

Vincent, Geoffrey, 140, 141, 141n

Vote: "backlash," 52n, 60, 60n, 272; "hidden," 88-92; by party identification, 276

Vote Profile Analysis (CBS), 10, 136, 143, 144-45, 154-55

Voting returns. See Election returns; Elections

Wages, minimum, 60

Wallace, George: campaign costs, 166-67; in primaries, 5, 54; southern support for, 53; support of Goldwater, 68; withdrawal of candidacy, 6-7, 46, 66

Wallhauser, George, 228

Walton, Russell, 49n, 50n

Waltzer, Herbert, 37n

Watson, Albert, 68, 229n, 243n, 244

Weisbord, Marvin R., 25n

Welfare, government: as campaign issue, 7, 11, 269-71, 279; candidates' differences on, 7, 11; Goldwater's position, 269; Johnson's position, 270; public attitude toward, by party and region, 271